ADVANCE PRAISE FOR

Building Community

Building Community is a welcome contribution to the world of sustainable community development. Jim Gruber has assembled a guide to essential research, case studies and tools to help citizens and community leaders address fundamental issues of participatory democracy. This vital resource for community building illuminates a path for reconstructing formidable problems into tangible solutions.

> — Dr. Mark Roseland, professor and director, School of Community Resources and Development, Watts College of Public Service and Community Solutions, Arizona State University, author, *Toward Sustainable Communities*

This book pulls together decades of invaluable field work to illuminate essential principles of practice for transforming "intractable problems" into challenges that together we can solve. This is crucial reading for all who feel compelled to lead, not because they have authority, but simply because they care deeply about their community and world.

> — Ronald A. Heifetz, MD, founder, Center for Public Leadership, Harvard Kennedy School, author, *Leadership Without Easy Answers*, co-author, *Leadership on the Line*

At a time when we are confronted daily with the limitations of national and global institutions to address the pressing challenges facing our planet, this engaging book reminds us of the vital role that strong local communities play in creating a resilient future. Gruber considers the challenging question—how can communities move from surviving to thriving?—and answers it in terms that are at once inspiring and pragmatic. Framed around 12 principles and illustrated with experience from communities in regions as diverse as rural New England, Andean South America, West Africa, and the Baltics, *Building Community* provides us with clear, approachable guidance on how to move in that direction.

> — Jessica Brown, executive director, New England Biolabs Foundation

Building Community is a remarkable guidebook on how to get controversial but critically important things done at the local level. It is also a highly insightful but down-to-earth leadership manual for individuals committed to making a contribution at the community level. As a decades-long practitioner of American democracy promotion abroad with a strong interest in comparative political cultures and in nurturing effective leadership, I was stunned by the extraordinary range of issues, countries, and situations addressed in this book's rich set of case studies. It is a must read for those seeking to make a lasting difference at the local level, while at the same time strengthening the building blocks of their democracy.

—Ambassador Adrian A. Basora (USFS, Ret.),
principal author, *Does Democracy Matter?*

Jim Gruber shares the lessons of a valuable career helping local communities learn how to solve their environmental and sustainability challenges. He identifies guiding principles that show how collaborative approaches succeed in communities across the globe. I am so impressed that I gave a copy to my mayor!

—Dr. David Blockstein, senior adviser,
Association for Environmental Studies and Sciences (AESS)

While the leadership principles presented in *Building Community* are used in addressing environmental issues, they would be valuable for problem solving relating to any persistent, systemic problem facing a community. Gruber highlights how these communities not only worked to resolve seemingly intractable problems, but also built community muscle. Make room on your bookshelf for this substantive work.

—David Mathews, president, Kettering Foundation

James Gruber has captured the essence of what it means to collaborate with a community of stakeholders in order to achieve sustainability. His "how to" blueprint contained in the twelve principles coupled with his insightful analysis of specific case studies, makes this a must read for students, academics, and practitioners alike.

—John MacLean, retired Keene New Hampshire city manager,
senior consultant, MRI

As we move through this century, functional communities will become critical for personal wellbeing. In this very user-friendly guide, Jim Gruber clearly maps out how people can create inclusive, vital communities. Packed with case studies and very helpful hints, this is a gem of a resource for anyone wanting to strengthen their own community.

— Tom Wessels, author, *Granite, Fire, and Fog,*
Reading the Forested Landscape, and *The Myth of Progress,*
faculty emeritus, Antioch University

Gandhi repeatedly said that to defeat systems of domination like British imperialism you need militant forms of nonviolent resistance, but to build just, thriving, and sustainable communities you need to organize many local, collaborative, inclusive, and constructive community initiatives and institutions. James Gruber's new book powerfully fleshes out this second path for community leaders today—with relevant research, stories from around the world, and hard-won wisdom distilled from Gruber's many years of practical experience.

— Dr. Steve Chase, International Center on Nonviolent Conflict

James Gruber, a highly experienced civil engineer, town manager, university faculty member, and consultant presents rich "case study" examples of successful community initiatives and projects that have made positive impacts nationally and internationally, countering the obstacles that lead to continued apathy and despair. Gruber provides guiding principles for essential leadership and building citizen engagement. More importantly, he provides a powerful antidote to withdrawal and isolation, while giving a gift of inspiration and hope.

— James H. Craiglow, President Emeritus,
Antioch University New England

Building Community is a roadmap and blueprint for working with local people in a collaborative manner so that everyone can make a significant contribution towards sustainable societal transformation.

— Dr. Esther Adhiambo Obonyo, Associate Professor of Engineering Design and
Architectural Engineering, director, Global Building Network,
a partnership with UNECE

To Patience

*In deep appreciation of your love,
brilliance, caring, and support that
made this book possible.*

~

BUILDING COMMUNITY

Twelve Principles for a Healthy Future

James S. Gruber, PhD, PE

new society
PUBLISHERS

Cover design by Diane McIntosh
All photos supplied by James S. Gruber
Printed in Canada. First printing May, 2020.

Inquiries regarding requests to reprint all or part of *Building Community*
should be addressed to New Society Publishers at the address below.
To order directly from the publishers, please call toll-free (North America)
1-800-567-6772, or order online at www.newsociety.com

Any other inquiries can be directed by mail to:
New Society Publishers
P.O. Box 189, Gabriola Island, BC V0R 1X0, Canada
(250) 247-9737

LIBRARY AND ARCHIVES CANADA CATALOGUING IN PUBLICATION

Title: Building community : twelve principles for a healthy future /
James S. Gruber, PhD, PE.

Names: Gruber, James S., 1950– author.

Description: Includes bibliographical references and index.

Identifiers: Canadiana (print) 2020016483X | Canadiana (ebook) 20200164880 |
ISBN 9780865719323 (softcover) | ISBN 9781550927252 (PDF) |
ISBN 9781771423212 (EPUB)
Subjects: LCSH: Community life. | LCSH: Social participation. |
LCSH: Community leadership.
Classification: LCC HM761 .G78 2020 | DDC 307b

Funded by the   Financé par le
Government   gouvernement
of Canada   du Canada

New Society Publishers' mission is to publish books that contribute in fundamental
ways to building an ecologically sustainable and just society, and to do so with the
least possible impact on the environment, in a manner that models this vision.

Contents

Acknowledgments xiii

Introduction 1
A Journey of Discovery 3

1. Challenges of Our Communities:
   Growing Local Leadership 9
   Local Communities: The Foundation of Society 9
   Challenges That Local Communities Are Facing 11
   Community Capital: What It Is and Why It Matters 12
   The Guiding Principles: How They Were Identified
       and How They Can Be Helpful 13
   How This Book Is Organized 16

2. Principle A—Involve Everyone 19
   The Cornerstone of Society 19
   Research Corner 20
   Why Public Participation Is Essential 21
   Case Study: Citizen-Powered Climate Action,
       Keene, New Hampshire, USA 25
   Case Study: Development without Dependency,
       Gran Sous, La Gonave, Haiti 32
   Notes from the Field 39

3. Principle B—Work Together 41
   Collaborative Partnerships 41
   Research Corner 42
   Social Capital—The Social Glue That Holds
       the Community Together 43

Leveraging Resources and Supporting Implementation . . .   43

Case Study: Community Gardens: An Immigrant Story of
    Food Sovereignty in Saskatoon, Saskatchewan, Canada   47

Case Study: Grow Appalachia and Rural Community
    Gardening, Kentucky, USA   53

Notes from the Field   59

4. Principle C—Protect Resources and Promote Fairness . . .   61

Community-Based Natural Resource Management   61

Research Corner   62

Natural Capital and Livelihoods   63

Case Study: Building a New Future for All Residents,
    Ixtlán de Juárez, Oaxaca, Mexico   66

Case Study: Reclaiming Wood, Bricks, Lives,
    and a Community, Baltimore, Maryland, USA   76

Case Study: Women's Empowerment Through
    Sustainability in India   87

Notes from the Field   92

5. Principle D—Be Transparent   93

Build Credibility Through Transparency   93

Effective Communication and Secrets   93

Research Corner   94

Case Study: Vital Communities of the Upper Valley
    Region, Vermont and New Hampshire, USA   99

Case Study: Regenerating and Transforming a Village's
    Land and Water Resources, Hiware Bazar, India   103

Notes from the Field   110

6. Principle E—Support Research   111

Asking the Right Questions and Separating
    Facts from Fiction.   111

Research Corner   112

Citizen Science and Citizen Technical Advisors   113

Local Community-University Partnerships   114

Case Study: Resilience to Food Insecurity, Bikotiba, Togo . .   116

Case-in-Point: An Outdoor Student Environmental
   Learning Lab, Keene, New Hampshire, USA 125
Case Study: Mobilizing the Local Voice to Support Protected
   Area Governance, Magombera Forest, Tanzania 126
Notes from the Field 136

7. **Principle F—Delegate and Empower** 137
   Devolution and Empowerment 137
   Research Corner 138
   Case Study: Community-Led Sustainable
      Development in Northern Ghana 142
   Case Study: Climate Change and the Minnehaha Creek
      Watershed: Where Will All the Water Go?
      Minnesota, USA. 148
   Notes from the Field 154

8. **Principle G—Earn Trust** 155
   Building Trust is Integral to All Community Work. 155
   Research Corner 156
   Essentials for Building Trust in a Community 158
   Case Study: Randolph Community Forest,
      New Hampshire, USA 159
   Case Study: Restoring the Strong People:
      The Lower Elwha Klallam Tribe and the Elwha River . . 169
   Notes from the Field 176

9. **Principle H—Embrace Feedback** 177
   Monitoring and Feedback: Using Nature as a Guide. 177
   Research Corner 178
   Seeking Feedback: How Do I Get People to Respond? 179
   Feedback and Accountability of Local Leaders 180
   Case Study: Healing Products and Healthy Business:
      The W.S. Badger Story, Gilsum, New Hampshire, USA . 181
   Case Study: The Conservation and Sustainable Management
      of an Inshore Fishery in Alanya, Turkey 187
   Notes from the Field 196

10. **Principle I—Practice Leadership**   197
Critical Leadership Actions   197
Research Corner   198
Case Study: Local Community Collaboration
in the Apuseni Mountains, Huedin, Romania   201
Case Study: Inner City Urban Recovery,
South Bend, Indiana, USA   207
Notes from the Field   213

11. **Principle J—Decide Together**   215
Moving from Them to Us   215
Research Corner   216
Common Characteristics and Challenges
of Deciding Together   217
Case Study: Bring Them Together—Young Achievers
School, Boston, Massachusetts, USA   219
Case Study: Wetlands Conservation and Sustainable
Livelihoods in the Ecuadorian Andes, Ecuador   225
Notes from the Field   234

12. **Principle K—Strengthen the Foundation**   235
A Strong Social Foundation   235
Research Corner   236
Community Norms—Or, What is Normal?   237
Building a Stronger Social Foundation for Your Community   238
Case Study: Getting Unstuck: A Congregation Moving From
Surviving to Thriving, Norwich, Vermont, USA   242
Case-in-Point: Connecting Underrepresented Families
to Their Local Environment, North Carolina, USA . . .   249
Case Study: Creating Local Community Foundations in
the Baltic Countries, Estonia, Latvia, and Lithuania . . .   251
Notes from the Field   258

13. **Principle L—Resolve Conflicts**   259
Preventing Conflict   259
Research Corner   260

Understanding and Addressing Conflict   261
Case Study: Community-Driven Regional Land Use
    and Transportation Planning in Southern New
    Hampshire, USA   265
Case Study: The Hunter, His Herbs, and Community
    Biodiversity in Fian, Ghana   272
Notes from the Field   281

14. **A Toolbox of Leadership Strategies**   283
Collaborative Leadership and Empowerment.   283
A Collaborative Planning Approach.   283
Notes from the Field: Planning, Organizing,
    and Facilitating a Community Meeting.   300
The Way Forward.   301

Notes   305

Index   327

**About the Author and the Contributing
Case Study Authors**   335
About New Society Publishers   338

Acknowledgments

This book was truly a community effort of many dedicated and hard-working individuals. I first acknowledge and recognize my wife, Dr. Patience G. Stoddard, for her many hours of assistance, encouragement, editing, and keeping me on course. The original doctoral degree research for this book was completed with the support and mentorship of Dr. Tarzan Legovic.

I was very fortunate to have an *Editorial Team* of exceptional graduate students at Antioch University New England who researched, wrote case studies, and edited this book. They are: Jacques Kenjio, Charlene Phillips, and Shaylin Salas. I could not have written this book without their incredible dedication and brilliant work. Thank you.

My *Senior Advisors* on this book were instrumental in providing critical advice and suggestions that helped throughout the writing process. These include: Mead Cadot, Jan Fiderio, Paul Markowitz, Rick Minard, Dr. Peter Palmiotto, Jim Rousmaniere, Michael Simpson, Peter Throop, Dr. Nicole Wengerd, and Tom Wessels.

The 26 *Contributing Case Study Authors* were critical for enhancing the value of this book by sharing their first-hand practical knowledge of communities that are moving towards a healthy and sustainable future. Each of these individuals and their biographies are listed on the Contributing Case Study Authors page. I would like to thank each of them for their valuable contributions.

Lastly, I do not have room to recognize all of the friends, colleagues, and partners that I had the opportunity and privilege to work with in different communities across the US and around the world that are described in the case studies and stories that I share. These include the faculty, students, and staff of Antioch New England Institute and the Environmental Studies Department at Antioch University New England. I tried to recognize at least some of them in the case studies and stories that I have shared.

Introduction

> *If you want to go fast, go alone.*
> *If you want to go far, go together.*
> —African Proverb

This book is written for those who care about enhancing the health and vitality of their community. If building healthy and thriving communities is something you are passionate about, actively involved in, or aspire to pursue, my hope is that you will use this book as a do-it-yourself guide. It focuses on building a healthier society that engages and involves all its members. The stories and case studies it presents illustrate the many ways that community members, as well as elected and appointed leaders, have engaged in actions and practiced leadership that made a real difference in their communities.

The contributors to this book believe that strong local communities are the foundation, the tap roots, of a healthy, participatory, and resilient society. In this age of ever-changing technology, mega-corporations, and economic globalization, livelihoods are at risk, natural resources are being depleted, and climate change is damaging the very planet upon which we all depend. National leaders and global corporations are failing to address this growing crisis. However, throughout the US, and in many other nations, local communities are finding innovative ways to thrive while protecting natural resources, enhancing the livelihood of their community members, and growing social vitality. Perhaps rather than looking to national governments, corporations, or new technologies to solve our environmental and social problems, we should learn from successful communities in order to find paths to a more sustainable future. These communities include not just local governments but also groups of individuals that are working together for the common good, such as neighborhood associations, schools, local and Indigenous groups, faith communities, businesses, and nonprofit organizations.

I have found that this often challenging yet rewarding work is somewhat like building or renovating a house. Many of the guiding leadership principles we will discuss are critical for establishing or reinforcing the existing foundation of a community. Without a strong *foundation*, future gains can easily collapse. The principles shared here also address ways to improve the *plumbing and wiring systems* of a community, including free-flowing energy and communication, information sharing and dissemination, and numerous feedback loops. You know what happens in a house when the sewer pipe is blocked! No community (or house) can stand without a viable *structure*, which is strong, but also resilient enough to be modified when necessary to meet the needs of the future. Houses (and communities) most importantly provide *shelter* for all within—shelter that can weather difficult times. And, finally, a thriving community is a *home*; a home where there is trust, collaboration, social justice, and where conflicts or disagreements are resolved amiably.

This book will share our research and reflections on each of the *12 Guiding Principles*. It includes explanations and short examples—illustrations of each principle along with 25 *Case Studies* from around the world from knowledgeable contributing authors/practitioners, and *Notes from the Field*, which list practical do's and don'ts. No, we cannot give you all of the answers to the questions you will have but we hope that this book will provide you with tools and resources for practical, effective leadership and collaboration that can guide you in your own important work of helping to build a community that people can truly call home.

A Journey of Discovery

As the primary author of this book, I hope that sharing some of my personal journey may help you to understand how I came to realize how local communities can thrive and make a transformative difference in the lives of their members.

Local Challenges and Failures of "Expert" or "Top-Down" Approaches

The toxic leachate from the landfill, located in a wetland, was seeping into the ocean off southern Massachusetts. Swimmers on a nearby town beach were getting ill with "swimmers' itch." Sewage from the basements of homes was flowing (by illegal connections) into stormwater manholes and nearby streams. One dark, stormy, rainy night, as the town engineer, I got a call at 2:00 a.m. from a resident who yelled into the phone: "Your water is flowing through the first floor of my house!" I soon discovered that their house had been built on a lot created by digging into an abutting wetland. It was raining and the water from the wetland was flowing through the lower floor of their home. As a young town engineer working for this coastal New England community, I tried to draw upon my engineering training. I concluded that many of these technical community problems could be solved, at least in part, by engineering, new ordinances, and town policies using a simple top-down expert approach. Many of these environmental problems were, indeed, *partially* solved or reduced through these technical fixes. Yet there were systemic issues, linked to community values and norms, that had allowed this plethora of adverse health and environmental conditions to be created. Sometimes it felt like I was playing a game of whack-a-mole, because every time something was fixed another problem would pop up. My central question was: Can I help this community vision and plan for ways to enhance their own health and vitality rather than just reacting to poorly thought-through actions? This was not part of my engineering training. I was ill prepared to help this community understand its challenges, assess opportunities for a different path, and then engage residents in actions that they recognized were needed to enhance their quality of life.

This expert-driven approach to solving local community problems and planning for the future, which I had been taught and had often observed, has historic roots. It was the foundation of the United States' urban renewal efforts (and also similar efforts in Central and Eastern Europe and other parts of the world) during the 60s and early 70s. During this period of urban renewal, federal funding and expert local planners supported tearing down historic downtown buildings and struggling neighborhoods and replacing them with large low-income housing units, space for strip malls, and parking garages. It was reported that by 1965 nearly 800 cities, in every state, were participating in urban renewal. This resulted in tearing down housing units with mass displacement of families, such as in New Haven, Connecticut, where 30,000 people were forced to find new homes.[1] Historic downtowns were completely leveled and replaced with nondescript buildings and parking garages. Poor or disempowered minority populations were frequently impacted the most. The experts did not seek or allow the input or involvement of citizens. This "renewal" effort resulted in entire zones of poverty where the sense of community had all but evaporated, crime flourished, and people felt trapped in a downward spiral of hopelessness.

Recognizing that the expert-driven, top-down model for improving the quality of local communities has not only failed to deliver, but sometimes actually caused more harm than good, was a valuable lesson for me in rethinking my approach. Five years later, I was ready to learn and explore new ways of leading that truly engaged community members and supported needed change. I soon discovered this required giving up some control. I could no longer be the expert in the room.

Adaptive Leadership and
How This Can Be Applied to Leading Change

Helping people face *their* challenges, *their* "problematic reality," and then supporting *them* when *they* undertake work that *they* realize needs to be done is the focus of Adaptive Leadership. This type of leadership work does not sound like rocket science but I have found it is challenging to practice. It requires giving up control and no longer functioning like an expert, but instead serving as a resource and a support system and then trusting the path (or paths) the community decides to take. These principles of Adaptive Leadership are described by Ron Heifetz[2] in his book *Leadership Without Easy Answers* and in other later publications.[3] In the 1980s, I was fortunate to take his course on leadership at the Harvard Kennedy School of Government (HKS). This course transformed my approach to working with local communities and its lessons are embedded in the concepts and applied approaches described in this book. Upon graduation, I entered the realm of town management in Vermont and New Hampshire, frequently seeking to build local community empowerment through an Adaptive Leadership approach to doing my job. Local community leadership is not easy: resources are limited but needs are not, special interest groups try to set self-serving agendas, and change is difficult and sometimes scary for residents. I found that listening, really listening, was essential in this new paradigm. I also found that the more direct involvement people had in the change, the more likely it was to succeed. The wise African proverb that says, "If you want to go fast, go alone. If you want to go far, go together," captures what I discovered after ten years of working with local communities.

Over and over again, I have witnessed the reality that practicing this kind of leadership can build the capacity for citizen-driven change that would not have been possible with an expert-driven approach. Later, I share the example[4] of how the town of Hartford, Vermont, working with its four neighboring towns was able to close two old seeping landfills and build a model community recycling center. This change from a landfill to the "un-shopping center" was led by nearly a thousand volunteers from ages 8 through 80. This incredible three years of work led by the local citizens, and eventually supported by the local government officials, was nationally recognized and given an award presented by Hillary Clinton as well as recorded in the US Congressional Record.

Building Community Capital
and Providing Support to a Wide Variety of
Communities at Home and Abroad

After deciding to move on and apply what citizens, dedicated local officials, and affiliated non-governmental organizations (NGOs) had taught me during my time in managing local governments, a colleague, Delia Clark, and I partnered with Antioch University New England (AUNE) to form Antioch New England Institute (ANEI). The Institute's goal was to support the sustainability of local communities and schools across the US and, eventually, in other countries as well. Its mission was to promote a vibrant and sustainable environment, economy, and society by encouraging informed civic engagement. To achieve this mission, we focused on building community capacity or community capital—the term community capital represents different forms of capital in a local community. These are described and discussed in Chapter 1.

My colleagues and I were fortunate to be able to recruit graduate students and faculty members from the university and to work with many active and dedicated partners to undertake work in the USA and ten other countries. A number of stories and case studies in this book are based upon ANEI experiences. Its local community capacity-building efforts ranged from working with US schools on community-based environmental education programs and training local elected town councils, to assisting in building the civil sector capacity of the three Baltic countries through the development of local community foundations. Each of these efforts embraced developing broad and deep partnerships, working directly with local residents, and practicing many of the Guiding Principles that serve as the foundation for this book.

Identifying Guiding Principles for Effective Leadership Approaches for Helping Communities Thrive: An International Research Study

As I consulted with groups that varied from local neighborhood associations to the Bulgarian Ministry of the Environment, I found that while specific issues varied widely, an adaptive management approach and certain community change processes seemed helpful in most situations. I began to think that certain core principles may transcend social and cultural norms and boundaries. When I decided on a research focus for my doctoral work, I set out to see what could be learned by studying communities that were successfully thriving despite often difficult and challenging circumstances.

This research was inspired and envisioned years earlier during my participation in the World Bank Foundation's 1998 international invitational workshop led by the late Elinor Ostrom (Nobel Laureate in economics) in Washington DC on the theme of community-based natural resource management. The workshop was designed to provide a platform upon which to share and learn from effective community-based programs from around the world that supported the local economy and conserved or improved local ecological conditions. Later, I was able to draw upon the hundreds of submitted cases from this workshop and other effective local initiatives to identify common approaches and factors that led to successful outcomes.

This book was written in order to share what was discovered from this workshop and my follow-up international research efforts. Eventually 12 categories evolved from all of this research data, which are here referred to as the *12 Guiding Principles*. These Guiding Principles are a compilation of what many local community leaders, from five continents, have found to be essential for growing healthy communities. These findings[5] have since been published in peer-reviewed papers, taught in graduate classes, used by local governmental officials, and applied to assisting local communities in the USA, Eastern Europe, and South America.

I hope this book will provide you with the practical leadership and practitioner tools that are needed on your journey of supporting the health and vitality of your local community. Today, more than ever before, this timely and critical work is needed to help find paths to a more sustainable future.

CHAPTER 1

Challenges of Our Communities

Growing Local Leadership

> *Our true destiny…is a world built from the bottom up by competent citizens living in solid communities, engaged in and by their places.*
>
> — DAVID W. ORR

Local Communities: The Foundation of Society

How can local communities thrive or become more successful?[1] I believe that any useful approach should include: 1) growing social vitality, empowerment, justice, equity, and trust within the community; 2) enhancing the livelihood of community members; and 3) improving local environmental and ecological conditions. In this book, there are 25 case studies as well as 19 brief examples of communities that are moving from surviving to thriving. These stories of diverse communities are located in 17 counties and 11 states in the USA. For example, the case study from Baltimore, Maryland, shares how an inner-city neighborhood with thousands of vacant and abandoned homes was able to reclaim wood and bricks through deconstruction while also reducing unemployment and helping to revitalize blighted neighborhoods. In Saskatchewan, Canada, locally initiated community-based gardens helped immigrants address food insecurity and built community connections. The case study from Hiware Bazar, India, illustrates

Credit: James Gruber

Figure 1.1. A university community of international students, faculty, and families.

how a village was transformed from a drought-prone and water-scarce impoverished settlement into an economically, environmentally, and socially strong community. These and many other inspiring stories of communities moving from struggling towards thriving, are told by knowledgeable contributing authors throughout the book.

I have found that there are many books, publications, and websites about improving local communities that give expert advice on *what* needs to be done, but pay far less attention to *how* this can be accomplished in a way that builds the strength of the community and a strong democracy. Today, many people in the United States seem to have lost faith in the value of our democratic traditions and citizen-empowered change, and instead favor a top-down, expert-driven, more "efficient" approach, frequently stating that we need to "run local communities like a business." It appears that this mindset has also become more common in other countries around the world. Frequently, these citizens do not see that they have an essential role to play in the leadership of their community. In my many years of experience in local government in the US, international consulting, and now as a researcher/ professor, I have not found this top-down/expert-driven approach to be successful in helping communities thrive. In fact, I have found the opposite to be true.

This book emphasizes *how* local elected, appointed, and volunteer leaders can help their communities thrive. It provides specific guidance based upon the 12 Guiding Principles, and offers specific tools on how to apply the requisite leadership and collaboration skills.

Challenges That Local Communities Are Facing

Today, local communities are facing many of the same challenges that state and national governments are facing (or, sometimes, avoiding). This includes the climate crisis, which is impacting our food systems and creating serious health risks for seniors and the vulnerable, through record summer temperatures, droughts, severe storms, and other climate impacts. Many jobs have been lost or are now unstable due to technological changes and globalization shifting manufacturing to other parts of the world. Local communities are also struggling to help refugees, impoverished and at-risk families, and the homeless. And the litany goes on and on.

There are real stresses in meeting the critical needs of a local community with limited financial resources. I remember how this stress was palpable for our town's staff and elected leaders. At the same time, volunteerism was decreasing and we were forced to pay for help that had previously been done by volunteers. Research by Robert Putnam[2] and others have described many factors contributing to citizens' decreasing involvement.

What to do? Where to turn? How can a local community, particularly one without wealthy members and adequate resources, turn itself around when it is struggling not just economically, but also environmentally and socially? Local community leaders face these concerns every day. These unsung heroes, who jump into critically needed local community leadership roles, have rarely received formal training in public and nonprofit administration, fund raising, or leadership. My hope is that the Guiding Principles and illustrative case studies in this book will provide a resource for you and other dedicated and brave individuals.

Community Capital: What It Is and Why It Matters

I will start with explaining the term *community capital* and how this concept will help you more effectively approach and enhance your community building efforts.

Communities have different forms of community capital (also referred to as community capacity and community wealth). This concept of capital can be illustrated by a manufacturing plant. The investment in building a manufacturing plant (referred to as *built capital*) along with the ongoing inputs of materials, labor, and energy, results in a flow

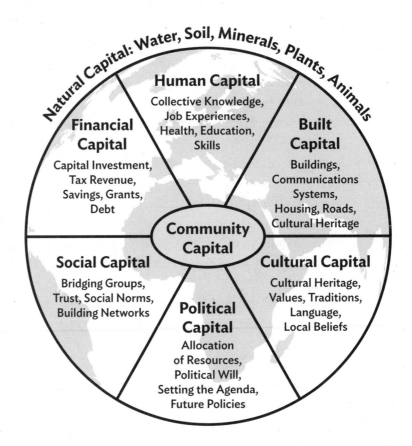

Figure 1.2. Graphical representation of the Seven Forms of Community Capital.

of manufactured products or goods. Other forms of community capital provide different types of flows or outputs. For example, a healthy forest is a form of *natural capital* that can provide a flow of lumber, oxygen, purification of water, and other ecological products and services. Preserving and enhancing different types of a community's capital is essential in building and maintaining a healthy community.

Community practitioners and researchers have organized these different forms of community capital into three to eight categories. I will use seven categories that I have personally found easiest to work with and most helpful for communicating with others. These types of community capital are well documented by a number of authors.[3] Figure 1.2 is a graphic representation of these. Growing community capital will help your community move towards having "healthy ecosystems; vibrant regional economies; and social equity and empowerment."[4]

Each of these seven forms of community capital are shown above with a working definition and brief comment based upon a wide range of ideas from other researchers and authors.[5] It is important to emphasize the importance of investing time, energy, and resources to grow each of these forms of community capital. The Guiding Principles will provide ideas on *how* you can approach this challenge through reaching out to and collaborating with the members of your community.

The Guiding Principles:
How They Were Identified and How They Can Be Helpful

The 12 Guiding Principles (shown in Figure 1.3) include successful approaches and strategies for communication and facilitation, conflict resolution, negotiation, managing and facilitating multiparty stakeholder processes, adaptive management, managing complexity, participatory decision making, building local community capital, and many other local community leadership and management skills. In general, my research has documented that many of these principles transcend a wide range of local cultures and economies and appear to be transcultural in their application.

Forms of Community Capital

- **Natural Capital: Renewable and nonrenewable natural ecological systems such as streams, forests, ground water, soil, and air.** Sustainably managing the natural resources and services provided from natural capital (including limiting the harvesting and use of them) is essential if you wish to maintain the source of natural capital and its ability to provide for the future. Other forms of capital (see below) can be considered embedded in and/or dependent upon the community's ecological or natural capital system. Drawing down or damaging the natural capital systems will impact the other forms of community capital.
- **Human Capital: The collective knowledge, education, skills, job experiences, health, self-esteem, and motivation of the community members.** Investments in these areas will grow a community's human capital.
- **Social Capital: The shared social norms, trust, and networks that impact how individuals and groups get along.** A form of positive social glue. High social capital requires the investment of time and energy. It includes networks of bonding and bridging between individuals and groups.

- **Political Capital: The ability of individuals and groups to influence the political agenda within the community.** This can include the ability to help set the agenda, future policies, and allocation of resources. High political capital of citizens is supported by participatory democracy and broad empowerment of all members of a community.
- **Cultural Capital: The local beliefs, values, traditions, language, history, and cultural heritage of a community.** Cultural capital can give community members their sense of identity and sense of place.
- **Financial Capital: A community's monetary assets invested in other forms of capital or financial instruments.** Forms of public financial capital can include savings, debt capital, investment capital, tax revenue, and grants. Private philanthropic capital can support community investments that yield public goods.
- **Built Capital: The built manufactured and infrastructure capital of a community such as water and wastewater systems, roads, machinery, electronic communication systems, buildings, and housing.** Under- or over-expanding built capital can adversely impact other forms of community capital.

How the Principles Were Identified

There was no magic wand or grand vision that developed these principles. I had an opportunity to listen to and read what local practitioners, local community leaders, and researchers found to be common in many, if not most, communities that were healthy and thriving, or at least beginning to thrive. The initial data was available from a workshop facilitated by the late Nobel Laureate Elinor Ostrom.[6] Sorting through all this information, which included hundreds of case studies from the workshop, as well as academic research papers, and some site visits, and then organizing the findings into 12 categories, required

Figure 1.3. Twelve Guiding Principles for a Healthy Future.

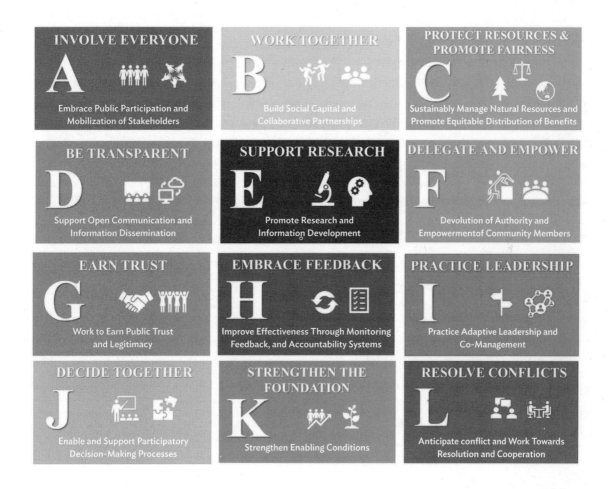

INVOLVE EVERYONE
A
Embrace Public Participation and Mobilization of Stakeholders

WORK TOGETHER
B
Build Social Capital and Collaborative Partnerships

PROTECT RESOURCES & PROMOTE FAIRNESS
C
Sustainably Manage Natural Resources and Promote Equitable Distribution of Benefits

BE TRANSPARENT
D
Support Open Communication and Information Dissemination

SUPPORT RESEARCH
E
Promote Research and Information Development

DELEGATE AND EMPOWER
F
Devolution of Authority and Empowerment of Community Members

EARN TRUST
G
Work to Earn Public Trust and Legitimacy

EMBRACE FEEDBACK
H
Improve Effectiveness Through Monitoring Feedback, and Accountability Systems

PRACTICE LEADERSHIP
I
Practice Adaptive Leadership and Co-Management

DECIDE TOGETHER
J
Enable and Support Participatory Decision-Making Processes

STRENGTHEN THE FOUNDATION
K
Strengthen Enabling Conditions

RESOLVE CONFLICTS
L
Anticipate conflict and Work Towards Resolution and Cooperation

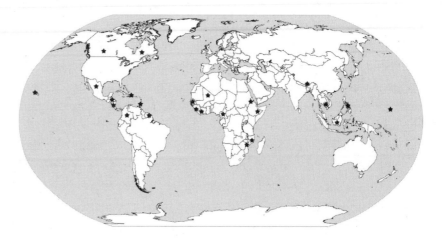

Figure 1.4. Location of initial research cases that were foundational for the Twelve Guiding Principles.

several years of work. Figure 1.4 shows the location of the initial 24 sites where local community data was analyzed. I see myself primarily as the messenger of this information, not the creator. The goal was to minimize any interpretation and overly broad statements, and to present, in an easily comprehensible form, what these community leaders and researcher were finding. The synthesis of the data forming the 12 principles is explained in each one of the core chapters. Two research papers that provide more technical background information are also available.[7]

How This Book Is Organized

This book includes 14 chapters. The following 12 chapters (2 through 13) each cover one Guiding Principle. Each chapter starts with a brief *Review of Guiding Principle*. This is followed by the *Research Corner* that provides five characteristics of the principle plus related research. I then offer one or two brief examples or stories to further illustrate the principle. Two *Case Studies* and shorter *Case-in-Points* are provided. Each chapter ends with *Notes from the Field*, which provide practical *Do's* and *Don'ts* in a list of suggestions or best practices.

The 25 case studies come from a wide range of communities that are beginning to thrive, and include those from regions with local economies considered developing, transitional, or developed, in the US and

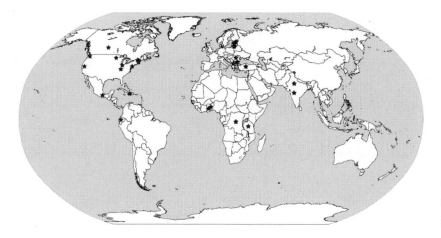

Figure 1.5. Location of the 44 sites of case studies and brief examples in the book.

other parts of the world. Each case study primarily illustrates the guiding principle discussed in the chapter. Also, other principles are noted where relevant. These case studies, from knowledgeable contributing authors, share specific and effective approaches on how a community can move from struggling towards thriving.

The last chapter, Chapter 14, provides a *Toolbox of Leadership Strategies*. This includes a *Collaborative Planning Approach* model for local convening, visioning, priority setting, planning, and implementation processes. I provide specific leadership tools and techniques for how to work effectively, step by step, with community groups. These approaches are based upon successful initiatives in the US and internationally. I end the book with a few concluding thoughts in the final section *The Way Forward*. Comprehensive End Notes for each chapter and an Index are provided in the back of the book.

CHAPTER 2

PRINCIPLE

A

Involve Everyone

Embrace Public Participation
and Mobilization of Stakeholders

> *Alone, we can do so little; together, we can do so much.*
>
> — HELEN KELLER

The Cornerstone of Society

Public participation is the cornerstone of healthy and sustainable communities. Similar to the first amendment to the US Constitution that includes freedom of speech, active involvement of the public is critical—no, crucial—to provide the conditions that hold a community together. Some say that expert-driven societies have efficiency in operations but I claim, and have experienced, that this top-down approach is very ineffective at meeting citizens' needs. Healthy systems of governance require dynamic feedback loops that are not possible without embracing public engagement including a broad diversity of stakeholders. I will share a brief story of what happens without allowing citizen feedback.

Watermelons and Toilets

One fall day in the 1990s, when I was working with the Bulgarian Ministry of the Environment on developing a new national solid waste policy, I saw a large pile of watermelons for sale in downtown Sophia. Next

19

INVOLVE EVERYONE

Embrace Public Participation and Mobilization of Stakeholders

Five Charcteristics

1. *Effective public participation is integral to all forms of healthy and sustainable communities and other community-based environmental initiatives.*
2. *Public participation processes should empower citizens and raise knowledge levels.*
3. *Public participation will directly impact public trust, confidence, and legitimization.*
4. *Seek diversity of stakeholders including citizens, NGOs, local and regional governments, private sector, and those with programmatic, operational, scientific, and legal knowledge.*
5. *Provide for participation of stakeholders at all stages: information gathering, consultation, visioning and goal setting, decision making, initiating action, participating in projects, and evaluation.*

This principle is cited by many authors as one of the most essential for successful local community-based initiatives and governance. Research data from communities from around the world identifies the importance of these characteristics for effectively involving the public and engaging stakeholders. Researchers have found that public participation should occur at all stages of local community planning and development.[1] Effective and inclusive public participation needs to include stakeholders with a wide range of knowledge, perspectives, and expertise such as programmatic, operational, scientific, and legal.[2] Local community leaders also need to work proactively to include the "non-experts" for they too have much to offer. Public and multi-stakeholder involvement should be included in all elements of local governance: information gathering, consultation, visioning and goal setting, decision making, initiating action, participating in projects, and evaluation. This involvement, to be effective, also needs to be transparent, open, inclusive, and fair.[3,4] Others have found that effective public participation will empower citizens if it involves all affected parties, including minorities, or those that may be marginalized in the community.[5,6,7]

to it was an equally large pile of toilets, also for sale. This odd juxta-position caught my eye. Having traveled back and forth to Bulgaria for nearly three years, I immediately knew why this was logical and it illustrates what happens in a top-down, expert-driven society, which all of Eastern Europe suffered under until 1990, when citizens drove out the totalitarian communist system.

The first time I used an Eastern European (Russian-Soviet inspired) toilet was in Latvia. The design appeared to be standard across Eastern Europe (and I assume Russia). The waste presented by the user sat on a small internal shelf above the water. The toilet, then kind of flushed, but did not have a vapor U-trap and vent that prevented the sewer fumes from entering the toilet room and house. The experts "solved" this unpleasant situation by having the toilet in a small separate room with an airtight door that they designed so that the fumes would not enter the home. Problem solved, or at least reduced, except when you had to open the door to use the toilet. There was no option for another toilet design. The efficiency of having only one toilet, mass-produced, ruled the day. Society at that time was not permitted to provide feed-back to the government. It is important to note that those who com-plained could find themselves banished to Siberia, as one monument in Madona, Latvia, attested by recognizing these brave individuals. Once the expert-driven, centrally planned social system collapsed and the residents were able to scrape up enough money, they bought Western toilets, along with a watermelon. They finally had freedom of choice.

Why Public Participation Is Essential

When I attended the Kennedy School of Government, a school that was dedicated to embracing the importance of public participation in democratic governance, the classic article by Sherry Arnstein[8] from 1969 on public participation was read and discussed by public admin-istration students. In her article, she describes an eight-rung ladder of citizen participation that moves from what is referred to as "manipula-tion" up to partnerships, delegated power, and finally to citizen control.

A change in mindset may be required to move from getting people on your side or selling them on your ideas (the lowest rung) to including local people in a substantive and meaningful manner, and sharing decision-making authority (the highest rungs). Community-based initiatives that are effective need to focus on working at the highest rungs of this ladder.

Involving everyone might seem like an easy and logical approach for those in formal and informal local community leadership roles, yet it is often more difficult than it sounds. It requires truly embracing public participation and proactive mobilization of a wide range of stakeholders, and perhaps even some that you have not always respected or were able to collaborate with in the past. Not an easy task!

Fully embracing public participation includes broad involvement; and sharing information and sharing knowledge means sharing power. This is, perhaps, the hardest challenge for formal leaders. Public participation is not just informing community members of what you, as a local leader, are doing; it requires involving members through all stages of local decision making and implementation. Try to be open and engaging in the early information-gathering phase, visioning, and goal setting, but don't stop there. If the goal is to initiate change that the community will fully embrace, you will need to involve community members throughout the decision-making process, ask and encourage them to participate in initiating actions, and finally, seek candid feedback throughout this change process.

Involving a wide diversity of stakeholders is also essential. Think about all those individuals who rarely are involved in local community efforts. Is it because they have small children and there is no childcare if they attend a meeting? Are they a disempowered minority that is anxious to participate? Are they seniors, physically challenged, or among those who cannot drive or attend late night meetings? Think about holding meetings or information-gathering sessions in places where community members often meet or other places that are accessible.

Finally, I have found that if you truly embrace public participation, you will have some challenging discussions, face some difficult issues, and the decision-making process is likely to be slower. However, the public's trust and confidence in local leaders will likely grow and there will be broader support for implementing changes that the community will accept and embrace.

Siting a Solid Waste Landfill

No one wants a landfill in their town or near their home. This was certainly true in the environmentally conscious state of Vermont. The term NIMBY (Not In My Back Yard) captures this response, when eleven local Vermont governments formed a regional solid waste district[9] to more effectively recycle waste, compost some waste, remove household hazardous waste for reprocessing, and educate its citizens on resource conservation. However, there was still some waste that needed to be buried (since incineration of this residual waste would create air pollution). Where would this waste be buried?

One common approach is to stealthily site a landfill then announce the decision (usually on a Friday afternoon). However, this regional community authority decided to undertake the challenge through a fully transparent public participation process. They set up a process to find the most environmentally appropriate location for a new landfill. Siting factors such as height above the water table, distance from a school or water body, and minimum distance from homes was debated and agreed to in a public session by representatives of all 11 towns in the region. Then engineers were hired to assess every acre of the 11 towns using the 15 or more siting factors to eliminate all but 20 potential sites. These sites were situated on a map, and then published in the regional newspaper and another public meeting was called to solicit input from all residents.

Yes, this was a large meeting, and some individuals even chose to bring along their lawyers. All information and documents, including from the engineers, were made public. The new regional solid waste board was committed to embrace public participation and transparency throughout this challenging process.

The meeting started with the Chair stating that this waste district was formed to help all 11 communities solve their waste problem. He quipped, "Please do not refer to this as our waste, it is your waste." He also asked those present to provide information about why a particular site would not be suitable for a landfill, information that they knew and waste district did not. By the end of a long, but civil meeting, all but a few sites had been eliminated, subject to confirming the newly received information. Within six months, all parties, including the town that would host the new landfill site, reached a unanimous agreement. The site was purchased and permitted.

This brief example illustrates that it is possible to face difficult and challenging community problems and collaboratively find sustainable approaches through an honest, transparent, and engaging public participation process. Solutions are then owned by all who have stepped forward to participate.

The Case Studies

The following two case studies focus on Principle A. The first case study, *Citizen-Powered Climate Action*, discusses how Keene, New Hampshire, has transformed over the last 40 years to become a leader in climate change adaptation and adopted a plan to become carbon-neutral by 2030. The second case study, *Development without Dependency*, shares the story of how—through partnerships, broad public participation, and self-direction—a rural community in Haiti is leading the way for other "communities living in poverty...[to] decide their own future and manage their own development."

Note, all applicable Guiding Principles are shown in ( ) at the end of a statement.

CASE STUDY	Citizen-Powered Climate Action, Keene, New Hampshire, USA

by Shaylin Salas

Prologue

This case study explores Keene's recent pursuit of a 100 percent renewable energy goal. Keene has become widely known for its creative and participatory problem-solving attributes in dealing with a variety of social, environmental, and economic issues. When communities feel like there is power to their voice, unprecedented action and change are more likely to follow. This high level of participation has, on many accounts, enhanced the effectiveness of city processes and inspired innovative, local solutions. Driven by extensive public engagement this robust energy goal is already on its way to becoming a reality.

Introduction

I arrived in Keene in January 2018 to begin an Environmental Studies master's program at Antioch University New England. I was nervous about making this move for many reasons, one being that I grew up in—and enjoy—larger urban cities. But to my surprise, Keene has a vibrant energy that is both exciting and comforting. The city is the social and financial hub of this rural region and the community here is active and strong. As an excerpt from the latest Comprehensive Master Plan explains:

> From the early decisions on placement of the community meeting house and planting elm trees in Central Square—now recognized as one of America's Best Great Public Spaces (2009 American Planning Association)—to addressing contemporary issues like climate change and community sustainability, the community [of Keene] continues to be recognized within the region, the state, the nation, and throughout the world for its innovative, practical efforts and solutions.[10]

In the past five years Keene has been recognized by national organizations for its climate change planning. The National Climate Assessment

2014, for example, highlights Keene for being the first pilot community in Local Governments for Sustainability's Climate Resilient Communities program for climate planning. It was acknowledged for its "long, steadfast history of climate protection."[11] Similarly, the US Climate Toolkit 2017 refers to Keene as a leader in planning for climate change and extreme weather.[12] But what is it about the culture of this city that enables it to innovate locally relevant climate change solutions?

Although small (approximately 24,000 residents), Keene is not a suburb of somewhere else. It is its own place. It sits in a valley surrounded by hills, and there are no major highways leading to it. Situated over an hour's drive away from the state's larger and more industrial cities, Keene is the economic and cultural center of the Monadnock region's population of over 100,000 people. This role has promoted a sense of self-reliance that has effectively enabled community members to use their voice and power to drive community livelihoods and social vitality.

General Overview

From what I have gathered, Keene has nurtured open and collaborative public participation for decades. In the 1970s, through the co-leadership of its city manager, mayor, city council, and many dedicated citizens, the community transformed its downtown from having many empty store fronts, deteriorating buildings and sidewalks, and few visitors to a thriving city center that is now the envy of most small cities. Individuals and community groups funded the new trees that line both sides of its wide Main Street and now, all summer long, outdoor cafés and restaurants serve patrons under their shade. Most recently, in 2017, a community action group organized a city-wide campaign that mobilized a range of residents and organizations through active outreach and public events to urge city council to adopt courageous climate and energy goals. Two years later, Keene council passed the group's sustainable energy resolution. The resolution was a community-wide commitment to pursuing a 100 percent renewable energy transition

Credit: Patricia Martin

Figure 2.1. The Clean Energy Team at city hall on the night Keene city council passed the sustainable energy resolution.

which will eliminate all fossil fuel use for electricity by 2030 and for everything else such as heat and transportation by 2050.

This resolution rests on the foundation of about 20 years of work to increase community resilience and climate change mitigation. In the late 1990s, Keene began focusing efforts toward building energy efficiency and reducing greenhouse gas emissions. The city recognized that these actions provide many local benefits, including decreasing air pollution and reducing energy costs. So, in 2000 Keene joined more than 300 cities and counties around the world in the Cities for Climate Protection Campaign and committed to greenhouse gas emission reduction targets. In addition, the city has replaced all of their traffic signals, airport beacons, parking facility, and downtown street lights with light-emitting diode (LED) light fixtures. They have built four roundabouts to improve traffic flow and reduce idle time. They have designed a methane recovery system at the landfill which powers the recycling center. They have designed tax breaks for residential wood, wind, and solar installations. Just months ago, they installed 2,010 solar panels on the Public Works building. They have an ongoing internal paper recycling program as well as an anti-idling program. And lastly, they have been using hybrid vehicles in the city fleets for over 14 years.

Moreover, Keene was the first in the state to adopt a Climate Action Plan (2004) and one of the first in the nation to adopt a Climate Adaptation Plan (2007). These projects, and dozens more, represent the ways that Keene has contributed to the growth in awareness and responses to climate change at the regional, state, and federal level.

I came to Keene with a passion for climate justice, and a hope to be involved in the local renewable energy movement. That opportunity presented itself early last year at a public screening of the 2018 *Fossil Free Fast* conference. At the end of the screening, a member of a local community group (called the Clean Energy Team) stood up and announced their related mission and how to get involved. It turned out that their next meeting was the following evening. I went, of course. By the end of it, I was completely hooked on their vision of achieving 100 percent renewable energy for this region and inspired by their small but mighty group. In under two years, this team had built a coalition, begun a city-wide campaign, designed the sustainable energy resolution for Keene, and then successfully got it passed.

Goals, Approaches, and Challenges

The goal of this effort was to design a bold, community-driven response to the challenges of climate change. The Clean Energy Team, initially called the "Climate Action Team," changed their name after seeing potential in the renewable energy commitments emerging around the world. Moreover, such a commitment could complement the city's existing climate and energy projects. The team started by talking to local individuals and organizations to find out if a 100 percent renewable energy goal was something that the community could get behind (A-B-D). After receiving a clear majority response of interest, the team went on to identify potential allies. They approached each potential ally seeking to learn about their thoughts on and experiences with clean energy, while also asking for endorsements to the 100 percent vision (B-H-K). After one year, the team had collected hundreds of signatures of support, 11 endorsement letters from various organizations, and a solid network of community partners.

This partnership approach is similar to that of the energy plan development thus far. The city's first step was to build relationships with neighboring towns setting similar energy goals and, at the same time, nurture an inclusive and engaging local planning process (A-B-J). City staff dedicated time to visit these nearby towns to learn about their process. They also hired an intern (me) to design the communications and outreach plan as well as kick-start some of the engagement activities. An early activity included conducting community interviews (A-D-H). Staff and community partners working closely on the plan put together a list of contacts for four broad energy consumer categories: residents, businesses, housing providers, and institutions. We developed these categories based on our assessment of who and what we had in our city and the belief that they were representative of our key stakeholders. Together we built an interview design and set of questions; then I went out to conduct the interviews. (E-H).

In climate-related community and partnership building efforts, there should be careful consideration of inclusivity and of the specific communities that are impacted by change the most (A-C-G-K-L).[13] To apply this in my work, I used the federal Environmental Protection Agency's Environmental Justice Screening and Mapping Tool.[14] The tool combines US environmental and demographic information to determine which community groups in which locations are most vulnerable to climate and environmental changes. In Keene, I found that these groups included the elderly (individuals over the age 64) and low-income households. I shared this information with city staff and community partners, and then did my best to include representatives of these groups in the interview and other outreach processes (D-E-K-L). So far, interview results have been overwhelmingly positive as well as informative. Additional engagement methods for this effort include online outreach, a general public survey, stakeholder focus groups, public community meetings, and free educational workshops.

One challenge that we have encountered has been in reaching a critical stakeholder group: landlords. Considering that 41 percent of Keene residents rent their homes,[15] developing a specific strategy for local landlords and their tenants is going to be crucial to serving this community's residents. We are realizing that the summer season is not an ideal time to meet with this group because of planned vacations, summer renovations, and preparations for students arriving for the upcoming school year. Nonetheless, with a tight time frame on the development of this plan (two years), we have been pushing hard on this effort. I have made many phone calls, sent dozens of emails, and met with a number of local landlords in hope of reaching a representative group. This work is ongoing, but we are gradually making contact with more and more of the city's landlords.

Outcomes

Overall, I was pleasantly surprised by how easy it was to meet and interview community members. For two months, I was averaging three interviews per week. I found that people were not just willing to talk with me, but excited to learn and collaborate in the process. The interviews have brought two important results thus far: (1) greater shared knowledge about community needs and energy-sourcing, and (2) stronger relationships. When I asked a community member how the city could help her company in reaching the energy goals she said, "I guess it's more us being more involved with the meetings and kept informed on what the city needs from us to assist with the transition."

Credit: Jim Murphy

Similarly, I was told by the representative of one community organization, "If the city wants to reach out to us to be part of a group that pulls together a strategic plan or any other work they have to do, we'll try to be there the best we can. We definitely support it!" And a representative of a business networking organization offered, "If you need help reaching anyone…just let me know, and we are happy to connect you." I left nearly all of my interviews encouraged by the support and strong willingness to participate.

In summary, through this experience I have learned the power of people who feel that they have a voice in their community. And when I say "people" I mean the small and local business owners, the non-profits dedicated to serving low-income families, the new homeowner devoted to environmental sustainability while living paycheck-to-paycheck, and the champions that fight for a better tomorrow after their day jobs end. Individually they are powerful. Together they are an immovable force.

Reflections on Principle A: Involve Everyone

In Keene, community voice and participation bring direct results and, often, a lasting impact. Public engagement is not only welcomed but encouraged and regularly occurs at multiple stages of any formal city process. This does not mean that decisions are easily arrived at or

Figure 2.2. The 2017 Climate Rally hosted in Keene Central Square.

that certain issues do not reveal factions and discord. Nonetheless, in the year and a half that I have witnessed this city in action, it is clear that Keene citizens are empowered by the accessibility of their local government and the tangible power that their voice holds. Moreover, strong civic participation has fostered a sense of trust, compassion, and confidence among this community. Whether it is climate action or another issue, you will find that the people are the true source of effective planning, implementation, and positive change.

 CASE STUDY | **Development without Dependency, Gran Sous, La Gonave, Haiti**

by Chad Bissonnette and Heather Heckel

Prologue

The collaboration between Roots of Development (Roots), a US-based NGO, and the Peasant Association for the Development and Advancement of Gran Sous (APDAG), highlights the value of pursuing sustainable development through broad community participation. Roots and APDAG seek to shift away from the dependency many communities have on international aid and focus more on local capacity building and development that is designed, managed, and sustained locally.

Through this process, the rural community of Gran Sous, on the island of La Gonave, Haiti, has achieved access to clean water, solar-powered energy, enhanced resilience, and the opening of multiple businesses. This case highlights our recommendations for a community empowerment process.

Introduction and General Overview

One evening, after a new clean water system had been constructed by the community, I (Chad here) took a walk down to visit it. Arriving at the water facility, I found an older man sitting in a chair. After greetings, he shared that he had decided to "watch over the water." The community-driven process of deciding to prioritize water, removing old debris-filled pipes, and creating a spring water facility that would serve over 10,000 residents, had taken nearly a year. But knowing someone cared enough to watch over the water was the moment I was certain that we had created genuine community ownership and sustainable development.

In 2007, I moved to Gran Sous following a study abroad visit. Over time, I observed international organizations trying to address varied development challenges. Their approaches often began with a "community consultation," followed by large infrastructure projects using foreign staff and supplies. Unfortunately, the projects were often underutilized and poorly maintained.

I also observed Gran Sous' strengths. Social capital and resilience were strong, with community members supporting each other in daily life and during times of crisis. Though access to quality formal education was low, knowledge of culture, community, and geography was high.

Conversations with community members about their development goals and community strengths led to the founding of APDAG and Roots. Together, we decided to pursue the vision of "a world in which the very communities living in poverty are the ones leading the fight against it; a world in which impoverished communities decide their own future and manage their own development."

Goals, Approaches, Challenges, and Outcomes

The water project began with community volunteers going door to door to invite everyone to participate in goal-setting discussions (A). Together, the community selected clean water as their first priority and began studying clean water access and organizing community members for construction (J-E). Roots provided funding for materials and hiring of technical engineers.

During the water project, community members decided to establish a formal community association they called the Peasant Association for the Development and Advancement of Gran Sous (APDAG). Members

Figure 2.3. Community members install clean water system in Gran Sous.

Credit: Chad Bissonnette

began participating in a variety of capacity-building trainings on topics like community organizing, conflict resolution, and effective project management.

As with many groups, APDAG faced inclusion challenges. Women were especially underrepresented, facing time and cultural barriers to volunteering. APDAG leaders consulted with women in the community to identify paths for broader participation, leading to the formation of a women's committee called GFDAG.

Additionally, APDAG encouraged broad community participation and awareness by:

- publicly sharing meeting notes, project proposals, budgets, and inviting community members to participate in evaluations
- striving for consensus decision making
- establishing multiple committees to engage community members with different interests
- collecting data on gender and age of training participants

Goal Setting

In the community empowerment model, goal setting is a long-term process, involving extensive discussions within the community and among partners. Goals may change to reflect new circumstances and learning. Goal setting includes a focus upon local leadership and local sustainability.

For example, in 2009, the women's committee considered providing scholarships for school fees. Through discussions, the community realized it could only maintain scholarships with foreign donations. So the group reconsidered the goal, resulting in a decision to open a women-run community store. The 85 Women's Committee members began with business development trainings, conducted by the Haitian NGO, Women in Democracy. This project provided:

- skill building for women staff including budgeting and management
- local access to supplies
- a source of funding for school fees—addressing the original challenge sustainably
- role modeling of entrepreneurial opportunities

One member of the women's group, Carline, reflected on how this experience changed her: "I was scared of a computer. Didn't want to even touch it. Now, whether it be Microsoft Word, Excel, etc., I can manage myself. And won't let the opportunity pass me by."

Roots' funding focuses on this community-investment process, emphasizing capacity-building trainings and initial investments that empower the community to sustain projects long-term. Roots seeks to avoid a donor-driven mentality, instead advocating that:

> The level of priority a project is given, or the way a project is carried out should not depend on the amount of money the supporting organization or institution is willing to allocate to it. Instead, the amount of money allocated to the project should depend on the amount necessary to complete the desired project, in its entirety and in a way that it is most effective.

Credit: Chad Bissonnette

Figure 2.4. Members of the Women's Committee participating in a training in Gran Sous.

Challenges

The community-led development model faces several challenges. First, a focus on empowerment processes requires significant time. Second, the number of people reached is relatively small compared with traditional international aid. Third, the value of community investment and capacity building can be difficult to explain to donors. This challenge is intensified by pressure to produce data-driven monitoring and evaluation. (How does one measure the long-term impacts of training 85 women in business skills or the values of community discussions and participation?) Fourth, ensuring inclusive participation can challenge traditional cultural practices and it can take years to fully involve under-represented populations.

Finally, as with any community, interpersonal dynamics and leadership issues arise and can impede progress. As APDAG has become well known, their "community" is expanding as they interact with a wide range of partners. Maintaining a focus on the local association's leadership and ensuring that power is not ceded to outsiders is an ongoing challenge.

Outcomes

Together, the communities have had significant development achievements including clean water, sanitation, opening of local businesses, solar power systems, internet access, housing construction, and significant growth in professional capacity. This process has strengthened social ties, trust, women's leadership, civic engagement, and pride (G-I). Additionally, communities have sought and built partnerships with government leaders, nonprofit organizations, businesses, and other Haitian stakeholders (B).

An unanticipated outcome was the community's increased resilience to environmental and political instability. The resilience benefits of local communities managing their own development became clear after the devastating 2010 earthquake. APDAG's personal connections enabled the purchase of food and supplies immediately after the crisis. And distribution was handled within the community; leaders identified those in need using local knowledge. Conflict, delays, and a sense of desperation were absent in Gran Sous and neighboring communities, because local knowledge and local leadership were used to plan emergency relief and follow-up with those most impacted. Involving the whole community and diverse stakeholders (A) led to the ability to adapt and learn in times of crisis (I).

Further evidence of success is illustrated by requests from neighboring communities to participate in their own self-development paths. In 2019, Roots is working with leaders from all 11 counties that make up La Gonave, representing the 100,000 residents that reside on the island. Some communities are collaborating to create larger economic opportunities including a plastic waste recycling business partnership that removed over 2,000 pounds of plastic waste in May 2019. Association leaders have also been invited to share their approach with mainland communities.

Scaling-up was facilitated by:

- social ties between communities and personal observations of projects

- intentional sharing of knowledge and lessons learned by both Roots and APDAG
- each community developing their own association
- long-term commitment and financial support from Roots

Reflections on Principle A: Involve Everyone

APDAG's work illustrates the importance of involving a broad range of community members consistently throughout the development process (A). It also highlights that effective public participation enhances the community's ability to work together (B), to be transparent (C), to empower and build skills (F), and to learn and adapt (I).

Core lessons include:

- Public participation and participatory decision making, building on social capital and local knowledge, is key to effective project implementation and sustainability.
- Effective community engagement requires intentional inclusion of under-represented populations.
- The process of enabling communities to drive their own development involves community discussions, collective goal setting, capacity trainings, and partner collaboration.
- Outcomes may be difficult to quantify or "market" to donors.
- Organic scaling-up can occur through relationships among communities and intentional sharing of best practices.
- This community-driven process requires funding and resources for capacity building, in this case provided by an external partner.

Principle A—Involve Everyone

We offer some *Do's* and *Don'ts* for Principle A: Involve Everyone. Some of these words of advice from our colleagues who have worked for many years with local communities may also apply to other principles. Please recognize that they may not all be appropriate for every situation of involving community members in change initiatives.

Do (Or Consider Doing)

- Develop a full list of stakeholders and ask others, "Who is missing?" Don't forget youth, seniors, young parents, minority groups, those who are physically limited, and competitors.
- In seeking involvement with others, think about sharing information with them at places they frequent, such as the senior center, community kitchen or food shelf, local school, places of worship, library, etc.
- Try to do outreach to community members through multiple community networks and organizations, and through multiple approaches, such as websites, letters, news articles, newsletters, and even talking to citizens at the local recycling center. If community members hear about events or new initiatives from three different sources, they are more likely to participate.
- Include community members at the beginning and throughout a new initiative.
- Seek feedback through different approaches that allow those who feel uncomfortable or insecure to participate (anonymous feedback forms, electronic attendance, etc.).
- At public input meetings, listen!

Don't (Or Think Twice)

- Don't claim or imply that you have all the answers (unless you truly do…which is quite unlikely).
- Don't assume an email or mass mailing to "everyone" will get a significant number of individuals to show up, especially those who are not the same old characters. A neighbor asking a neighbor is usually far more effective that the local government extending a broad generic invitation.
- Don't use jargon or acronyms. This makes those "out of the know" feel inadequate and frustrated.
- If holding a public hearing or listening session, make sure those with formal authority are not sitting high on a stage or behind a large table. The physical space will directly impact the quality of community members' sharing and feedback.
- Carefully design the agenda and process so that all community members will have a timely opportunity to share their thoughts. Avoid long technical presentations.

CHAPTER 3

Work Together

Build Social Capital and Collaborative Partnerships

> *Community connectedness is not just about warm fuzzy tales of civic triumph. In measurable and well-documented ways, social capital makes an enormous difference in our lives.... Social capital makes us smarter, healthier, safer, richer, and better able to govern a just and stable democracy.*
>
> — ROBERT PUTNAM

Collaborative Partnerships

Working together. This seems so obvious and essential for a community to thrive, yet it is not always easy. I hope to share a few ideas along with a brief story on how this can be achieved drawing upon the concepts of social capital and collaborative partnerships. Collaborative partnerships can serve as a catalyst for building social capital and healthy vital communities. Nearly all successful community building efforts that I have been involved with over the last few decades had a foundation of collaborative partnerships. These partnerships were also able to leverage and share resources, share knowledge and skills, and collectively enhance the outcomes of our efforts.

WORK TOGETHER

B

Build Social Capital and Collaborative Partnerships

Five Characteristics

1. *Networks and partnerships are integral to building social capital and serve as a catalyst to finding innovative strategies and solutions.*
2. *Collaborative partnerships are key to leveraging resources and supporting implementation.*
3. *Stakeholder trainings, workshops, and other collaborative learning opportunities can build social capital and commitment.*
4. *Seeking agreement among key environmental NGOs, governments, and private sector to work collaboratively and to share resources and responsibilities is paramount.*
5. *Ownership by community members and other stakeholders enhances design, implementation, and operation, supports cohesion, and encourages long-term commitment.*

Social capital, also referred to as "community-based capacity,"[2] describes strong social networks, healthy community norms, and trust between community members.[3] Social capital is enhanced through participatory processes that allow the community to learn together as well as engage in all aspects of communal projects or decisions. Participatory visioning, problem solving, and decision making will oftentimes encourage the building of trust among community members and a sense of local ownership.[4]

The importance of cultivating social capital and developing collaborative partnerships is frequently cited as an attribute of successful initiatives. They are critical in leveraging resources and supporting appropriate implementation.[5] Collaborative partnerships can be formed through governmental or organizational agreements with the intent of sharing resources and responsibilities. These partnerships have the potential to be the source of efficient and innovative strategies.[6]

Social Capital—The Social Glue
That Holds the Community Together

We have found that you cannot "get" social capital for a community. It must be grown. Social capital is a term coined by Robert Putnam from his study of recovering post-World War II Italian communities. On his website, Dr. Putnam states: "The central premise of social capital is that social networks have value. Social capital refers to the collective value of all 'social networks' and the inclinations that arise from these networks to do things for each other."[1] Some common examples include building a community garden or a village playground, collaboratively planning a bike path, or constructing a greenhouse for a retirement center. It is essential that any social capital building activity or event represent all stakeholders of the community including the minority population, the elderly, youth, newcomers, and others.

We Can Do It Ourselves: A New High School Greenhouse

My local regional high school needed a new greenhouse to serve the growing number of students interested in horticulture and agriculture. Unfortunately, several ballot efforts to raise the necessary money from taxpayers failed. Instead of giving up, community leaders decided that we would meet this need by fundraising and building it ourselves. It took many organizers, fundraising efforts, planning sessions with local builders, and hundreds of volunteers. Then, during one intensive weekend, people of all ages and abilities came together and built a new greenhouse and agriculture classroom. Not only did the agriculture department gain an educational resource it urgently needed, but also the community's social capital grew. The next ballot request for school improvements, including energy conservation retrofits, was easily passed.

Leveraging Resources
and Supporting Implementation

Collaborative partnerships can bring resources, connections, innovative and creative ideas, and other benefits to a new community effort. However, we suggest that you approach each new partnership as cautiously as you might approach dating. The partnership can be life transforming or can quickly go sour. We have found that it is essential that each partner shares similar core values and that each needs to receive both a benefit from the partnership, as well as provide a tangible contribution to the overall effort.

Under "Research Corner" you can find a list of the specific characteristics of this Guiding Principle along with what other researchers have found. I will share a short example of the importance of building social capital and collaborative partnerships in the effort to build a healthier and more vital community. What follows is a brief story of building social capital and a broad collaborative effort to convert the town of Hartford's old leaching dump into an Environmental Community Center for Recycling and Waste Management (nicknamed by town residents *The Un-Shopping Center*[7]) without drawing upon the financial support of property tax revenues.

Vermont's First Un-Shopping Center

It was a cold Vermont Saturday morning in January, about 15 degrees Fahrenheit with some light snow flurries when the new Un-Shopping Center was dedicated. Rather than the typical three or four local officials anticipated at most public building dedications, approximately 1,200 residents were present in a celebratory mood. Why? Because by incorporating the creativity of our local citizens and youth into the fabric of this new center, they had gained ownership. It was *their* Community Center for Recycling, and many citizens expressed a personal joy for their contributions as well as offering a pledge to actively participate. Now, 25 years later, as I reflect on this positive event, I realize that it was all because of the project team's dedication and commitment to social capital and collaborative partnership development during the previous five years. Here are a few milestones along the way that illustrate the dedication of these community citizen-leaders.

It began when the engineers who were hired to evaluate the town dump stated that the do-nothing option was no longer available. The old landfill had to be closed in the near future at a cost of over one million dollars. This amount of money was neither planned for nor available. As a town administrator, I realized that this crisis could be an opportunity to leverage change and begin a comprehensive recycling program. Unfortunately, only one member of the local town council had any interest in recycling. To facilitate a major paradigm shift, we looked to community members to form a guiding team to explore options, build support for change, and lead the community in the direction that they decided. This group, including a citizen leader of a local condo association, a local business leader, an environmental educator, a regional planner, a local recycling business owner, and many regular citizens who wanted change, came together to plan a better future.

Six months later they filled a public hearing room to present their ideas to the Board of Selectmen (town council). Although, at the beginning of the meeting, 80 percent of the Board expressed no interest in recycling, by the close of the testimony, the proposed radical change was unanimously endorsed by the Board. The elected leaders were following the citizens who had gained a broad authorizing environment (or informal authority) through building social capital and new partnerships. This citizen leadership group had gained ownership of their proposed approach to move towards zero waste and to include all of the citizens of the community in the process.

Soon hundreds of citizens, organized into neighborhood recycling teams, were going door-to-door asking their neighbors to participate in the new curbside recycling and to support the new Un-Shopping Center that would include composting, recycling, the Good Bye (reuse) Store, and the management of household hazardous waste. But even more importantly, over a thousand school-age children and youth were involved.[8] They developed the signs, artwork, and information for the new center. All of these young people would share in the "ownership" of this new center.

Throughout this process it was critical for those in charge of building the center (town managers, officials, and even the planning team itself) to give up some control if they really wanted others to step up. One illustration of sharing decision making is when the adults thought that the entry to the education center should show the problem by having artwork depicting garbage covering the walls. The high school students, who were to do this artwork, responded by stating, "You said this is our project to plan and complete. We do not want to show garbage, we want the artwork to illustrate a tropical rain forest with the animals that we want to protect." Those in charge responded, "This is your project, so yes!" The result was an incredible mural of a rain forest that became the gem of the center! Today, this center is still serving the community, 25 years after its opening, and is still valued by the community members.

In closing, I believe that the social capital and collaborative partnerships that were nourished and grew through this effort have continued on to today. This social glue helps hold the community together, including during difficult times, and has been essential in helping to address other needs. Since that time, this community has spearheaded innovative programs for housing for the homeless, energy conservation, urban renewal, education, support for at-risk families with children, and bikeways that could not have been adequately addressed by the staff of limited local government and through property taxes alone.

The Case Studies

The following two case studies both include community gardening. One case study from Saskatchewan, Canada, explains how a small community garden project expanded to provide, not only fresh vegetables to local community members, but also a series of educational opportunities that created a network of support for new immigrants. The other case study from the Appalachian region in Kentucky demonstrates how dedication to collaboration at local and regional levels and working with multiple partner sites can help a struggling region to thrive, one garden at a time.

CASE STUDY	Community Gardens: An Immigrant Story of Food Sovereignty in Saskatoon, Saskatchewan, Canada

by Ranjan Datta and Jebunnessa Chapola

Prologue

Food insecurity within immigrant and refugee communities in North America is a significant challenge. New immigrants and refugee communities experience higher rates of food insecurity than any other immigrant or non-immigrant community. This case study offers insights from a community-based garden, providing tangible strategies for newcomers (including immigrants and refugees), and other vulnerable or marginalized populations to build community and community connections.

Introduction and General Overview

Canada receives approximately 330,000 new permanent residents each year and recent immigrants are more likely to be food insecure than non-immigrant households.[9,10] Food security is linked to how immigrants perceive membership, reconstruct identity, and integrate successfully.[11] According to Food Secure Canada quoting La Via Campesina, "Food Sovereignty is the right of peoples to healthy and culturally appropriate food produced through ecological sound and sustainable methods, and their right to define their own food and agricultural systems." The Food and Agriculture (FAO) Organization of the United Nations has defined food sovereignty as "a basic human right…[It] is a precondition to genuine food security."[12] David Boult, a community-based food security researcher,[13] defines food security as a condition where all community residents obtain a safe, culturally acceptable, nutritionally adequate diet through a sustainable food system that maximizes community self-reliance and social justice.[14] The impact of food insecurity on new immigrant youth is particularly troubling, as 50 percent of all new immigrant and refugee children face it on a regular basis.[15] The health implications stemming from these conditions are many, including increased rates of anemia, delayed physical and social development, high prevalence of diabetes, and increased rates of obesity.[16,17]

The vision of our cross-cultural community garden was to develop community. By starting small and growing steadily, we were able to grow our garden and our knowledge. In 2012, we started with ten garden plots and gardeners from three different countries: 10 families, 18 adults, and 5 children. By 2018, our garden space had extended to 120 garden plots with over 25 countries and cultures represented among members, including 400 university students (single, married without children, and parents) and 60 children. Another six sharing plots were created: two for sharing foods with local people, two for sharing with other students, and two for neighbors without access to garden space. Many of the children were there daily, particularly during weekends and the three months of summer when schools are closed. Our gardening-affiliated activities (i.e., various informal educational workshops and social events) have brought us into contact with many volunteers, educators, Indigenous elders, and scholars from the University of Saskatchewan. The garden, situated in the city of Saskatoon, provides a collaborative space to residents living in university-owned apartments on campus.

Goals, Approaches, Challenges, and Outcomes
Goals

As international students and new immigrants in Canada, our love and appreciation for the process of gardening and for the cultivation of community inspired us to begin this program. We also sought to address the ways that we engaged with our community garden in light of poverty, lack of food, isolation from a community of people, severe weather, cultural shock, and the passion for food sovereignty which we have been carrying with us from our childhood (C-L-K). We have been involved with this garden, along with our children, for the last eight years. Using Participatory Action Research (PAR) as a research methodology, this study was developed from eight years of relational cross-cultural community garden activities.[18,19] Our goal is to create a shared space where children and adults grow their own food, learn how to create food security in their own community, and share their cross-cultural learning with larger communities (A-B-J-K).

Approaches

1. Seeking Indigenous Knowledge in Community

Redefining food sovereignty through the building of meaningful relationships with Indigenous communities has been a major focus of our work. Learning Indigenous histories and the importance of native plants from Indigenous elders, learning about how to care for our land, grow food, build and maintain community networks, and hearing the stories that many Indigenous elders, knowledge keepers, and youths shared when they visited our garden has changed the way we grow our food. We have learned that we are all guests here. It is our responsibility as newcomers to know the Indigenous people of this land, and show gratitude for their sharing their land with us while offering friendship to live here peacefully.

2. Educational Programs

Providing the space and educational resources for our community to grow food has had incredible impacts. For instance, one gardener said: "I spent ten dollars to buy seeds from the superstore. In the long run our small size of plot produced more than $200 worth of fresh vegetables." Another gardener commented, "We could not afford to buy fresh vegetables from the superstore. I was sad for our children that they are not getting enough nutrients due to poverty. However, the community garden gave us the access into organic, fresh vegetables. We could preserve our home-grown vegetables for six months." Year-long garden activities and engagements with the food production system ensure food sovereignty.

3. Cross-Cultural Participatory Activities

Cross-cultural community garden activities are a fantastic way to forge relationships between new immigrants, Indigenous, and non-Indigenous people. By creating common experiences between gardeners, our community garden transfers knowledge one to another, deepening understanding. We as coordinators, with the help of other gardeners, initiated many cross-cultural participatory activities (singing, dancing, recitation, sharing positive experiences about gardening, etc.). We have learned that garden activities can teach us all how to deal, work, and interact with people from different cultures. Having cross-cultural activities in the garden, where we educate ourselves and others, helps us all to better understand and respect each other. For instance, for the past eight years our community garden's year-end, cross-cultural harvest celebration (Figures 3.1 and 3.2), has exposed the community to the cross-cultural heritage of the world, with people sharing about their diverse food culture. Celebrating traditional foods is an important way to connect with culture and create a sense of belonging.

Challenges

There were many barriers and challenges, both for students and for new immigrant community members. We have seen that many new immigrants and international students are not able to spend adequate time working in their garden because they are involved with multiple "survival" jobs to feed their families and pay tuition and fees. It is difficult for gardeners to keep up the enthusiasm due to many of life's challenges. By encouraging one another, community gardeners, community activists, and scholars are overcoming these challenges, and supporting each other to hope, engage, increase participation, and continue to build food sovereignty in this little corner of the world (J-D-I-F-C).

Additional challenges include:
- It takes a long time to build trustful relationships among gardeners.
- Continuous inspiration is needed from each other for growing foods, building networks, and promoting engagement.
- Funding is also needed to facilitate various activities in the garden.

Outcomes

Building meaningful relationships with Indigenous communities, creating a shared educational space, developing our own food sovereignty, and empowering the community are a few of the outcomes of our community garden program (L-E-F).

Credit: Ranjan Datta

Figure 3.1. Year-ending cross-cultural harvest celebration.

Food sovereignty through a community garden is not only a tool for food security, but also a source of informal and formal educational spaces that provide information about the societal, social, and psychological benefits of having community garden access for people. For instance, one of the children gardening with us said, "We have a kid's plot where I learned to dig the soil, and make compost by myself.... I know most of the seeds' names and saw the process of food growing since I was three years old." And a gardener immigrant from Saudi Arabia shared: "We learned to eat exotic herbs, for example: dandelion tea and dandelion flower salad from a community activist." Clearly, the act of engaging with food, and engaging with those who know a lot about food, makes for meaningful connection.

Food sovereignty, for us, is not just about growing food. It is also an opportunity to advocate for community empowerment. For example, we've both served as cultural coordinators of this garden for five years, and have had numerous opportunities to lead community-based activities in our city and beyond, including:

- community engaged planting (community members come together to discuss, learn, and sow different types of plants)
- land-based education for children (kids learn directly from grand-

Credit: Ranjan Datta

Figure 3.2. Community gardeners with harvests.

parents and Indigenous knowledge keepers about the importance of native plants, and culturally significant stories about species of plants and insects)

• art

• women's empowerment (immigrant women have decision-making power regarding their choice of food, teaching their children about the land, networking opportunities, and sharing food)

Reflections on Principle B: Work Together

Our cross-cultural community garden helped us not only create a new community of food security, but also created opportunities for many other community-based activities within the university community and beyond (growing food together, learning together, networking, and sharing). These activities have raised awareness about why we grow our own foods and how the process of growing food is interconnected with our learning, networking, and creating food sovereignty, as well as being vital in creating an alternative model for producing food. We learned that an active community gardener does not need to depend on superstore or market-produced food only, and they are ensured access to healthy and safe food through this model. Achieving food sovereignty requires knowing how to grow food, understanding the importance of growing food, having the awareness of cross-cultural community and its inherent value, and having the willingness to learn.[20] Our garden helped us learn these principles first hand. As a new immigrant family with three little children, we did not know the potential social learning benefit of this effort. Over time, however, our community garden helped us grow not only our own healthy foods, but our understanding of what community can be.

The valuable takeaway lessons are that community gardening not only develops gardening skills but also encourages the development of other community-based activities, enhancing cross-cultural networking skills, and raising the awareness of food sovereignty. Together, we found ways to think about and work for localizing food systems, value food producers, work with nature, transfer the food-producing knowledge to the next generation, and make decisions locally. We now know one approach that we can make positive change through and bring hope into our lives and the lives of our community members.

CASE STUDY | Grow Appalachia and Rural Community Gardening, Kentucky, USA

by Elyzabeth W. Engle

Prologue

In the past century, the industries and economies of rural America have undergone rapid changes. This has resulted in social, economic, and environmental consequences for rural families and community well-being.[21,22] The region of central Appalachia exemplifies many of these challenges, including high rates of persistent poverty, outmigration, food insecurity, human health issues, social stigmatization, and environmental degradation.[23,24]

Although daunting, these challenges are embraced as opportunities for action by many grassroots initiatives across the region.[25,26] One such initiative is the Grow Appalachia program headquartered in Berea, Kentucky, which promotes community food security and economic building across the six-state region of central Appalachia. Through traditional foodways and organic agriculture, Grow Appalachia and its partners form community-driven programs and resource-sharing networks to empower local people and places.

Introduction

Appalachia covers 700,000 square miles of the eastern United States, stretching along the Appalachian Mountain range from northern Alabama to southern New York.[27] Since the 1960s, this region has been the target of several federal programs focused on economic development and poverty alleviation. While some progress has been made overall, these programs and policies have also intensified social, economic, and environmental inequalities within the central Appalachian coalfields of southern West Virginia, eastern Kentucky and Tennessee, and southwest Virginia.[28,29] To address these issues, a number of grassroots initiatives have arisen throughout the region[30] (C).

While searching for an applied research project on the community development outcomes of rural, localized food systems, I was introduced to Grow Appalachia. This project ended up being the foundation of my doctoral dissertation research in Rural Sociology and the Human Dimensions of Natural Resources at Penn State University (2016–2018).

The organization's directors kindly invited me to observe their annual gathering of garden program site coordinators in February 2016. This marked the beginning of a multiyear research partnership in which I have conducted interviews, field observations, and program-wide surveys to capture how Grow Appalachia is contributing to this region's efforts in sustainable growth. The reflections shared here evolved from that collaborative research process.

Grow Appalachia was founded in 2009 in partnership with John Paul DeJoria's Peace, Love & Happiness Foundation and Berea College, a liberal arts college nestled in the foothills of Appalachia. Grow Appalachia is a Strategic Initiative of Berea College with a mission to "help as many Appalachian families grow as much of their own food as possible." Their efforts foster new social and economic opportunities through promotion of organic gardening and heart-healthy food practices, income and market creation, and a rejuvenation of the region's historical ties to subsistence agriculture.[31]

Grow Appalachia started with five partnering organizations, or "partner sites." Each partner site is a place-based nonprofit organization that utilizes Grow Appalachia resources to build local gardening programs. During the year of our initial study (2016–2017), Grow

Appalachia had 32 partner sites located throughout the Appalachian regions of six different states: Kentucky, North Carolina, Ohio, Tennessee, West Virginia, and Virginia. They included social service organizations, educational institutions, cultural heritage centers, and economic development organizations (A-B). Each partner site engaged anywhere from 10 to 150 households in their gardening program.

In 2016 alone, Grow Appalachia distributed $611,000 in resources to 1,300 families in 61 Central Appalachian counties. In turn, these families produced an estimated 650,000 pounds of organic produce to be consumed fresh at home, preserved for winter months, or shared with family, neighbors, and local charities.[32,33,34]

Credit: Kathleen Gansen

Figure 3.3. Site coordinators and gardener participants sharing a summer harvest in eastern Kentucky.

Goals and Approaches

To accomplish their mission, Grow Appalachia provides their partner sites with financial and technical assistance to support gardening education and implementation, as well as other community-wide assets, like farmers markets, commercial kitchens, and summer meal programs for youth. Each partner site has a community-appointed site coordinator who manages reporting, grants, markets, educational workshops, and the distribution of resources.

Throughout the years, site coordinators have also participated in annual gatherings, trainings, and semi-annual regional meetings to encourage network development, resource sharing, and collaborative learning (B). I had the chance to sit at conference tables with many site coordinators and listen to them describe their goals, challenges, and successes—from heartbreaking stories about gardeners working through chronic illnesses to the joy of introducing children to new vegetables.

Some site coordinators had been gardening for decades before joining Grow Appalachia, while others were learning for the first time alongside their program participants. The site coordinators also represented a variety of education levels, professional experiences, and ages (A). But what they all shared was their dedication to their home communities, as well as their ability to see strength and opportunities where others might be overwhelmed by need or limitations. When asked how partner sites were selected, one Headquarters staff member replied:

> Number one, I want them to be an organization that is in and of those communities so we don't work with branches of large non-profits or NGOs.... What we work with are those organizations that have grown up in those communities, have been managed and staffed by those communities, and who are embedded in those communities. (F)

This embeddedness allows Headquarters to put the programs almost fully in the hands of the partner sites. Although broad guidance—such as organic production methods—is provided by Headquarters, site co-ordinators hold great local decision-making power. Their pre-existing local knowledge and social capital also enable accelerated partnership formation and program implementation.

Challenges and Outcomes

Grow Appalachia's community-led approach and financial support have enabled effective relationship building both within and across central Appalachian communities. For example, one of Headquarters' requirements is that each partner site offers at least six educational workshops each growing season, including garden planning, food preparation, and season extension. But site coordinators can tailor these workshops to their community. As observed by one Headquarters staff member:

> These communities tend to be pretty class-ridden where the rich folks and the poor folks don't mingle a whole lot.... [But] if we offer classes that don't cater to one or the other but welcome everybody, we find for example avid environmentalists and coal miners sitting in the same room learning how to can tomatoes. Folks ordinarily wouldn't talk to each other on the street, but if they're talking about canning tomatoes—there ain't no politics there. (D)

Many site coordinators have shared how working with Grow Appalachia made it possible for them to build new and stronger relationships with other organizations, both within their home communities and across the region (B). For example, one Tennessee partner site has leveraged the program to bring together university extension, K-12 schools, senior centers, and correctional institutions. Although establishing and maintaining these relationships has been time consuming and political, it has also resulted in intergenerational learning and greater community reach. As the site coordinator explained, "You have to do what it takes to work together. You need their services, they need you, and you need to have a unified front for the community to see that. How are you going to build community-based agriculture if you're not a community working together?"

The success of these individual programs weighs heavily on the individual site coordinators, who often have additional part- or full-time jobs. The in-person regional meetings held throughout the programmatic year provide an important space for coordinators to find relief over shared obstacles, swap stories about challenges, and support one another. As one relieved site coordinator put it at their regional meeting, "I now know that I'm not alone."

Reflections on Principle B: Work Together

Grow Appalachia looks a little (or a lot!) different at each partner site, but many of the values remain constant, including a dedication to collaboration at local and regional scales. The leadership development and financial support provided by Grow Appalachia enables site partners to do impactful work both in and beyond their home communities. Grow Appalachia also functions as a networking hub, bringing together organizations so they may learn from each other while swapping stories and sharing tested solutions.

Figure 3.4. A quilted Grow Appalachia logo square displayed at a Grow Appalachia-supported farmers market in eastern Kentucky.

Credit: Elyzabeth W. Engle

Additionally, Grow Appalachia's community-driven, hands-off approach lets those with local knowledge build programs in a place-based manner. In a region long affected by top-down political and industrial control, this program enables the creation of grassroots-driven, collaborative spaces—spaces that are especially important in rural places where geographic dispersion exacerbates social, economic, and environmental issues. Through Grow Appalachia, communities are finding new ways to work together and thrive, one garden at a time.

Principle B—Work Together

Below are a few suggestions on how you can collaboratively grow social capital and more effectively work together as a community.

Do (Or Consider Doing)

- ✔ Seek a small early success. If planned and implemented through an inclusive process, small wins build confidence, foster future collaborations, and cultivate ownership by all involved.
- ✔ Planning, organizing, and fundraising for an event should model collaborative decision making so that all voices are heard and positive relationships can be built. This will help grow social capital.
- ✔ Consider organizing a vision-to-action type of forum (described in Chapter 14) to bring community members together. These forums focus on the needs of a community and action planning to enable community members to make decision about where they want to focus their time and efforts. These events frequently result in positive changes and set the stage for other efforts in the future.

Don't (Or Think Twice)

- ✘ Don't undertake simple top-down or "expert" planning and organizing of a community building event. It is likely to fail. If you have an idea, first share it with others in your community who you believe are trusted and respected to see if others are interested in co-leading or collaborating.
- ✘ We urge against pushing an idea without support from others. This is akin to pushing rope—it does not work. Try something new, but start small, and learn as you proceed. Build a following of supporters through this process.
- ✘ Don't jump to placing trust or resources in a partner or collaborator who you don't know or others in the community do not fully endorse. Trust needs to be developed and your reputation will be linked to that of your collaborators.
- ✘ Don't seek to quickly create social capital, new relationships, or partnerships. These need to grow naturally through genuine and honest working, sharing, and playing together.

CHAPTER 4

PRINCIPLE

C

Protect Resources and Promote Fairness

*Sustainably Manage Natural Resources
and Promote Equitable Distribution of Benefits*

> *Universal responsibility is the key to human survival.*
> *It is the best foundation for world peace,*
> *the equitable use of natural resources and,*
> *through concern for future generations,*
> *the proper care of the environment.*
>
> — THE DALAI LAMA

Community-Based
Natural Resource Management

Local community sustainability, while including the conservation of natural resources, also requires the recognition of the local livelihoods of its members. Effective sustainability practices should enhance the ecological resources that a community depends upon and ensure that these resources support the needs of its residents now and into the future. This may require thinking and planning with a longer time frame than is typical in many local communities today. It will also require addressing equity—where some have far more resources than they need, others often do not have enough to survive. Indigenous and minority communities in the US have a long, troubled history of unfair treatment and oppression including issues of economic inequity

PROTECT RESOURCES & PROMOTE FAIRNESS

C

Sustainably Manage Natural Resouces and Promote Equitable Distribution of Benefits

Five Characteristics

1. *Environmental justice is a social imperative that includes recognizing local values.*
2. *Seek to improve (or minimize negative effects upon) the local economy.*
3. *Recognize need for linkages between conservation and the local economy based upon equity, local needs, and financial and environmental sustainability.*
4. *Seek equitable and fair distribution of local benefits, potentially including compensation for protecting natural resources.*
5. *Recognize that regulating access to natural resources and graduated sanctions can help ensure equity.*

Researchers have found that for local communities to sustainably manage their ecological resources, support the local economy, and embrace social vitality they need to recognize and understand the interdependent relationships between natural resource protection, local social values, and the livelihoods of community members.[1,2,3] These linkages should take into consideration equity, local needs, and sustainability.[4,5,6] To promote equity, communities need to seek fair distribution of benefits as well as the sharing of hardships or challenges for those who may have their access to resources regulated or are subject to sanctions.[7] Examples include tight fishing quotas or limits to irrigation water.

All local societies are dependent on the ecological products and services that they receive. There are no exceptions. This was eloquently described by Jared Diamond in his book *Collapse*,[8] which includes many examples, including Easter Island, where the local community's failure to recognize this critical linkage led to the society's collapse. This ecological dependency is further described in Thomas Homer-Dixon's book *The Upside of Down*[9] where he discusses many societies that have collapsed, including the Roman Empire, through the depletion of critical resources including ecological products and services such as food, energy, and building materials. Homer-Dixon, however, goes on to describe successful renewal processes that valued and conserved critical ecological systems and their services. In addition to conserving resources, communities need to grow and develop the resilience of the critical ecological systems on which they depend in order to have a long and sustainable future. This is particularly essential during this critical time of climate change.

and lack of environmental justice. This, unfortunately, is also the case in many other parts of the world. However, some communities have addressed this concern successfully, using an approach that is increasingly being recognized and is commonly referred to as community-based natural resource management (CBNRM). I will share three case studies of successful community change efforts that are effectively managing natural resources and promoting greater equity in the distribution of benefits.

Natural Capital and Livelihoods

It is important to emphasize that there is a direct connection between the conservation of environmental and ecological systems and a sustainable local economy. Environmentalists and ecological economists frequently use the term "natural capital" to describe our natural environmental systems. This term describes the world's global stock of natural assets or ecological resources. Similar to human-built capital, such as a factory that produces cars from the inputs of steel, energy, etc., our ecological "natural capital" produces valuable and critical goods and services such as lumber for our homes, the water we drink, the food we eat, and the oxygen we breathe from inputs from the sun, air, minerals, and other living organisms. Without this natural capital, humans could not exist. When we poison our water, deplete our soils, and contaminate our air, we are undermining our life support systems. Vital and healthy communities need to protect and conserve the natural capital on which they depend. This is often presented as a false trade-off—either protect jobs or protect the environment. However, in the longer term, the economic well-being of a community and its members depends on protecting and preserving its ecological resources.

Lake Ohrid and Pogradec, Albania, and
Ohrid and Struga, Macedonia

Traveling through and working in local communities in Central and Eastern Europe in the early 1990s just after the collapse of the totalitarian centrally planned communist systems, provided me an opportunity to experience this principle first hand. This was a very difficult time for these local communities and the welcoming people that I met. Many experienced a lack of food, household materials, and energy to heat their homes along with widespread unemployment (or employment without pay for teachers), and the collapse of many local currencies. On one journey I had an opportunity to travel to Lake Orhid, an ancient lake that is the border between Macedonia and Albania (Figure 4.1). This journey provided a visceral experience of what happens when ecological systems that a community depends upon are destroyed. The incredible success of the following 20 years demonstrates how a critical ecological system near collapse can be turned around, and become a model of positive, community-driven change.

As a member of a small environmental advisory group, I was there to listen and to participate in a dialogue with local residents and leaders from the three towns located on the Macedonia and Albanian shores of this lake, with a focus on how to address the acute environmental deterioration of the lake. Crossing the border from Macedonia into Albania required walking through a guarded border with UN Peacekeepers. Though Albania's armed civil war had "ended" only six months before our visit the road to Pogradec was still strewn with burned-out cars and all public or commercial buildings that we saw had been burned and were standing as charred hulks. Moreover, we were advised

Figure 4.1. Shore of Lake Ohrid showing traditional fishing boats and youth.

Credit: James Gruber

that our safety could not be ensured after nightfall. During our initial meeting with the mayor in the partially burned city hall building, we learned how dire the situation was: toxic waste piles from an old abandoned Chinese steel plant were poisoning the lake; the main river in the town was washing municipal solid waste into the lake; unexploded landmines were still scattered along the lake shoreline; local builders were digging up the shoreline for free sand and gravel; and some of the fishermen were using hand grenades to catch fish.

An afternoon session with both Albanians and Macedonians focused on assessing the situation and then finding common ground between the neighboring communities who had had virtually no contact for the last 50 years. They all recognized that this lake was their primary ecological resource and it was critical for their livelihoods and their quality of life. They both stated, in their own language, that Lake Ohrid was to them "a gift from God." All who were present acknowledged that the lake's environmental sustainability was essential if the future needs of local community members were to be met. At the end of this day of intense meetings, they committed to change their practices and work collaboratively together.

While being driven at high speed back to the border after nightfall, we were told to duck down in the back seat due to snipers. Fortunately, we all arrived safely at the Macedonian border. Nonetheless, the experience left me questioning whether this early effort to break through long-term distrust and find common ground could possibly result in substantive actions after all these years of mistrust and cultural differences.

It turned out that this meeting was the beginning of an ongoing collaborative process, which has in many ways transformed the lake and the community surrounding it. Today, the local economy of these communities is directly supported by the improved conditions of the lake. For example, ecotourism has grown; enforced fishing quotas protect the fisheries; the lake is now referred to as having a "pristine lake environment"; and this "gift from God" is now a UNESCO World Heritage Site. Yes, there are still future environmental concerns such as non-point pollution and managing fish catches. However, Lake Ohrid and these three communities, though cooperation, collaboration, and embracing change, are now economically stronger, ecologically recovering, and socially healthier.[10]

The Case Studies

These three case studies reveal how creative approaches to sustainable resource management can strengthen justice and empower people. The first case study of a developing rural community in the mountains of Oaxaca, Mexico, reveals how by regaining control of their land and deciding to manage the forest cooperatively and sustainably, the Zapotec people helped reverse years of environmental deterioration and injustice. The second case study from Baltimore, Maryland, shares how an inner-city neighborhood with thousands of vacant and abandoned homes was able to reclaim wood, bricks, and other valuable materials through deconstruction (rather than demolition) and at the same time help address problems related to blight and unemployment and contribute to neighborhood recovery and revitalization. The third case addresses the intersection of recycling and educational opportunities for disadvantaged girls in a city in northern India.

CASE STUDY	Building a New Future for All Residents, Ixtlán de Juárez, Oaxaca, Mexico

by James S. Gruber

Prologue

The Indigenous local community of Ixtlán de Juárez had been economically and socially repressed and marginalized for many years by the Mexican national government and wealthy industrialists. During this dark period, the natural resources that were the economic foundation of this Zapotec community were exploited and removed by those external powers, a clear example of environmental injustice. Only after what some referred to as a local revolution, could they regain control over their community and the ecological systems that supported it.

Rather than privatize the land, it was decided that nearly all of it would be managed as a "common" or "common-pool resource" for the community members' immediate and future needs. The resulting actions reversed the previous years of environmental injustice and built a new future for all residents of Ixtlán de Juárez where the sustainable yield of natural resources would be equitably shared.

Introduction

One early spring in Montreal, at a meeting of the North America Council for Environmental Management, I heard about Ixtlán de Juárez—a "mile-high" forest community in the Oaxaca region of Mexico. This local Indigenous Zapotec community, started in the 15th century, was turning around decades of national-government-driven ecological, economic, and social exploitation and was now recognized as a successful model of community-based resource management. My new colleague, Francis (Paco) Reyes, a lawyer and previous manager of the Forest Commission for the States of Oaxaca and Guerrero, offered to help organize and host a visit for me and to serve as my interpreter. My quest was to understand how, in a few decades, this change occurred. What was their approach? What strategies did they use, and how are these strategies related to the key principles of community-based resource management and sustainable development? I was not disappointed!

General Overview

That November, I arrived in Oaxaca, at the peak of the Day of the Dead (Dia de Muertos), a holiday celebrated by people of Mexican and indigenous heritage in honor of those that have died and to support their future spiritual journey. This cultural experience was a precursor to the coming days I spent in the Ixtlán high forest region with this vibrant Zapotec community.

The following day, Paco and I drove nearly two hours up the winding mountain road, passing by a recently established military base for combating the growing drug trade, and finally arrived at Ixtlán de

Juárez. After meeting with C. Luis Pacheco Rodriguez, the community president, I had an opportunity to view and read about the last 50 or more years of the community's rich history. Hanging on the wall behind his desk was the World Wildlife Fund's Gift to the Earth award for the sustainable management of their forest. Pictures of generations of community leaders circled the walls, along with framed newspaper clippings of their numerous successful initiatives. This was an active and engaged community that had struggled since the early 1980s to turn around previous exploitive actions from the national government, actions that inflicted ecological, economic, and cultural harm on this Indigenous forest community. Although this town is located in Oaxaca, one of the poorest states of Mexico, the local economy of Ixtlán is healthy and growing with an emphasis on social, gender, as well as economic equity. It was reported that the average income of the residents of this community is roughly twice the average of others living in the greater region.

The town of Ixtlán de Juárez, at 6,660 feet elevation with a current population of about 2,500, was founded in the latter half of the 15th cen-

Figure 4.2. Town Hall, Ixtlán de Juárez.

Credit: James Gruber

tury by the Indigenous Zapotec people. By the mid 1940s, the forests in this region were subject to timber exploitation by the private paper mill Tuxtepec.[11] Intensive land and forest exploitation were in full swing by the mid-1950s when the federal government pushed to establish a timber industry in the region by providing a 25-year concession to a state-controlled company, Fapatux. Their actions during these 25 years resulted in serious exploitation and degradation of the forest in the Sierra Juárez region from 1956–1981. This also led to widespread poverty and social injustice. Starting in the early 1980s major protests and resistance to the national government's authority and these national contracts eventually resulted control of the land being transferred to the local communities in 1986, including the town of Ixtlán de Juárez. This was the dawn of a new era that allowed local community-driven decision making on land management and conservation.[12]

Goals, Approach, and Challenges

We had an opportunity over the days that followed to conduct personal interviews and survey community leaders and residents. We asked about their goals, approach, and challenges or barriers they encountered along the way.

They described the goals of their community as:

- managing the forest with sustainable management and harvesting practices
- developing alternative sustainable economic activities to replace the short-term reduction in revenues from previous exploitative forest practices
- continuing to reduce pollution and environmentally damaging activities in their forest and on their land, and
- appropriately managing sensitive ecological areas within their land

Their overall approach has a core focus of raising the knowledge and skill levels of community members (D). They expressed the importance of community members gaining a better understanding of their ecological systems and gaining the requisite knowledge and skills for effectively managing these resources. In order to achieve this major paradigm or mind shift, one participant stated that they needed "to gain confidence/trust of the people/persons who had previously bad experiences from other government agencies." (A-G) Terms such as "building a sense of credibility," "approval," "acceptance of the project," and "support/approval by the community" were woven throughout their responses to our questions about their approach to leadership and their change process (B-F-G). Clearly, the credibility of their community leaders (that included trust and confidence in their work) was central to being able to facilitate this change process (I).

Several individuals stated that acceptance of the project by local community members was dependent on linking the conservation of their natural resources with future sustainable economic and social growth (C). They also stressed the importance of educating community members so that they could gain an understanding of the importance and value of their natural resources (D). They emphasized that this change process required a gradual approach with trainings and hard work for all of those involved (A).

The community leaders stressed the importance of organizational systems and social norms and values. The community's organizational systems that they mentioned included:
- how the community was organized, including their participatory decision-making process (J)
- the policy-making committee's organizational structure (I)
- the furniture manufacturing project's industrial structure (I)
- their internal organization, regulations, and evaluations (H-I)

The responses that are associated with the community's social norms and values were:
- the high level of honesty and responsibility (G)
- community values like honesty and equity (C)
- and the confidence and trust in the leadership by the community members (G)

When asking these individuals the question, "What was the most difficult barrier/challenge that the community had to overcome?" the responses primarily focused on the difficulty of initiating and carrying forward a community-wide change process. The challenges that they described included issues of sustainability, adaptive leadership, and an adaptive capacity change process (I-J). Clearly, the local community had complex social and ecological conditions and their leaders had to develop innovative solutions without a clear template or guide (E-I). One individual interviewed, when referring to the greatest challenge, stated it was "not knowing or 'the unknown.'"

Outcomes

This community and their communal forest of 47,716 acres today have an international reputation for effective community-based conservation and sustainable development efforts over the last 30 years.[13] The Sierra Norte highlands region, northeast of Oaxaca, is now one of the best-preserved biospheres in Mexico. This region, dominated by humid pine and oak forests, is home to hundreds of bird species and thousands of plant species. The Forest Stewardship Council (FSC) and its European equivalent certify that the forest's lumber is now sustainably harvested. Ixtlán established a modern and well-equipped on-site furniture factory that manufactures green-certified local wood furniture. The community has also established an ecotourism program that includes lodges, a dining facility, trail systems, and related amenities. During the last 30 years they have established an international reputation for sustainable and green-certified forestry practices and as a center for ecotourism.

During my visit I noted that there was a broad and deep dedication by community members to have a successful community-driven approach (A-B-F-J). The changes to date included a major shift from the previous, non-sustainable extraction of logs from the forests to a new sustainable approach that included ecotourism, generating and replanting seedlings, green-certified forest management/harvesting, and developing value-added final products such as their "green-certified" furniture (C). This community is committed to look outwards towards tourists and customers for their furniture. They are also growing in their awareness of global competition—that they were competing for visitors as a small niche of the global market. Although there is a growing awareness that they have made major strides forward, they are also now aware of how much further they may need to go to achieve a sustainable natural resource-based economy. Two specific priorities they described include enhancing the quality of their wood products and becoming more sophisticated in the ecotourism trade (E). Finally, they are aware of a growing impatience by some members of the community for raising the current living standard rather than the current priority of investing in their future (C). "The community of Ixtlán de Juárez has learned not only to manage their resources; (they) have found that if you unite and organize their efforts, the realization of its objectives will be achieved sooner or later," Jesus Alberto Belmonte of the National Forest Commission said during the opening of the furniture plant. I provide two brief examples to illustrate specific actions they have taken towards achieving their goals.

Example A: From a Forestry Nursery to Producing Green-Certified Furniture

Over a period of 20 years, the previous non-sustainable forest harvesting practices were converted through an integrated systems approach. This systems approach included: 1) establishing and operating a tree nursery and tree planting, 2) limiting cutting and sustainably managing their forest, and 3) manufacturing and selling green-certified furniture. This shifted their economic base from exploitative raw resource extraction (selling logs) to producing and selling a value-added product (wood furniture).

During the 1990s the Ixtlán de Juárez forest commune worked towards certification of their forestry practices by the Forest Stewardship Council (FSC) and the Pan European Forest Certification organization (PERC). These certifying organizations examine environmental,

Credit: James Gruber

Figure 4.3. Green-
certified lumber
furniture factory.

economic, and social factors for sustainably managing forests (C). The
community was able to acquire FSC green forest certification for 38,919
acres out of the total of 47,716 acres that they control.

They established a local band-saw mill, a wood kiln dryer, and a modern furniture factory that would use the newly certified green lumber
(Figure 4.3). Consequently, all their manufactured furniture is FSC certified. The manufactured products they produce include doors, desks,
chairs, windows, bookshelves, and related school and office furniture.
These are sold primarily to schools and the government. This strategy
of manufacturing and selling value-added green-certified wood products has been successful with sales steadily increasing. The 26-year-old
manager of this furniture factory impressed me during our interview
with his high level of dedication along with his entrepreneurial mind
set. Enhancing the quality of their wood products is a high priority for
him, that he linked to working cooperatively and raising the level of
knowledge and skills of all the workers (B). He emphasized this point

by stating, "The most important [factor], without doubt, is the people. The machines can be rented, selected, but if we don't train and attend to the people, the work won't get done" (H).

Another initiative, established in 2006, is the Regional Forestry Nursery. In a partnership between the state government of Oaxaca and Ixtlán de Juárez, this automated high-tech nursery produces 500,000 trees a year to address the previous deforestation of approximately 495,000 acres in the state of Oaxaca.[14] The initial capital costs were supported by international donors (K). The nursery samplings are used for the restoration of ecosystems and commercial tree plantations.

Good planning realizes that the natural and cultural resources are the foundation of ecotourism.

— Ecotourism Manager, Ixtlán de Juárez

Example B: Ecotourism—Competing on a Global Scale

The leadership of Ixtlán de Juárez, with the support of the community members, initiated ecotourism in 1996 as a core component of an integrated program to sustainably manage their forest. The Sierra Norte highlands region has unique ecological assets and has been recognized as a well-preserved biosphere. The Ixtlán region also has an international reputation as a unique Indigenous community. This may

Figure 4.4.
Ecotourism lodge.

Credit: James Gruber

be due in part from the internationally well-known book *Journey to Ixtlán* by Carlos Castaneda. Today, this ecotourism program is well established with housing, dining facilities, trails, a training center, and guided tours on the flora and fauna (Figure 4.4). The ecotourism program is designed to protect the unique biodiversity of this humid pine and oak forested region. It supports conservation and preservation as well as providing a means to generate income in a sustainable manner (C). A participant who was active in developing the tourism program shared the importance of raising the awareness and understanding of all community members. He advised, "Walk with the community and explain to them the potential that ecotourism would bring." (D)

A senior member of the community closed our interview by stating, "We are a successful community because of the community's participation, the common grounds, and the conservation of our natural resources and environment for future generations." (A-B-C)

Reflections on Principle C: Protect Resources and Promote Fairness

This case study illustrates nearly all of the 12 principles, some to a greater extent than others. I will focus here on how this case illustrates Principle C—Protect Resources and Promote Fairness.

An early step in this process of change was recognizing the linkage between conservation and the local economy. A senior member of this community stated that one of the most difficult early challenges that had to be overcome was "gaining the community's openness and acceptance of the project as one of sustainability with economic and social growth and the conservation of resources." Convincing community members of this critical connection between strengthening conservation, social vitality, and economic livelihoods was essential for building towards a sustainable future.

The community also decided to regulate access by limiting all forest cutting to protect certain critical natural resource areas. This protected their water supply as well as critical habitat of flora and fauna. Ecotourism was established to support the economic needs of the community and has provided local employment and income to many.

In order to limit forest harvesting to a more sustainable level, the community built and now operates a wood furniture factory that produces value-added products. These products are sold to schools, other governments, and furnish their ecotourism cabins. This enhances economic return and reduces harvesting of natural resources.

Equity also includes gender equity, and as stated by the National Forest Commission: "Ixtlán is not only an example of caring for the ecosystem and sustainable development, (but) also provides a broad view of gender equity."

In closing, I believe that their embrace of Principle C: Protect Resources and Promote Fairness, helped provide a moral compass that was seminal in building a strong community that could work together, face everyday challenges, and, together, make the hard decisions that are often needed for a community to thrive.

 CASE STUDY **Reclaiming Wood, Bricks, Lives, and a Community, Baltimore, Maryland, USA**

by S. Hines, N. Srinivasan, L. Marshall, and J. M. Grove
Adapted by J. Kenjio

Prologue

This case presents a "multi-faceted approach to solving the complex problems of inner-city vacant homes, unemployment, and the need to protect forests in an age of climate change and can serve as a model for other cities."[15] In Baltimore, a city with thousands of vacant and abandoned homes, reclaiming wood, bricks, and other valuable materials through deconstruction has been proven to "help remedy problems related to blight and unemployment and contribute to neighborhood revitalization."[16] This successful community-wide effort to increase environmental, economic, and social benefits, as well as sustainability and resilience, relied on the willingness of a team of partners to face large-scale challenges while engaging in collaborative problem solving. It not only succeeded in recovering valuable and reuseable resources but also resulted in a positive systemic change that improved the lives of local citizens. This case study draws upon an interview with a key stakeholder as well as published accounts of this initiative.

Introduction

It's not a well-kept secret that Baltimore has had its fair share of challenges. Hard-hit by suburbanization and a loss of manufacturing jobs after World War II, the city has lost over a third of its peak population. This loss has exacerbated economic stagnation and racial segregation, raising the need for creative revitalization. I (Jacques Kenjio) first visited Baltimore in 2017, and what I saw left an indelible mark on me. Entire blocks of row homes, that must have been bustling with people and activities a few decades earlier, now stood empty along with vacant storefronts and businesses. I saw people (mostly African Americans) roaming scanty streets soliciting and exchanging what appeared to be recreational drugs. This experience made me wonder two things: How did this city come to this state? And what was being done to address these problems?

It's within this urban landscape that the US Forest Service and a diverse group of community partners are piloting an effective approach that appears to address many of these problems simultaneously. Their creative integrated approach to urban renewal focuses on the reclamation and innovative reuse of wood and bricks. Recognizing that many post-industrial cities face challenges similar to Baltimore's, the community partners believe that because of their ongoing success with this urban revitalization initiative, there is potential to replicate their approach in other stressed urban areas with similar challenges.

General Overview

The city of Baltimore, established in 1730, is one of the oldest post-colonial cities in the United States. Baltimore's rapid development in the 18th century was primarily ignited by the industrial revolution and commercial trading.[17] The growth of industries resulted in the extensive demand for labor. This resulted in the influx of immigrants and slaves from different parts of the world such as Acadia (now Canada's

Maritime provinces), Ireland, Santo Domingo (today Haiti), Italy, and Poland.[18] Over the course of that same 18th century, Baltimore became the second major port of entry into the US (after New York City) following the arrival of over two million immigrants through its harbor.[19] In 1820, Baltimore had the largest population of African Americans in the United States, most of whom were slaves. During and after the Second World War, Baltimore's manufacturing sector exploded as the city benefited from the introduction of factories that produced and tested military equipment like planes, ships, and tanks.[20] This explosion was also followed by a large increase in population—especially of African Americans. Housing shortages therefore became critical as the incentives and demand for suburban housing was restricted to a certain group of privileged people. African Americans were systematically denied access to privileged suburban neighborhoods through the process of redlining.[21] This discriminatory practice resulted in racially and economically divided neighborhoods.

The more recent problem of neighborhood vacancy can be traced back to the loss of manufacturing after the 1950s and to discriminatory housing practices and racial segregation. Today with its continuous urban depopulation, Baltimore, home to over 950,000 people in the 1950s, now houses approximately 610,000 residents.[22]

Goals, Approach, and Challenges

While the US has very few old-growth forests remaining and, therefore, it is generally not desirable to harvest those that remain, there is still an abundance of old-growth wood available for use—it just happens to be locked up in Baltimore's many abandoned row homes (Figure 4.5).

Wood accounts for more than ten percent of the annual waste material in the US. Out of the 70.6 million tons of wood waste generated in 2010, 42 percent comes from demolition activities.[23] Trees from urban forestry operations, especially those that have sustained damage from pests or infections, also produce considerable amounts of waste. Much of this can be reclaimed,[24] making the recovery of this wood a major

Credit: USDA Forest Services

Figure 4.5.
Abandoned row homes
in Baltimore. By clearing
abandoned row homes,
land is made available
for green areas and
other community uses.

opportunity for addressing triple bottom line issues that include people, profit, and planet.[25] According to research done by the US Forest Service, reclaiming the wood from the national waste stream could replace 30 percent of the annual consumption of hardwood trees in the US.[26] Diverting wood from the waste stream preserves valuable material and prevents it from taking up space in already-overflowing landfills (C-K).

The United States Forest Service (USFS) championed the urban wood reclamation initiative in Baltimore. Rather than using a simple approach of demolition and recovery, the Forest Service chose to work closely with organizations and members of the community to co-create a transformative process that could directly benefit the community as well as recover natural resources. These leaders in Baltimore support "knowledge co-production,"[27] which involves researchers working together with communities, stakeholders, and practitioners to produce actionable knowledge (E-A). This co-production of knowledge approach led to the establishment of partnerships with multiple stakeholders (Table 4.1).

Table 4.1. List of Key Partners and Their Roles in the Baltimore Urban Revitalization Initiative.

Key Partners	Mission	Role Played in This Initiative
United States Forest Services	This federal agency manages and protects US national forests and grasslands. Their mission is to sustain the health, diversity, and productivity of the nation's forests and grasslands to meet the needs of present and future generations.	Early champion of the urban wood initiative project and established partnerships. The USFS is currently leading two complimentary approaches: the identification of national buyers and the creation of access to capital.
Maryland Department of Housing and Community Development	They work with partners to finance housing opportunities and revitalize places for Maryland citizens to live, work, and prosper.	They partnered with Humanim Inc. on the idea of deconstruction with the goal of fighting urban blight caused from vacant houses.
Maryland Department of Natural Resources	Their mission includes preserving, protecting, restoring, and enhancing the state's natural resources.	They provided support for the creation and management of community parks, urban forest assessments, and the diversion of deconstruction waste from landfills.
Baltimore Office of Sustainability	Their mission is to strengthen communities through collaborative social, environmental, and economic planning and action.	They partnered with Humanim's enterprise (Details Deconstruction) on the urban wood deconstruction initiative in an effort to create employment opportunities for residents, reduce the quantity of waste directed to landfills, and salvage materials for reuse.
Humanim Inc. and Details Deconstruction	Humanim Inc. is a multi-enterprise nonprofit organization with a mission to support and empower individuals who face social or economic challenges by building pathways to economic equity, opportunity, and independence.	Through their different enterprises they were able to collaborate effectively with the USFS to sustainably remove the vacant homes. Details Deconstruction (a subsidiary) started hiring and training local residents suffering from high unemployment and incarceration rates to deconstruct vacant buildings. Once the buildings have been deconstructed, the salvageable materials are taken to Brick & Board to be processed, aggregated, refurbished, and sold.

Table 4.1. (cont'd.) List of Key Partners and Their Roles in the Baltimore Urban Revitalization Initiative.

Key Partners	Mission	Role Played in This Initiative
Room & Board	A modern furniture and home décor retailer committed to sustainable practices and American craftsmanship that creates contemporary designs for modern living rooms, dining rooms, and bedrooms.	Room & Board joined the project in 2017. Through their partnership with the USFS, they are repurposing the wood salvaged from the deconstructed houses into furniture, flooring, wall cladding, and siding.
Camp Small	Camp Small is the city's wood waste collection yard whose mission is to sort and distribute a variety of wood products for the city.	Under the Camp Small Zero Waste initiative, this wood waste collection yard became a wood sorting, processing, and distribution site in Baltimore.
Parks & People Foundation	This nonprofit organization transforms and restores the land following deconstruction into green spaces like parks and playing grounds. They engage with communities to visualize designs for the land after deconstruction.	They partnered with the USFS to engage with the Easterwood community in 2016 to design the Easterwood/Sandtown Park and Playground.
Quantified Ventures	This is a social impact investment advisory firm that simplifies the process of financing innovative and evidence-based environmental, health, and educational outcomes.	Quantified Venture used social impact investment to scale up both the fresh cut and deconstructed urban wood.

The multifaceted approach to Baltimore's complex problems relied on holistic goals:

- creating livelihoods, improving lives for minority population in their neighborhoods
- supporting the US wood-processing and manufacturing industry
- enabling ecological restoration
- serving as a model for creating a circular, self-reinforcing economy in urban areas

It was also hoped that by achieving these four goals, through an inclusive, multistakeholder effort, growing this effort in the future could be supported by attracting much-needed private investment and economic development for the city (C).

The Multifaceted Approach to Baltimore's Vacancy Problem

The foundational approach toward solving Baltimore's vacancy problem involved the creation of collaborative partnerships, knowledge co-production, open communication systems, and the establishment of strong support systems between different stakeholders (B-E-D-A). Open communication loops between the different actors were vital in managing prevailing challenges (D-H). "Communications between the different partners were enhanced by in-person meetings, brainstorming ideas, and visiting deconstruction sites as a team."[28] The involvement of communities at different stages of the urban revitalization process not only ensured that the needs and desires of the residents were observed, but also fostered a sense of trust and stewardship among the residents (A-B-I-G-F). For example, Parks & People engaged community members in visualizing designs for the vacant lots after deconstruction.

The leadership team in this case study was formed through "...organic interest expressed by the different stakeholders in solving the Baltimore vacant home problem."[29] Collaborative partnerships involving stakeholders of diverse backgrounds and areas of specialties can create networks of problem-solving approaches that improve communities, solve presenting problems, and generate outstanding outcomes. "Creating partnerships with both private and public organizations was a viable way to remove these vacant homes."[30]

The major challenge identified by proponents of this urban revitalization initiative was deciding to remove the vacant buildings by deconstruction rather than demolition (L). Demolition had been the standard method for eradicating vacant buildings in Baltimore because it was quicker, cheaper, and less labor intensive.

However, in 2012 when the urban wood project began, the leaders prioritized the deconstruction method because it was sustainable, created more jobs, and was more economically feasible when all factors were considered. Through deconstruction, up to 90 percent of the materials in a vacant building was repurposed, hence diverting waste from landfills, and reducing the exploitation of natural resources—including forest products (C). Multiple endorsements from different stakeholders facilitated the decision process (I).

There was wide support for proceeding with this innovative deconstruction approach because of the significant socioeconomic and environmental benefits of implementation. This decision was not only favorable to the city of Baltimore, but also to the stakeholders involved in this broad partnership. For example, while Parks & People Foundation would need to spend $250,000 to build a park on land that had buildings demolished, it would only need to spend $50,000 on a cleaner site that had buildings deconstructed (C).[31] Moreover, "deconstruction with its added need for labor, has the ability to ameliorate some of the difficulties citizens returning from prison face in finding jobs."[32]

Outcomes

In less than ten years of operation Baltimore's multifaceted revitalization initiative has been successful at multiple scales. The city, which originally had over 16,800 vacant homes,[33] has removed "350 vacant homes through deconstruction since the beginning of the project in 2012."[34] The USFS and its partners have devised a plan for significantly scaling up the number of house units deconstructed to 250 buildings annually. This goal will generate more employment opportunities, salvage (recycle and reuse) more building materials, and transform more deteriorated row-house city blocks into healthy and vibrant neighborhoods.

Materials such as bricks and wood salvaged from deconstruction have been repurposed and resold bringing revenue to the city. Through Details Deconstruction and Brick & Board, Humanim Inc. (see Table 4.1) has developed one of the largest markets in the US for reclaimed brick from Baltimore.[35]

The initiative has created jobs for Baltimore residents which has also helped reduce poverty levels, reduce high incarceration rates, and improve lives. "My wife and I have just bought a house.... this is the first time I have owned anything that I can call mine, it came from working.... I am living my best life right now,"[36] said a Baltimore resident and employee of Details Deconstruction. In 2018, after six years of operation, Details Deconstruction has trained and employed 165 low-income residents.[37] Multiple greenspaces and public and recreational grounds (like parks) have been created which has improved the social vitality, well-being, safety, and happiness of Baltimore residents. "These parks are restorative which brings life to a community… contributes to a sense of wellbeing, public health…beauty and a sense of tranquility."[38]

Figure 4.6. Employees of Details Deconstruction and Brick & Board at work.

Credit: Humanim

This community was able to transform some of their neighborhoods from an unsafe state of urban decay to a welcoming neighborhood with open green spaces, pocket parks, and maintained homes. Parks & People Foundation constructed multiple parks and playgrounds including the Sandtown Park and Playground and the Harlem Park. In some instances, the lots left from deconstruction are "developed into new and affordable housing units for the residents of Baltimore."[39]

By 2018, Room & Board had launched almost a dozen products made of reclaimed yellow pine under the brand name Urban Wood Project: Baltimore. Room & Board has also developed partnerships with local manufacturing companies like Open Works, not only to produce furniture out of reclaimed pine, but also to create meaningful employment opportunities for those with employment barriers. Room & Board also financially supports the city through its donations to Parks & People Foundation for the creation and maintenance of parks and playgrounds.

Reflections on Principle C:
Protect Resources and Promote Fairness

My experience with the Baltimore community has taught me one lesson: successful measures to increase sustainability and resilience depend on the willingness of those involved to take on large-scale

Credit: USDA Forest Services

Figure 4.7. Deconstructed lots provide opportunity for community green spaces. Row home removal is enabling the creation of green community in Baltimore, including this one near McKean Avenue.

challenges and engage in collaborative thinking to produce innovative solutions.

This case study also demonstrates that addressing economic inequality and racism can go hand in hand with effective resource conservation. There are some valuable takeaway lessons to be learned from this community effort. During an interview with Sarah Hines, one of the community leaders in Baltimore, she said that:

> It has been a very rewarding and powerful experience for all of us as a community...in order to solve complex problems one needs to think creatively and holistically...identify where the barriers are and work as a team to remove them. The federal government should embrace the role of a catalyst by creating ideal conditions for success at a community level.[40]

I personally believe that the ongoing urban revitalization initiative in Baltimore depicts a brilliant example of a bottom-up, citizen empowerment approach to addressing urban blight.

In my view, their embrace of Principle C: Protect Resources and Promote Fairness has provided an excellent prototype for urban economies in other US urban areas as well as world cities facing similar problems. The different stakeholders were able to sustainably manage the forest resources of the greater Baltimore region and effectively collaborate with one another in solving a complex urban problem, while building a strong and vibrant community. It is no surprise that this initiative received the Mutual of America Partnership Award in 2018. Their official statement said, "Mutual of America proudly recognizes Humanim, Inc. and its partners for their pioneering work with Baltimore City Deconstruction Project, providing employment opportunities to underserved residents while reducing urban blight, reclaiming materials and increasing green spaces."[41]

CASE STUDY	**Women's Empowerment Through Sustainability in India**

by Tazeen Beg and Mirza I. Beg

Prologue

Women in India have always been marginalized in terms of not receiving an equitable distribution of resources, especially in the realm of education. This phenomenon is even more prevalent in economically depressed communities. The reasons are manifold, including cultural, religious and, of course, financial differences. However, this did not deter an "educationally privileged" group of women in Aligarh, a university town in India, from starting Ismat Literacy and Handicraft Centre (ILHC or The Centre), a school for girls of all ages, with the purpose of imparting free education and vocational skills.

Mr. Tushar Gandhi, the great-grandson of Mahatma Gandhi and a noted writer, visited The Centre in March 2017. Highly impressed by its role in educating girls from impoverished neighborhoods, he was amazed to see the multifaceted skills of the students in creating the handicrafts from used, recycled materials displayed at the exhibition.[42]

Introduction and General Overview

In the fall of 2017, we visited our alma mater, Aligarh Muslim University (AMU) in Aligarh, India. A well-wisher of The Centre invited us to ILHC, located within the precincts of the university. The Centre was established in 1997 by Dr. Jamila Majid Siddiqui, a retired faculty member from AMU's Medical College and the president of the AMU Ladies Club. The Ladies Club's Charitable Initiative provided the initial funds for the founding of The Centre as a means of providing education to underprivileged girls coming from areas surrounding the university. This school is in a small building provided rent free by the university with some lessons also held under a tree in the yard, on the verandah, or even in the kitchen. Mrs. Sabiha Lari, the current coordinator of The Centre, gave us a tour of the premises highlighting the challenges but also sharing the girls' achievements with pride. We were overwhelmed by the sheer enthusiasm and excitement of the girls who are willing to attend school even if they sit on the floor!

Credit: Sabiha Lari

Figure 4.8. Finished recycled products on sale at the annual exhibition.

The students at this Centre are girls of all ages who had never been to a school or even thought of getting educated. Their education, including textbooks, is free with a nominal fee charged for the vocational courses. Along with their regular classroom experiences at The Centre, young women are taught computer skills, tailoring, embroidery, and cooking, along with other vocational skills. In addition, they learn about sustainability and environmental conservation from utilizing recycled resources from the local community and turning them into beautiful handicrafts, the sale of which helps raise additional funds for the school (C).

Goals, Challenges, Approaches, and Outcomes
Goals
The primary goal of The Centre is to educate girls from economically depressed communities and help them to become independent members of their society. We, the authors, believe that vocational training is fundamental to the promotion of independence and self-sufficiency in girls. The Centre's approach is to create beautiful handicrafts from used materials by recycling and reusing them. This was key in raising environmental awareness among this population, which was another goal of The Centre. Students are learning that current generations need to preserve resources for future generations in order to achieve the goal of sustainability. Finally, the education and vocational training offers an opportunity for girls to achieve their own incomes and degrees, and the sense of empowerment and independence that comes with that kind of success (F).

Challenges and Approaches
The main challenge was recruiting girls for The Centre given a lack of community involvement. Some of these girls work as home helpers and contribute towards the family income, so it becomes difficult for

them to attend school instead. At other times, the families are so poor that they are unable to afford education for these girls even if they want to. Also, free government schools are sparse and may be far away from their homes. Families needed to be convinced that this schooling would significantly improve their daughters' chances for a good life. However, when these girls and their reluctant parents were given the added incentive of vocational training, the task of recruitment was made much easier. The Centre grew as the name spread with more families volunteering to send their girls for education (G).

Recruiting capable teachers was also an early obstacle. Finding trained teachers to work with minimal salaries, or none, was understandably difficult. Some retired teachers from the community eventually volunteered their time for free. As the school became more established and girls began to graduate, seven of its own graduates were hired as primary teachers by The Centre. They were trained through the government sponsored Nursery Teachers Training and English-Speaking Program. They have now been admitted to a nationwide training program in Science, Math, and English for three years sponsored by a private company, Wipro Ltd. These young women, who are all from underprivileged backgrounds, have demonstrated hard work and dedication to achieve their posts as teachers.

Finding an affordable space for The Centre could have proved a major hurdle. However, the university stepped up and offered to provide a building on the campus free of charge. The building to house it was sanctioned by the then Vice Chancellor of the university, Mr. Mehmud Ur Rehman. While the building has served The Centre well, with the expansion of classes and increased enrollment, creating space for more classrooms is an ongoing challenge.

Yet another challenge was the unwillingness of people to pay for a finished product made of used materials. It did not take long for the attitude of the customer base to change once they saw the beautiful handicrafts and creativity of these girls. This change can be seen in the success of the annual Handicrafts Exhibition and Festival started a few years ago, which has become quite an attraction with good sales.

Outcomes

ILHC started with 30 girls being given a non-formal education in the school (15 received vocational training also). It has now grown to about 250 girls currently enrolled for classroom education from kindergarten to Class 10. The results of the girls' engagement in The Centre and their education has begun to show. Some of them have passed the Private High School Examination offered by the university with good grades and were further guided to pursue higher education through distance learning. Some girls have enrolled in the local college for undergraduate degrees.

The Centre's vocational training program has been very successful since its inception. The various items handcrafted by the girls include decorative items like book and pen holders, frames, envelopes, gifts bags, trinket boxes, jewelry, and paper flowers. These gift items are more special as they are all made by hand with personal attention to detail. In addition to these gift items, students prepare and sell pickles, jams, and snacks and cater food as part of their culinary training, which generates revenue for The Centre and helps support it. The basic computer skills program provides them with the necessary prowess to deal with the modern world.[43]

Figure 4.9. Young women emulating scientist Isaac Newton, astronaut Kalpana Chawla, and author J. K. Rowling.

Credit: Sabiha Lari

And finally, there has been a reduction in the paper, plastic, and metal waste that would have gone to the landfills. The Centre was the venue of a charity camp held by the Ladies' Club in July 2014, where food packets were distributed to poor families and solar lanterns were given to outstanding students. The use of solar lanterns was demonstrated as a source of sustainable and renewable energy.[44] (C)

Reflections on Principle C:
Protect Resources and Promote Fairness

The Ismat Literacy and Handicraft Centre promotes social equity through the education of young women, while protecting natural resources through its sustainability efforts by reducing, reusing, and recycling waste from the neighborhoods where these women reside. The Centre recognized the needs of this marginalized section of its community and stepped up to empower women by helping them become more self-sufficient both socially and economically. Through sales of their handcrafted products, the girls are being compensated for protecting natural resources. The revenue generated through the sale of these items covers some of The Centre's financial needs, thus promoting self-sufficiency and a sense of empowerment. Women run the entire operation at ILHC. Many girls, who had never been to a school, have graduated and gone on to pursue higher education. Thus, the opportunity offered by The Centre gives these girls from low-income families a chance for a brighter future.

Principle C—Protect Resources and Promote Fairness

Do (Or Consider Doing)

- ✓ Identify local and national policies, rules, and procedures that have directly or indirectly supported discriminatory practices, such zoning regulations or "red-lining" for home mortgages.
- ✓ Seek legal and political help to change policies, rules, or procedures that promote unfair practices.
- ✓ Consider the need for new laws, regulations, or policies that can regulate access to limited resources or protect livelihoods of traditional communities.
- ✓ Build effective partnerships across jurisdictional lines that can work together to address complex challenges or environmental and socially linked problems.
- ✓ Learn from other successes, but modify, when appropriate, for the unique conditions of specific communities.

Don't (Or Think Twice)

- ✗ Don't create a new effort for conservation or enhancing equity without understanding who is already working in these areas. Then, consider working with them, adding additional resources as needed.
- ✗ Don't assume facts, no matter how strong, will by themselves change attitudes and build support for change.
- ✗ Don't assume change will happen quickly.
- ✗ Don't be discouraged if you are criticized or attacked by the media if you are actively promoting a more equitable and just approach to sharing ecological resources. It may mean you are making progress.
- ✗ Don't ignore the legitimate needs and practices of local or Indigenous communities.

CHAPTER 5

Be Transparent

*Support Open Communication and
Information Dissemination*

> *A lack of transparency results in
> distrust and a deep sense of insecurity.*
>
> — THE DALAI LAMA

Build Credibility Through Transparency

Today's massive misinformation or "fake news" that is disseminated through trolls, algorithms, and other digital manipulations is undermining our local communities. People struggle to discern what is true or factual from what is misinformed or actual propaganda. A proactive commitment to transparency can build the credibility of community leaders and can push back against this massive, online misinformation. Enhanced transparency can grow the credibility of community leaders and build stronger social capital across your community.

Effective Communication and Secrets

What does it mean to be transparent or to fully support open communication and information sharing? Is it appropriate for government or local community leaders to hold secrets from its citizens or members, and if so, when? These are difficult questions that have been studied and debated for centuries. When working in European Eastern Bloc

BE TRANSPARENT

D

Support Open Communication and Information Dissemination

Five Characteristics

1. *Well-designed communication systems provide information sharing that supports multiple social networks and raises the collective level of knowledge and awareness.*

2. *Linkages provided between different information and knowledge systems support learning, decision making, and change.*

3. *Effective communication supports openness and transparency.*

4. *Information sharing is promoted between experts and non-experts through multiple approaches including: seminars and workshops; printed, electronic, and mass media; and projects.*

5. *Expectations and limits are clearly stated.*

Effective communication is crucial to any level of information sharing, especially that which is needed to affect community-based planning and implementation. Moreover, this communication must be open and transparent in order to provide accessible information to the people most affected by the decisions being made, which can, therefore, foster trusting relationships with and among these groups.[4,5] Similarly, accessible knowledge supports the learning and adaptive capabilities of the community.[6] Community initiatives that embrace open and readily understood communication between partners, stakeholders, and community members will most likely include effective information dissemination and build harmonious social cohesion.[7]

countries, I had an opportunity to personally see and experience what happens when governments operate behind a veil of secrecy. This systematic secrecy allowed the totalitarian abuse of the citizens and kept them powerless. I also had to face these questions while supervising town departments, including the police department. The citizens have a right to know as well as to have their privacy protected.

Padded Doors—Why Transparency Really Matters

During my first trip to Bulgaria in the early 1990s, every mayor's office and every city council chamber that I entered had this strange black padding covering the entire outside, and sometimes the inside, of the entry door. The doors looked somewhat like the back of a black leather couch with buttons, sitting on its edge. One council chamber had two doors, inches apart, both with black padding on both sides of both doors. It was odd. I asked my interpreter, "What's with these doors?" He responded, "It stops the sound!" I soon realized that any important government office always had a black padded door to ensure that no one outside could listen as decisions were discussed and decided inside. It was a visceral image of how totalitarian regimes depended on secrecy to control and repress their citizens.

There is a direct connection between secrecy and power.[1] The capacity of government to keep its actions secret and to penetrate the secrets of its citizens is power[2] that all too often becomes abusive. This is what I learned from the recovering communities in Bulgaria, Latvia, Albania, and other countries in the 1990s who had recently thrown out their communist oppressors. The values associated with openness and access to information for participants, along with the rights for personal autonomy and privacy, are fundamental to a democratic society[3] and for healthy local communities. During my previous ten years of local government leadership in the US, I found that it is far better to err on the side of being excessively open and transparent, proactively promoting open communication and sharing of information as long as, at the same time, one ensures that the privacy of individuals is respected.

A Tale of Two Public Hearings

A public hearing can be imagined as a Norman Rockwell painting with a serious and earnest local citizen standing up in a town hall asking the town council a question. A local public hearing could be a formal or informal meeting with the citizens, an all-members event of a community group, or a congregation-wide gathering for a church with the goal of information sharing. These hearings typically occur at least annually or when there is a major new proposed project, law, or expense. On one hand, hearings can be an effective *transparent approach* to support learning, decision making, and change, as well as a dialogue and opportunity for all to listen to each other. On the other hand, they can also serve as a mechanism designed to sell others on an idea that was already decided by those with formal authority or power—a one-way sharing of selected information.

The following story of two public hearings illustrates the difference. One took place in Veliko Tarnovo, the historic capital of Bulgaria, and the other in Sullivan County, New Hampshire. They both focused on the planning of future solid waste management for their community or region.

Public Hearing One

The Chair of the Board of the solid waste authority opened the meeting by welcoming the 30 to 40 citizens present and read a statement of his legal authority to have people arrested if they spoke without his permission. There were a number of armed police officers on all sides of the room. I had been asked by the Chair to be an independent consultant, as an expert on solid waste, and to facilitate the discussion on the current mass-burn incineration system as well as the potential for future waste management and recycling options. Local residents had requested this meeting. When the Chair gave me the floor, my first step was to develop ground rules for this public discussion. One citizen politely proposed limiting the police presence to two armed officers since they felt intimidated. The Chair refused and indicated he could have as many police officers present as he wanted. We never made it past the ground rules and the public meeting went downhill from there. It was clear that those with formal authority did not seek nor want public input into their decision-making process. There was no transparency or learning, and any trust between the citizens and the Board proceeded to deteriorate. The meeting bitterly ended early.

Public Hearing Two

I was asked to help guide the governmental agency that was organizing a public hearing on proposed new solid waste management policy. When asked how they could have the best possible public hearing, I strongly suggested that they welcome all participants and state their goals for the hearing. I also suggested that they focus on listening, not defending each of their ideas, that they record what was said, and thank everyone for their participation and feedback.

They showed me a large auditorium with a high stage separated from the seating by an orchestra pit that they thought would work. I asked if they would consider the smaller city council meeting room where all of the council member tables and seating for the citizens were on the same level. They agreed, noting it might be a bit tight. I have found that physical space does matter in how we communicate with each other.

The meeting opened after 50–60 local citizens filled the room. No police were present. The Chair started the hearing by reading a statement that said, in part: "The issue of solid waste management can't just be managed by regulations but also by people themselves. We like to involve all members from this society in the process of decision making, to meet the needs of the public in a better way."[8] He then asked for input on the draft policy ideas that had been publicly provided prior to the meeting.

There were many angry citizens who brought up the past lack of transparency. All members of the agency really listened. The Chair stopped an assistant as soon as she started to rebut a statement, allowing for disgruntled views to be heard in their entirety. Then, after an hour of expressing their concerns, citizens began to share ideas about how to improve the policy. Toward the end of the second hour, people thanked the agency staff for being open and for hearing them, and they expressed their support for many of the ideas that had been offered. The hearing ended after two hours with a newly shared appreciation of all in the room, support for the new policy ideas, and smiles. By embracing an open and transparent process, the agency gained public trust and raised the level of knowledge and awareness of all who were present.

Two Hearings: Postscript

Public Hearing One: Within six months of this failed public hearing in Sullivan County, New Hampshire, over 20 police officers provided security at the next public meeting with this solid waste authority and there were only five citizens in attendance. Six months later, the solid waste district was dissolved by the vote of local governments. The mass-burn incinerator is now shut down. Local New Hampshire citizen groups are finally implementing recycling programs.

Public Hearing Two: Six months later, after conducting other public hearings in the country, the Bulgarian National Assembly passed a sweeping new solid waste policy[9] that promoted effective waste management and recycling across the country. Within six months of passage, over a hundred local communities voluntarily implemented recycling programs. This new, more transparent approach to governance, five years after the fall of the totalitarian communist government, was uniting the citizens and their government.

The Case Studies

The first case study of the Upper Valley, a socially and economically diverse region in New Hampshire and Vermont, presents a local foods event offered by a grassroots nonprofit organization that successfully strengthens the region's community capital through sharing information among businesses, schools, and residents of all ages.

Sometimes transparency in the dissemination and sharing of information can be transformative. The second case is of Hiware Bazar,

India, where effective communication of environmental pressures and needs led to a dramatic change in the landscape, the economy, and the well-being of the region.

CASE STUDY: Vital Communities of the Upper Valley Region, Vermont and New Hampshire, USA

by Jacques Kenjio and Shaylin Salas

Prologue

At the heart of the Upper Valley region of New Hampshire and Vermont is found Vital Communities: a local nonprofit organization that unites citizens, organizations, and local towns. They work to bring this rural region together and address challenges while, as explained in their mission statement, "bridging boundaries and engaging the whole community to create positive change." Vital Communities engages residents in a wide range of programs and community-based initiatives to enhance energy conservation, develop alternative transportation, offer community education, provide leadership training, address local food insecurity, and meet many other community-identified needs. This case study illustrates how Vital Communities approaches their role as a catalyst of community connection and empowerment through one of its highly touted local food and farm initiatives: Flavors of the Valley.[10]

Introduction and General Overview

Vital Communities was born 25 years ago out of the League of Women Voters project "Upper Valley: 2001 and Beyond."[11] This brought together local communities, ranging from rural villages to semi-urban towns and from economically struggling former mill towns to well-off university and retirement communities, to identify common values and create a shared vision for the future. Today, renamed Vital Communities, they bring their mission of cultural, economic, environmental, and social well-being to 69 cities and towns in New Hampshire and Vermont. This case study showcases an annual event that the Food & Farm program of Vital Communities,[12] Flavors of the Valley,

Credit: Vital Communities/Rob Strong Photography

Figure 5.1. Community residents and vendors at the Flavors of the Valley, 2019.

to illustrate their approach to bringing residents together to build a healthier future.

We attended this event in the spring of 2019. The first thing we noticed as we approached the venue at a local middle school was children's laughter filling the air as they participated in a planned activity. The school gym, where the vendors were set up, smelled of freshly made foods and was glowing from all the smiles in the room (Figure 5.1). We were quickly welcomed with a cup of carrot ginger soup; and then with a sweet pancake; and then a slew of organic juices. We tried everything from cookies, baked by young students of a local culinary school, to carrots freshly picked from a local farm.

Flavors of the Valley "has grown from a small tasting expo held in a small event venue to a large event, today with 46 vendors and 1,000 attendees."[13] This event was created in response to farmers and food vendors wanting to find new ways to connect with consumers in the region. Vital Communities opens their vendor registration to anyone and everyone that produces local foods in the Upper Valley region. They use this opportunity to build strong and sustainable relationships with local businesses by inviting them to meet and share who they are and the food they produce.

Goals, Approaches, Challenges, and Outcomes
Goals

Having interviewed the Vital Communities communications manager,[14] we identified the main goals of the Flavors of the Valley event as:

- a marketing opportunity for local farmers and farm-based businesses
- a platform to promote healthy mutual social relationships between community members and business owners
- a community engagement platform for volunteers to assist in community building

In order to achieve these goals Vital Communities undertakes a subset of approaches at different levels. Our interviewee explains that "the keys to success to grow an event are to hold it regularly, to organize it well, to budget correctly and create a fee structure that supports the event, and in the case of an event that supports farms, to be sure that the farms benefit from the event."[15]

Vital Communities solicits feedback and adapts changes to this event each year (H-I). Through these efforts, the organization has developed clear and open communication with community members as well as its farm partners. For example, at Flavors of the Valley 2019, there was a four-sided opinion map set up near the exit of the gym. Each side asked a different question, such as "What was your favorite thing that you tasted today?" and "What makes the Upper Valley special to you?" Participants engaged with voting stickers and/or markers to write their thoughts (see Figure 5.2) (A-B-E-H-I).

Flavors of the Valley 2019 involved more than 70 volunteers who helped before, during, and after the event. This aspect of community engagement is an important goal of the event, as well as allowing the organization to better leverage their resources while also building their network and partnerships (A-B-G). It also encourages a sense of

Credit: Vital Communities/Rob Strong Photography

Figure 5.2. Soliciting feedback from participants via an opinion map.

community ownership of the event, which has increased the quality of its design, implementation, and operation.

Challenges

Although this event has generally been successful, it has experienced some challenges. For example, low participation from vendors had been a challenge for a few years. An effective strategy has been allocating more staff time and resources to outreach and sourcing potential vendors. In addition, they have been very strategic in explaining the marketing implications and opportunities that this event presents.

Outcomes

Over the past 18 years, Flavors of the Valley has brought significant social vitality to the region. We heard from multiple vendors and participants that the event has been successful in bringing in a diversity of people from many different places. One of the participants said, "Certainly, it brings people out!... vendors come from far places...some people have tunnel vision; they need to get out and see people."[16] (A-B-K) The number of community participants and variety of vendors continues to grow each year.

Flavors of the Valley creates an opportunity for people to learn where their food comes from and who the farmers are who grow it. A local resident attending the event said, "The event is good for vendors, and a good reminder of where people's food comes from and who is around the community doing local work."[17] With almost no effort, community members can walk away with new relationships as well as new awareness of local food (B-C-K).

The event provides a platform for the local vendors to reach new customers (B-D). One vendor expressed gratitude for this opportunity: "Bringing people together around food and *local* food is great." Flavors of the Valley also supports strong relationships within the community as communication between consumers and vendors is established and sustained (G-H). A staff member of Vital Communities said that the event fostered relationship "safety and connectedness," something he had longed for since moving into the area (B).

Another outcome of this event relates to its zero-waste initiative. This initiative is both practical and educational as most of the materials (like cups and plates) used are recycled, composted, or reused (C-K). "Reducing waste is what we focus on.... People are attracted to the event for the food and then realize there's more and get a chance to learn things,"[18] said one of the volunteers.

Reflections on Principle D: Be Transparent

We believe that the transformative wind of change that Vital Communities brings to the Upper Valley Region through Flavors of the Valley is a catalyst of social vitality and community cohesion. It maintains a holistic planning process that includes outlining visions, goals, and best practices, as well as appreciating what already exists in the community. A key component of the event's success is its direct collaboration with the local businesses and farmers throughout the event's entire design, operation, and implementation. These ongoing partnerships encourage lasting and meaningful commitments to the event and to Vital Communities itself.

CASE STUDY   Regenerating and Transforming a Village's Land and Water Resources, Hiware Bazar, India

by Shilpy Arora

Prologue

Hiware Bazar, one of India's most prosperous villages, was transformed from a drought-prone and water-scarce settlement to an economically strong community. The fate of the village changed in the 1990s, after a young Popatrao Baguji Pawar, the area's only postgraduate, was elected village head. Pawar engaged residents in planning and executing various projects, including watershed management, building percolation tanks, and carrying out extensive tree-planting drives. He realized that there was a need not only to address drought-related issues but also to make residents self-reliant, and persuade them to participate in development work to help bring about social, economic, and environmental change.

The story of transformation that is Hiware Bazar illuminates how effective communication by a local leader brought residents together to address environmental challenges, paving the way to economic prosperity and social development—and, thus, a healthier future.

Introduction and General Overview

Located in the semi-arid foothills of the Sahyadris mountain range, in the Ahmednagar district of Maharashtra, Hiware Bazar is marked by agricultural plots dotting the undulating terrain. The average annual rainfall is not more than 14 inches. Farmers and their crops survive mainly on rainfall and groundwater. But in 1972 the village faced a severe drought as water retention was limited due to poor permeability of the local geology. Forest degradation created an additional stress on resources. Farmers in the village had no option but to migrate to cities

Figure 5.3. A recharge well to trap rainwater at Hiware Bazar.

Credit: Hiware Bazar Village Council

in search of employment. Those who chose to stay fell into depression or became addicted to alcohol. This fuelled many social and economic problems. Soon, however, the fortunes of Hiware Bazar changed. Those who left the village in the 1970s and 80s, looking for jobs in nearby cities like Pune and Mumbai, came back in the 1990s and 2000s. Within a decade, the income of villagers increased by around 20 times. According to a 1995 survey, 168 families out of 180 were below the poverty line. Today, no family in the village of Hiware Bazar falls in that category.

Now, the village has well-built, immaculate roads, concrete houses, an elementary school, and a community center, which are rare in Indian villages. Every home has a toilet. The village has a high school, a health center, and a well-maintained mother and child care hospital. There are 294 open wells, recharging groundwater. There is a ban on deforestation, digging tube wells, grazing animals, open defecation, and tobacco and alcohol consumption. Even though rain is still scarce, the village manages to maintain the water table at 65–80 feet (which was once recorded as high as 230–260 feet). It has been a remarkable turnaround.

Goals, Approaches, Challenges, and Outcomes
Goals

- To increase the water table in a low-cost, self-managed, and effective way in order to help farmers increase agricultural produce (A-B)
- To introduce and establish community farming to address the problem of labor and create an environment of social cohesion (B-C-D)
- To spread awareness to enforce a proper ban on water-intensive crops, and encourage all farmers to grow vegetables, pulses, and fruit that use less water (D-E)
- To help villagers look beyond agriculture and introduce floriculture and dairy farming (K)
- To improve the quality of grass with the help of soil conservation in order to make available fodder for animals that leads to an increase in milk yield

- To introduce and establish community engagement programs so that people assist in community building (A-B)

Approaches

Participatory governance. The village council (*Panchayat*[19]) drafts a comprehensive five-year development plan and involves all community members in drafting the plan. School children are involved in reading rain gauges and measuring groundwater levels. Women collect a monthly water tax on individual connections. Decisions on water budgeting, crop planning, and maintenance of water structures are taken during meetings of the village council. Besides, monitoring cleanliness and afforestation drives is a responsibility of village committees[20] comprising villagers and village officials. Participation by all the residents—rich, poor, young and old—creates a strong sense of ownership (A-B-D-F-H-J).

Using short-term funds for long-term development. In 1972, when the village was reeling under water crisis, the village council used the money provided by different government schemes for drought relief to work on reviving the forest and the catchments for village wells. The council then took up watershed conservation and soil conservation. Therefore, the short-term drought relief funds were used for sustainable long-term development(C).

Voluntary contributions. The council encouraged the community to work together and contribute towards labor-intensive work including tree planting, constructing wells, digging trenches around hill contours to trap rainwater, and building percolation tanks and check dams (A-B). The villagers worked as laborers to build check dams, trenches, and wells. The residents were encouraged to help the community through *Shramdaan*[21] (a voluntary contribution involving only physical labor). When government funding was inadequate, villagers volunteered physical labor so that the funds could be used to purchase good quality construction materials (K-L). To date, residents come forward to build community buildings and check dams through *Shramdaan*.

Investment in water conservation. After farmers' income stabilized, they began to invest in water conservation by building additional water storage structures. Many farmers invested in drip irrigation to conserve water and soil (C-D-E-I-K).

Change in cropping patterns. Farmers were made aware of the need to avoid water-guzzling crops like sugarcane and bananas. Millets, onions, and potatoes, which use less water, were promoted (D-E-I-K).

Expanding agricultural activities. Many farmers used their increased agricultural earnings to buy cattle. Since the revegetation program and as part of watershed development, there was an increase in the availability of good quality grass for cattle, and this helped to increase the milk yield. Dairying, therefore, emerged as an important source of income. Similarly, floriculture, which uses less water, also gained popularity among farmers (D-F-I-K).

Investment in education. The village invests a substantial amount of money in creating a good education system. The literacy rate of the village that was 30 percent about 20 years ago has now increased to 95 percent. In primary education, children learn about water and soil conservation. Today, children from other villages also come to study in the village school (D).

Transparency to gain trust. To make the process transparent, the village council makes revenue and expenditure accounts accessible to all (D-G-H-J).

Community-driven priorities and regulation. There is a strict ban on tree cutting, grazing, and digging of tube wells. The emphasis is on maintaining the ecological balance (A-C-H-L).

Challenges

One of the major challenges was to ensure that landless farmers reaped the benefits of development, as all the schemes primarily benefited those who owned land. Since landowners own most downstream land, they had easy access to water. On the other hand, poorer farmers living uphill/upstream had to wait for years to reap the benefits of groundwater recharge. Also, limiting access to pasture/forest land for grazing animals and a strict ban on deforestation had an impact on the livelihoods of the landless, who were dependent on the forest for firewood. Nevertheless, an inclusive approach by the village council helped address the challenge. Poor and landless farmers were involved in labor-intensive work and were paid by the council through the government's employment schemes. Moreover, the village council took steps to actively assist those who did not benefit directly from the program.

Outcomes

Improvement in water table. With the help of dug wells to tap the shallow aquifers and rainwater harvesting, the water table in the area has increased from 70–80 feet to 20–25 feet. This was despite an average rainfall of 14 inches in the village.

Increase in fodder availability. A ban on grazing increased the availability of good quality grass (fodder) from 1,650 tons in 1994 and 1995 to 5,500–6,600 tons in 2001 and 2002. As a result, there was an increase in milk production from 80 gallons per day to 925 gallons per day over that same time period.

Reverse migration. Reverse migration began in 1995. Over 200 families moved back to the village and invested in agriculture.

Increase in per capita income. The success of watershed development helped many families recover from debt and poverty. Per capita income of all families increased drastically within two decades. Today, the village boasts of having one of the highest per capita incomes in the country.

Figure 5.4. Evolution in the landscape of Hiware Bazare from 1995 (*left*) to 2017 (*right*).

Credit: Hiware Bazar Village Council

Sustainable development. The community realized that a ban on felling trees and massive afforestation, and effective water conservation programs helped in ecological restoration, thereby ensuring sustainable development.

Reflections on the Principle D: Be Transparent

Communication remains an effective tool in ensuring people's participation and mobilizing community, building their confidence to draft development plans and carry them out. The success story of Hiware Bazar shows how open communication can help in promoting action. Through effective open communication, villagers developed their own model of community participation in government programs such as social forestry. "Every day, I try my best to interact with a group of villagers, especially youngsters. It is crucial to make sure that people from all economic, social, and cultural backgrounds share their ideas and participate in the development work," said Pawar.[22]

It is important to note that informal modes of communication such as community meetings at village squares and at the village council building proved effective in this case. Sharing results helped achieve bigger goals. Various success stories emerged through the proper dissemination of information. Nine neighboring villages—Khor (district Buldhana), Sakhara (district Washim), Kothoda (district Yavatmal), Kingaon (district Aurangabad), Nivdungewadi (district Ahmednagar), and Bhagadi (district Pune)—replicated the model of Hiware Bazar. It should be noted that drought-prone and suicide-prone villages also benefited from the successful development programs of Hiware Bazar.

Interestingly, the information is still shared with the younger generation; oftentimes, the younger generations are not made aware of the steps taken by their ancestors who carried out development work in the past. However, as residents of Hiware Bazar involve youngsters, they are able to pass on the knowledge. Water awareness is an integral part of the school curriculum since primary education. The students are also involved in drafting water budgets and annual auditing.

Principle D—Be Transparent

Do (Or Consider Doing)

☑ Enhance transparency in your community by ensuring that information and data is from reliable, trusted sources and stop the spread of misinformation or fake news.

☑ Post a wide range of information on your website that may include: facts, figures, policy documents, codes, meeting agendas, and minutes. However, ensure that you have not violated any personal privacy rights of your community members.

☑ Post all meetings that are open to the public—in advance.

☑ Be open for input from community members at the beginning of every board or leadership team meeting.

☑ If you are in or working with a local government, make sure you meet all open meeting and open records policies.

☑ Publicize information on improvement as well as deterioration of natural capital or environmental systems that serve your community.

Don't (Or Think Twice)

☒ Don't assume that your community is too small to be hacked by bots. You are not!

☒ Don't have executive closed-door sessions on topics that really should be in an open session.

☒ Don't use "shop-talk" at public meeting with acronyms and jargon.

☒ Don't assume you are the expert and that the public or community members will not have anything new or of value to offer. They will!

CHAPTER 6

Support Research

*Promote Research
and Information Development*

> *If I had an hour to solve a problem
> and my life depended on it,
> I would use the first 55 minutes
> determining the proper questions to ask.*
>
> — ALBERT EINSTEIN

Asking the Right Questions and
Separating Facts from Fiction

Engaging in research and finding the information that is needed for building healthy communities starts with asking the right questions. I encourage every community to come together, at least once a year, to raise the questions that need to be asked. Let these questions guide your research and information gathering for the coming year. As community members gather information in response to these questions, try to ensure that the answers are factual and confirmed by those with the right knowledge and expertise; and that the answers reflect the full diversity of social values and perspectives of community members.

Community decisions based on a broad base of knowledge, information, research, and facts collected and assessed through a transparent

SUPPORT RESEARCH

E

Promote Research and Information Development

Five Characteristics

1. *There is a common information base that is accessible and useful.*
2. *Decisions should be based upon a broad but systematic body of information.*
3. *Integrated information includes technical, scientific, social, quality-of-life, economic, and other forms of local knowledge including Indigenous experiential knowledge.*
4. *Economic evaluation of environmental assets is a valuable information base.*
5. *Ongoing research is necessary to improve upon existing solutions including a role for community members in collecting scientific information.*

Thorough and ongoing research presented as accessible and shared information is integral to the success of any community-based initiative.[2] This research must encompass local knowledge, ecosystem understanding, and evaluations of environmental assets.[3] The data should be scientific and quantitative, social and qualitative, and include other forms of Indigenous local knowledge.[4] This diversity of data and knowledge is needed to effectively inform sustainable, community-wide decisions.

Engaged scholarship[5] involves co-creation of knowledge through the involvement of a wide range of stakeholders and community members as active participants in all stages of the research process. This approach to research, which focuses primarily on meeting urgent and important societal needs, has been embraced by national institutions[6] and is being adopted by universities around the world.[7] This acceptance is documented in the recently released UN report entitled "Global Trends in Support Structures for Community University Research Partnerships."[8] It has been demonstrated that this research approach can result in the science being applied, valued, and supported[9] and can directly increase the societal benefits of the research.[10]

process are core to a healthy community. But today, with so much spin and misinformation actively disseminated by special interest groups, how do you know what is true and what is false? Asking my colleagues and friends this question, they reflect that research and information that is based on science, has multiple documented (real) sources, has been vetted by peer-review journals, published by trusted publications, and/or is shared by reputable media is likely to be trustworthy.[1]

Today, more than ever before, separating facts from fiction is essential when a community makes important decisions that will impact its social conditions, environmental health, and/or economic vitality. But how can most communities afford the costs and time of conducting essential research and gathering trusted information? My recommendation is to consider two usually under-utilized assets: a local school, university or college, and community members themselves.

Citizen Science and Citizen Technical Advisors

Citizens can serve as scientists, technical advisors, and resources for gathering and providing numerous forms of local knowledge. For example, monitoring the quality and safety of the water in a community river or lake is now frequently done by citizen scientists working with a local nonprofit, school, or university that provides the testing equipment and technical support. When citizens are involved in conducting research or gathering information, there is a greater understanding and appreciation for this information. In my community, I have experienced how the findings of these citizen-scientists or citizen technical advisors are frequently trusted by members of that community more than similar information provided by paid "outside experts." The trust between neighbors is a critical resource for many communities, particularly when they need to gather information that they can trust and then use to address difficult challenges. Some communities gather every year to celebrate, to party, and to honor all of these volunteers for their valuable service to their community.

Local Community-University Partnerships

Students at many universities frequently seek research opportunities that could benefit local communities. This type of research, sometimes referred to as "engaged scholarship," entails the co-creation of knowledge by a university through the involvement of stakeholders and community members as active participants in all stages of the research process. The US Environmental Protection Agency's Sustainable Healthy Communities subcommittee has published a review of one type of engaged scholarship approach known as a Health Impact Assessment (HIA).[11] I will share one example of a university-local community partnership where the students, through providing their service, also learn how to apply their new knowledge in helping others. These types of partnerships are common across universities in North America and in many other countries.

Faculty at my university, Antioch University New England,[12] have supervised hundreds of local community research projects where students have worked closely with a local community. Their shared findings have been helpful and were completed at low or no cost to the community. This research can include special team projects, Master Thesis/Projects, and PhD Dissertations. I will share two examples from our Community Service Initiatives (a Master's degree project) completed by a small team of students.

Tools and Techniques for Shifting Towards Sustainable Businesses in Local Communities [13]

In response to a request from the Hannah Grimes Center, a local nonprofit business incubator, our graduate students undertook a sustainability assessment study of the Center along with providing recommendations. Following this, they researched and developed a variety of organizational tools that can be easily used by these start-up incubator businesses to increase their environmental sustainability. These included: an electricity use tracking and recording model; an environmental management assessment tool; an eco-efficiency tracking model; and a model for communication plan development.

Great River Consumer Cooperative Society[14]

This co-op's mission is to create a year-round retail farmers market featuring local meats, produce, baked goods, and food products. Their goals included the protection of vulnerable farmland from development by supporting local farmers through a year-round market, the improvement of regional residents' access to fresher, healthier foods, and the overall stimulation of the region's economy by keeping more of their dollars in their region. The research and road map recommendations by the students are already helping this community organization.

Washing Machines and the Bureau of Indian Affairs

What happens when research and information gathering is not adequately conducted prior to making local community decisions? What happens when this information gathering is conducted only by external experts, without including the knowledge of local community members? I am sure you can think of numerous examples. I will share one that stayed with me for many decades.

In the 1970s I had a Native American friend in college who was born and grew up on an Indian reservation. I truly appreciated her efforts (and her patience) with widening my understanding of another culture. I was very naïve. Unbeknownst to me at the time, I had grown up with white privilege—and in a community, that I later found out, had practiced covert racism by not allowing Hispanics or Blacks to purchase homes.

She shared with me a story of what happened one day when she returned home to her family on the reservation. In front of every family's residence was a new washing machine provided by the Bureau of Indian Affairs. She asked me "What do you think everyone did with their washing machines?" "Washed their clothes?" I quipped. She looked at me, paused, and responded, "We all used them for outside storage lockers. No one had running water." She continued by sharing that an official had visited the reservation and had noted that the "Indians" (Native Americans) looked dirty, so he ordered a washing machine to be delivered to every residence. This expert decision-making process (besides illustrating racism and arrogance) did not seek input and critical information from local community members and, as a result, totally failed.

The Case Studies

The following two case studies on supporting effective research include one from Togo, one from a community in Tanzania, as well as a brief case-in-point on the role of young student researchers in New Hampshire. Each case demonstrates how well planned, participatory research can not only produce useful information, but can also build legitimacy and empowerment by involving community members in the research itself.

 Resilience to Food Insecurity, Bikotiba, Togo

by K. M. Kibler

Prologue

Bikotiba, Togo, presents a compelling example of an Indigenous community working to understand the impacts of climate change pressures. This historically colonized, developing community contends with a corrupt national government, Indigenous political divides, disappearing natural resources, and unpredictable climatic changes. The people of Bikotiba recognize their climate pressures, but lack the support to mitigate food system challenges and adapt to these pressures over time.

I joined community members in seeking to assess families' resilience to food insecurity (the ability to overcome threats to food access, availability, and use).[15] Six research assistants and I developed, tested, and then implemented a system of interviews with over half of the homes in Bikotiba. The participatory decision-making process I describe in this case was necessary to create and employ *locally relevant* interviews. Ultimately, this participatory decision-making process allowed this research to best address the community's needs and demonstrated the relevance of the 12 community leadership principles described in this book.

Introduction

I arrived in Bikotiba, Togo, in 2011 as a United States Peace Corps Environmental Action and Food Security Volunteer, as requested by the community. I lived in the village and integrated into the community to share technical skills and build relationships.[16] I arrived in Bikotiba well intentioned and motivated, but inexperienced as a community partner. For two years I lived with a family, and gardened and farmed with community members. By the end of those two years, I was still well intentioned, I was newly motivated, and I had greater experience as a cross-cultural partner. For example, I helped women gardeners receive a grant to fence their land and thus protect their income. Some mistakes, embarrassment, and feelings of defeat along the way helped me develop humility, genuine relationships of trust, and thus a basic but privileged understanding of Bikotiba.

Four years later, the community welcomed me back as a researcher. I spent those years away strengthening my capacity to work ethically with Indigenous partners to understand complex food systems. Upon return, the community and I recognized that we could work together in sharing and creating knowledge about their food system. Volunteer research assistants (RAs) and I developed a participatory research process to best assess the community's food challenges.

General Overview

Bikotiba is a rural village of approximately 1,500 people in the small West African country of Togo, which is home to nearly eight million people. The French colonized Togo in the early 1900s, and it remained a colony until gaining its independence in 1960.[17] The national language is French while the local language in Bikotiba is Bassari, representing the Bassar city and ethnic group. Togo's economy has grown in recent years (4.7 percent in 2018[18]), due largely to international aid[19] that a wealthy minority monopolizes,[20] keeping it from reaching the extremely poor rural majority (who live on $1.90 or less daily).[21] The Organization for Economic Co-operation and Development lists Togo as an impoverished fragile state and in 2013 rated Togo lowest in overall life satisfaction of the 149 countries studied.

By 2030, 90 percent of global citizens living below the poverty line will reside in sub-Saharan Africa.[22] Further, between 2030 and 2050, studies predict that citizens living below the poverty line in West Africa will experience severe crop failure because of unpredictable rainfall, higher temperatures, and strained water resources.[23] Before our research study began, farmers in Bikotiba increasingly told me about unpredictable and intense rainy seasons, resulting in crop losses, financial burdens, and increased labor demand, which is consistent with climate predications for the region as demonstrated in neighboring Ghana and Burkina Faso.[24] In Togo, the staple subsistence crop is corn. Interview participants (average age: 47) told me that corn production boomed to an unsustainable scale throughout their or their parents' lifetimes; which is consistent with evidence of corn production as far west in Africa as Togo in 1959,[25] when corn thrived in Togolese soils. Participants say the possibilities corn offered decades ago resulted in unchecked production. This weakened soils and thus stimulated deforestation in search of fertile land. Participants still sought corn production decades after soils were stripped of nutrients, which is when chemical fertilizers came into play. The introduction of these chemicals continued the cycle of soil depletion, land conversion, and poverty.

The Togolese people struggle with many economic challenges and livelihood threats. They have been described as the unhappiest people in the world. However, I counter this with the joy, celebrations, cultural pride, and unbiased hospitality that I have experienced. When I walk through Bikotiba I hear laughter and joking, I see children singing and dancing, and I see acceptance to the degree that blood relation is a minute aspect of what makes a family. When I walk through Bikotiba, I am rarely called *anasara* (foreigner), indicating likely mistrust. More often, I hear children shouting *Saye*, the Bassari name the community gave me, which means "the second daughter." Or I hear *tante* (aunt), *soeur* (sister), or *fille* (daughter)—names that generally imply respect, trust, and friendship.

I have also witnessed some of the community's food challenges. When I walk through Bikotiba, the children that I see singing are of-

Credit: Katie Kibler

Figure 6.1. Participants demonstrating farming techniques.

ten malnourished, and stop to grab breakfast with dirty hands. People return to town carrying atop their heads a 110-pound sack of corn, or logs heavier than I can imagine; they arrive having walked to and from the farms that are on average five miles away.

Since 2011, participants have reported climatic changes. Which when asked, 82 of 125 participants defined it generally as scarce, unpredictable, or violent rain. This overwhelming concern about rain is logical because their livelihoods depend on it.

My first two years in Togo led me to continue research on their climate and food security challenges. I returned to Bikotiba four years later with a better understanding about food systems and an enhanced capacity to ethically engage—as well as reengage—stakeholders. Willing participants and I then set out to explore threats to their food access together (Figure 6.1).[26]

Goals, Approaches, and Challenges

Leaders in Bikotiba have often sought assistance to help with farming challenges, such as requesting Peace Corps Volunteers. When I approached the community to conduct this research, I distinguished my role as a researcher and my past role as a volunteer (D). As a volunteer I was dedicated to the community's needs, but as a researcher I also had personal goals. I explained that my goal was to understand their food access and farming challenges, and that my hope was to arrive at this understanding together. I added that I would share what we learned so other communities and scientists can learn from them, too (B-D). In light of the weather changes that they described to me, they were eager to identify the aspects of their food system that were making it harder to adapt to a changing climate. Participants and I set out to understand the threats to their food security, to share their stories, and to advocate the need for participatory decision-making research in communities (A-E-F-J-L).

This case study is not a perfect example of including participants in all parts of research. For example, they did not participate in the statistical modeling of resilience for my research. Still, this study importantly fostered participatory decision making to generate, implement, and understand *locally relevant* research of Bikotiba's food system (A-G-J). To accomplish this goal, at my request the community nominated six volunteer research assistants to work closely with me in this study (A-D-F-G-I-J). I first developed the assessment tool—a household interview—alone, based on my knowledge from two previous years living in Bikotiba. Then over the course of one month, the RAs and I practiced the interview with each other and community members (E-H). We revised the interview six times before settling on an acceptable draft to implement (H-I-J). The RAs worked to translate the intent of the interview questions (French) into the language (Bassari) they agreed was most relevant to participants. This drafting and practice process taught us a few important things:

1. My understanding of Bassari culture and society was significant but I still had much to learn, and always will. Sometimes researchers enter communities and spend little or no time getting to know the community personally; participants in Bikotiba expressed their familiarity and discomfort with such approaches. Without years spent building relationships in the community (G), it would have taken far more than six drafts to arrive at the final interview; I would also not likely have been welcomed into homes as readily, among other challenges.

2. In a participatory research process, when developing an assessment tool such as an interview, it is important to practice the interview with a few community members; this ensures it is relevant to the participants (F-G-H) and that all questions are clear. Researchers should budget sufficient time in their designs to test methods and assessment tools with participants.

3. Developing locally relevant assessment tools (G), when participants communicate across multiple languages,[27] will require more time; this ensures participants and researchers have developed a sufficient mutual understanding despite communication challenges (A-D). Many participants do not speak French and my French skills are imperfect as well. Thus, developing locally relevant projects means all stakeholders spend time developing a common language and understanding (B-D).

Once we settled on an interview that was relevant to both our research and community needs, RAs and I spent the next two months visiting 125 (or approximately 56 percent) of the homes in Bikotiba. Adult residents consented to questions about their family, farming methods and challenges, income, and other topics relating to food access. We ended each interview thanking participants in Bassari (which I speak and understand moderately well) and reminding them about upcoming community workshops, where we would discuss what we learned from the interviews (D-G).

In addition to generating data, it is critical for participants to validate data interpretations (A-G). Participants and I collaborated daily to develop the interview, implement it, and try to understand the results (A-B-G-J-K). I analyzed data along the way and RAs helped to confirm or offer insights to improve my interpretations (A-J-K). For example, RAs helped me to understand that participants cite the semi-nomadic Fulani tribes as crop pests (just like caterpillars), claiming they steal from the fields and let their cattle damage crops. When the study concluded, we invited the community to hear what we learned from the interviews and asked participants to confirm or correct how we understood the data (D-G-H-J-L). I believe this validation process enhanced the community's overall trust, appreciation, and interest in the research.

The greatest challenges in this case were social. When I returned to Bikotiba after four years, I was surprised by the degree of social divisions that existed in the community. I learned that during my time away disagreements had arisen because of tensions between the three districts that make up Bikotiba. The district designated as the village's chiefdom was not supported by the other two. It became clear that despite sharing traditional cultural values, this community has been politically divided for a long time. Unfortunately, these contentions limited the study's implementation and scope. Young men at the students' workshop expressed their elders' stubbornness in finding agreement over community issues. While this participatory research has encouraged some to find common ground, challenges managing conflict remain as an obstacle (A-J).

Outcomes

In a final community gathering, RAs and I shared key takeaways from the interview process using images (Figure 6.2). Images were essential because a majority of the population is reading illiterate. Participants appreciated the humility expressed in my poor drawing skills and they related to the images as RAs spoke in Bassari in more detail about key takeaways. We asked participants to share their reactions to our interpretations. RAs and I demonstrated that the four primary concerns community members expressed in the interviews were social disagreements, scarce rain, depleted soils, and the demand to treat corn with fertilizer. RAs and I outlined actions that the community could take in mitigating some of these concerns. Based on what we heard during the interviews and workshops, these included reforestation, a gradual return to predominantly eating traditional crops (millet, sorghum, cassava, and yam) versus chemical-intensive corn, and efforts to rebuild social cohesion.

I hope to follow the community's progress over time and continue

Credit: Katie Kibler

Figure 6.2. Drawings of
key interview takeaways
and potential mitigation
opportunities.

our research partnership. Still, the lasting impact of this participatory
assessment for the community is intangible. The greatest takeaway I
identify from this process is the new knowledge generated through the
participatory research process. Participants were interested in the interview results, particularly our observations about corn production.
For most families, three meals per day are comprised of corn, yet it
is the only crop requiring chemical fertilizers to meet yield requirements. Overwhelmingly, 108 of the 125 participants agreed that corn is
drought-intolerant. We asked participants how their parents farmed to
understand how farming has adapted over time. Of the 125 participants
questioned, 15 said their parents did not grow corn, 25 said their parents did not use fertilizer, and 17 said their parents farmed only for food
to eat rather than for making a profit. In personal conversations, most
participants told me that when corn was first introduced it became
so abundant (and lucrative) that their generation stopped producing
more drought-tolerant, traditional crops. Over time, with intensive
corn production, soils were depleted and now corn requires expen-
sive chemical fertilizer to achieve much lower yields. Even though
crops like millet and sorghum are more reliable, behaviors are hard to
change. Most participants just do not like the taste of traditional crops

anymore. From what we gathered, the people of Bikotiba cumulatively do not seem ready to shift their farming practices. Though I believe positive individual participant efforts grew from this experience, this community will require longer-term, local support services pointed toward challenges identified in this study.

Reflections on Principle E: Support Research

This case study demonstrates three important things:

1. All 12 principles in this book are represented to some degree in this one case study, which demonstrates their relevance.
2. When a community supports thoughtful, ethical, and locally relevant research, it is possible to develop context-specific assessment tools, such as interviews.
3. Despite challenges, this community successfully supported a participatory research process. Social and political disagreements limited the scope and reach of this study, but this study's outcomes created an important and reflective foundation for future research and resilience efforts in the community.

Despite the obstacles identified, I left Bikotiba in 2018 hopeful for several reasons. While the traditional political divides in this community will take time to resolve, this participatory research demonstrated to community members how those divides hinder their progress over time. By supporting this research process, the community can move forward with new knowledge and local insight. This study integrated a variety of findings to develop a systematic body of information relevant to both participants and a broader scientific community. Participants and I left our study with an understanding that the community could better assess their specific climactic pressures as well as take action with minimal external assistance. I left Bikotiba confident that young leaders, like the RAs, were motivated and equipped with what they needed to guide their community in further climate change research and adaptation efforts.

CASE IN POINT   An Outdoor Student Environmental Learning Lab, Keene, New Hampshire, USA

by Paul Bocko

The Rachel Marshall Outdoor Learning Lab[28] (RMOLL) came about when Antioch University New England faculty, Keene officials, and school district leaders visited the forgotten 2.5-acre section of Ashuelot River Park and envisioned a partnership. The partners saw much more than hard-scrabble land. Instead they imagined a learning lab for K-12 youth and the community.

The purpose of the learning lab was to provide students with the space and resources to conduct ecological research and make land management decisions. Projects included third grade students collecting data on bird migration, seventh grade students expanding habitat planting, and high school students researching invasive species eradication. All of the projects were based on historical and ecological inventories held by the city and community organizations. Proposals and results were reviewed by the RMOLL Education Advisory Committee and shared with the community in reports, public programs, and educational displays.

A few years following the start of the program, projects had outgrown the allotted space and were threatening the ecological integrity of the site. Given the research success and community value that the program was providing, the city agreed to donate 2,000 acres of unused city-owned green space. This generous donation encouraged more student field work. Projects grew to include documenting the succession of an abandoned pasture, macroinvertebrate water-quality testing, and nature writing.

The K-12 youth who participated in RMOLL walked away with a meaningful connection to nature and first-hand experience caring for it. Connection and exploration are the key concepts here. A teacher who participated in the program emphasized the purpose of the first field trip of any RMOLL project: "Just to be there and know the place."

She clearly understood that if students are to care for their surroundings in real time and in the future, they first need to scout the landscape and forge ties to it. This is what David Sobel wrote about in *Beyond Ecophobia*—giving children the chance to connect with nature well before we ask them to save it.[29]

In the end, thousands of students participated, hundreds of teachers led projects, and a formal partnership between the city, school district, and university was established. During the nine years of engaging programs, RMOLL was able to successfully engage youth in environmental research and conservation actions. It was also able to strengthen the way the City of Keene and the surrounding region interacted with and stewarded their natural, cultural, and built environments. The legacy and relationships formed there still live on today in successor groups and initiatives.

 CASE STUDY Mobilizing the Local Voice to Support Protected Area Governance, Magombera Forest, Tanzania

by Nicole Wengerd

Prologue

Protected areas (PAs) are not a modern concept. Societies have long recognized the need to safeguard natural resources. For thousands of years, indigenous communities have been setting aside land for hunting, grazing, collecting resources, and a variety of cultural pursuits and activities. In the Global North, the common practice of area protection was built on the belief that biodiversity protection is best achieved by isolating ecosystems from human disturbance. This approach promoted the ideals of a people-free landscape with a top-down, often government-led, exclusionary focus. It wasn't until the 1980s that a movement to decentralize control and shift to a more participatory, human-centered model of biodiversity conservation gained momentum. This new model emphasizes cooperation among stakeholders and views local communities as active partners rather than passive recipients of top-down directives.[30] This case study is set in the southern highlands of Tanzania, around Magombera forest, where I worked with four forest-adjacent communities. With the protection status and governance structure of Magombera forest pending, this case study details how the methods of Asset-Based Community Development (ABCD) can be applied to build a base of community-level information that mobilizes community voice in the PA planning process.

Introduction

Magombera forest sits to the east of the Udzungwa Mountains National Park and adjacent to the Selous Game Reserve, in southern Tanzania. In many ways, the story of Magombera forest is a familiar one. The forest is internationally known for its rich biodiversity, including populations of the endangered Udzungwa red colobus monkey, as well as the discovery of new species, including the Magombera chameleon. Its biological conservation value has been clearly documented over the years; however, it's less well-known that there are also four neighboring communities that rely on access to and around the forest for their livelihood and survival. Past approaches to address the conservation of biodiversity and, at the same time, the well-being of local people have produced mixed results.[31] The challenges are often embedded in issues of governance, not necessarily management. The difference between the two might seem nuanced, but the distinction is important. While management addresses what is done about a given site or situation, governance addresses who makes those decisions and how, implicating power, relationships, responsibility, and accountability.[32] Who counts? Who has influence? Who decides on the decision-making structure? And how are decision makers held accountable?

These questions are a big part of what inspired my dissertation research, which explored how an asset-based, biocultural approach[33] could support local stakeholder participation in protected area planning and management.[34] This case study details a portion of that research, focusing narrowly on how the methods of ABCD could be used to mobilize and share the voices of local stakeholders before developing a governance structure and seeking protected status designation.

The following will briefly outline the history of the site, followed by the goals for the study, the details of the approach, and the most pressing challenges. Lastly, the case will conclude by reviewing the broad outcomes and connections to Principle E (Support Research).

General Overview

Although the narrative of Magombera forest is familiar, the details of the situation are unique. Following the discovery of the Udzungwa red colobus in the 1970s, and other species of plants and animals that were either rare or unique to the area, the Tanzanian government agreed to add Magombera forest to the adjacent Selous Game Reserve, which was much more heavily protected. For reasons that are still unclear, the forest was never formally annexed, leaving it without a protected status. In the early 2000s, researchers and conservationists in the area learned of this error, which reignited efforts to secure protection for the forest. When I first visited the site in June of 2015, the protected status and governance structure was still in flux. One of the strongest advocates moving the protection agenda forward was a conservation project called the Udzungwa Forest Project (UFP). UFP operates in partnership with Flamingo Land, a United Kingdom-based theme park and conservation zoo, and the Tanzania Forest Conservation Group. During my data collection I was lucky enough to partner with members of the UFP team who had established relationships with the four forest-adjacent communities.

Goals, Approaches, and Challenges

The primary goals of this study can be summarized as follows:

- Utilize the methods of ABCD, specifically asset mapping, to identify the capacities and strengths of the local communities in the context of forest management.
- Use a community visioning process to organize and mobilize a unified voice for the four villages through a joint-forest management plan.
- Communicate that knowledge to the potential partnering stakeholders.

To achieve these goals, this research relied on an ABCD approach. An ABCD approach focuses on "discovering and mobilizing the resources that are already present in a community."[35] The approach shifts interactions with communities from a deficiency, needs, and problem-based orientation to an asset-based approach, built on a foundation of communities engaging and contributing around a shared goal by identifying and mobilizing existing assets (A-B-K-J).[36] A five-step guide for implementation was created to help communities facilitate the process of identifying and mobilizing community assets and capacities around a common vision or plan[37] (Table 6.1). The steps include participatory asset-mapping, building relationships, mobilizing community assets, building a community vision and plan, and leveraging outside resources to support asset-based, locally defined development (E-A-B-J-K-I).

Table 6.1. ABCD Methods[38]

Step	Kretzmann and McKnight Methods
1	Mapping completely the capacities and assets of individuals, associations, and local institutions.
2	Building relationships among local assets for mutually beneficial problem solving within the community.
3	Mobilizing the community's assets fully for economic development and information-sharing purposes.
4	Convening as broadly representative a group as possible for the purpose of building a community vision and plan.
5	Leveraging activities, investments, and resources from outside the community to support asset-based, locally defined development.

This study used these proposed guidelines as just that—guidelines. We utilized each of these steps to some degree throughout the process, although the strongest connection can be found with steps 1 (asset mapping), 4 (community visioning), and 5 (supporting locally defined development), which are presented below in more detail.

Asset Mapping (Goal 1)

The intention of the asset-mapping activity was to understand what capacities and assets existed in each of the communities, concerning resource use and management. We wanted the communities to be able to articulate what they bring to the table, to highlight why they should be included in the management decisions to outside stakeholders, who traditionally were the decision makers (J-I-K). We asked participants to identify assets at three levels (individual, association/organization, and local institution). Some examples of assets included witchdoctors (individual), an association for witchdoctors (association/organization), and the family (local institution). We then asked the participants to identify which of those assets, at any level, influence the use of resources from the forest (mapped prior to asset mapping). Knowing what resources are being used is important baseline information, but the value of this process was its ability to uncover *who* was most influential in *why* and *how* the participants used the resources (A-C-H). For example, at the local institutional level, participants said the family was the most responsible for why and how you would use resources from the forest, based on values and norms. This information was valuable because it emphasized the power of cultural norms and values. Another interesting finding was how frequently witchdoctors were cited as an influential player in resource use. Since they are not traditionally a group that would be included in forest management discussions, this information helped identify voices that have previously been absent at the forest management table.

The Details

In total, 94 participants contributed to the data collection process.[39] We spent half the day guiding an asset mapping inventory, which was facilitated by my two Tanzanian field assistants in each community. The asset mapping process was conducted in separate men's and women's groups to ensure that both of the groups were heard with no undermining of one by the other (E-F). The session opened by defining what is considered an asset. Once the concept was clear, an inventory of assets was collected using large poster paper, broken down into the following categories: individuals, associations/organizations, and local institutions. At the end of the session, the data were compiled into a database by myself and my lead field assistant. The database coded all the identified assets by category (individual, associations/organizations, local institution), then by village and gender.

Equipped with a complete list of resources and assets for each village, my field assistants guided an in-depth discussion on the connections between the two, with men and the women together in the same session (H-I-B). Starting with each of the resources listed, participants were asked which assets influenced or controlled the use of that resource. My field assistants and I then grouped the listed assets based on the frequency in which they were identified, both the number of times and number of resources. After each village grouping was complete, general themes of influential assets were identified based on the cumulative responses for all four villages. The themes were then used to inform a community visioning process, focused on joint resource management.

Community Visioning and Stakeholder Meetings (Goals 2 and 3)

The community visioning process was the culmination and application of the asset mapping activities. The intention was to give communities the time and space to reflect on how they wanted to engage with resources in the future, to make connections with assets from inside their communities in governance and management, and to ask hard questions about accountability. The other goal of the visioning process and the stakeholder meetings was to create a unified voice amongst the communities. The joint community vision (see details below) was an attempt to broaden their view from "my community" to "the communities of Magombera forest." For management purposes, there needed to be hard conversations and beginning negotiations about what resources communities relied on for their livelihood, and I thought that conversation was most productive if it happened amongst themselves first, before bringing in outside voices.

Figure 6.3. A community visioning in progress.

Credit: Nicole Wengerd

The Details

The visioning started with all the participants together identifying the most influential assets in terms of resource use in each category. Following this, in a focus group setting, participants used this information to outline a joint forest management community vision. Three questions were used to guide the discussion and focus on future community participation, highlighting the connection between resources, accountability, partnerships, and transparency (H-A-B-D-C).[40] The questions were grounded in principles cited in a vast body of literature on good governance, which focuses on both the effectiveness of conservation strategies (such as protected areas) as well as the equity in their management.[41] After each of the villages created a vision, two representatives from each village met for a two-day session to create one joint community vision based on information from the asset mapping process.

The joint vision created by community representatives was presented orally to both regional and national stakeholders by two representatives from the two-day session in two separate meetings. The first meeting was held with the regional stakeholders who represented the potential future partners with the community if a joint forest management governance structure was to be implemented, as well as the representatives from each of the villages. The second meeting was held with the corresponding national representatives from the equivalent offices and departments in Dar es Salaam,[42] but only included the two representatives presenting the joint community vision. Paper copies of the community vision were provided in Ki-Swahili to all who attended, which included the two representatives from each village, local government officials, and the outside stakeholders.

Challenges

While the process was informative and productive, no approach is without limitations or challenges. The challenges for this study fit into three broad categories: inclusiveness, education, and power. First, while in principle, ABCD is an inclusive process, in practice this can be more challenging to achieve, especially in communities where social hierarchy excludes or marginalizes some groups.[43] The second major constraint is formal education. This limitation specifically concerns stakeholder education. Depending on the application of the model, simply providing stakeholders with the opportunity to participate in decision making may not be enough for them to actually participate.[44] Power is another limitation in the ABCD approach. Stakeholder participation and decision-making processes do not take place in isolation but are embedded in a pre-established power structure.[45]

Outcomes

There were two primary outcomes. The first was a joint forest management community vision, and the second was the regional and national stakeholder meetings. Each is detailed below.

Finished Joint Forest Management Community Vision

The joint forest management community vision was a snapshot of what the communities wanted and how they saw themselves involved in the management process. The vision included a plan for resource usage, monitoring, and management, as well as discussion of key partnering stakeholders, the role of the communities, and how to improve communication and transparency. Having this document provided both a sense of legitimacy to the outside stakeholders, a unified voice in the process, and a living document that can be referenced to and altered in the future.

Stakeholder Meeting

The stakeholder meetings were an outcome in that they started the conversation about an asset-based, internally focused governance structure and management plan. The meetings did this by showing the unified engagement of the communities and by identifying their capacity to be part of the process. The regional stakeholders, in particular, praised the communities for the process, their hard work on the community vision, and offered valuable feedback. When asked in a survey if the process could improve communication between the communities and their organization or department, a stakeholder responded that they strongly agreed that it would because, "A common understanding on conservation issues…helps [me] to know that conservation is for all stakeholders at [the] grassroot[s] and my department." Another stakeholder commented on the "full participation of the communities" and how "well informed" all of the stakeholders would be as a result. They also offered valuable knowledge and ways to improve the vision. For

Figure 6.4. Presentation of the community vision to the regional stakeholders.

Credit: Nicole Wengerd

example, tailoring the community resource use vision to the specific laws in place. These interactions helped to create a more equitable narrative for negotiation and management.

Reflection on Principle E: Support Research

There are several principles that I think this case study could fit into, but Principle E (Support Research) truly captures what the ABCD approach tries to achieve: voice. That voice is carefully and systematically crafted by starting with the strengths and assets of a community. In this case, we were able to detail not only *what* resources were being used, but also *why* and *how*, and identify *who* influences that use. Using that information base allowed the communities to articulate their wants and needs in their future use of the forest to the outside stakeholders and traditional decision makers, as well as articulate what role they can and want to play in that process. At the regional stakeholder meeting, especially, we witnessed the value of integrating the community's knowledge and perceptions of forest resources with the more formal training of the managers.

This case study also illustrates how continuing research allows us to become more effective in achieving conservation outcomes. Identifying assets in the community allowed us to see not only the capacity of the villages to engage, but it also uncovered groups and individuals that could bring a valuable voice and influence in the management of the forest (e.g., witchdoctors). I think there are more opportunities like this to engage and shift the narrative of communities as threats to partners in management. Instead of looking at the people as a barrier, they can be viewed as assets.

Principle E—Support Research

Do (Or Consider Doing)

- ✓ Develop a common information base that community members have easy access to.
- ✓ Support citizen science where community members help monitor the health of rivers, wetlands, and other ecological resources.
- ✓ Seek out the knowledge of often disempowered members such as racial minorities, seniors, low-income residents, among others.
- ✓ Translate data into a more readable format such as graphs and charts rather than tables of numbers and include your sources for all information provided.
- ✓ Support research that is based on a variety of forms of knowledge such as: technical, scientific, social, cultural, and economic.
- ✓ When undertaking economic research, make sure to include the economic value of the community's ecological assets including the ecological services they provide.
- ✓ Support citizen science where community members help monitor the health of ecological resources, but have a knowledgeable individual oversee and coordinate the work.
- ✓ Consider partnering with your local university or college to gain needed information for your community.

Don't (Or Think Twice)

- ✗ Don't accept information that is from hearsay or from special interest groups that does not have credible documented sources.
- ✗ Don't accept information from social media unless there are documented and credible (multiple) sources to confirm that the information is true.
- ✗ Don't "kill the messenger" if the data contradicts your hypothesis or desired outcome.
- ✗ Knowledge is power. Don't control, delay, or hide disturbing or challenging information or knowledge from the community.

CHAPTER 7

Delegate and Empower

Devolution of Authority and
Empowerment of Community Members

> *It is when citizens stop waiting for professionals*
> *or elected leadership to do something,*
> *and decide they can reclaim what they have*
> *delegated to others, that things really happen.*
>
> — PETER BLOCK

Devolution and Empowerment

During our work to help build democratic institutions and civil society in the US and overseas, our project team (including colleagues from my university and other democracy-building NGOs) framed three levels of involving citizens in the work of their communities. The first level is sharing information, including the discussions and actions by those in leadership or decision-making roles. We discuss this under Principle D: Be Transparent. The second level is to ask for and actively seek input from the community members. This is discussed under Principle A: Involve Everyone. The third level, usually the most challenging for those in formal leadership roles, is to engage and involve community members in decision making *and* implementation of actions. This level of involvement, the focus of this chapter—F: Delegate

DELEGATE AND EMPOWER

Devolution of Authority and Empowerment of Community Members

Five Characteristics

1. *True sharing of power and responsibility (devolution of authority and responsibility) between government authorities, community groups, and the wider community will enhance local decision making and improve outcomes.*

2. *Most individuals affected by rules and regulations, including those who are often marginalized, should be included or represented in the group who make or modify the rules.*

3. *There are multiple layers of governments and enterprises related to the roles and activities of decision making, appropriation, monitoring, enforcement, conflict resolution, and governance, which are nested or situated within each other.*

4. *Devolution of control and decision making significantly changes the relationship between central governments and rural/regional areas, and if done effectively, it can engage and build the commitment of local community members.*

5. *Establishing clear rules, procedures, and regulations can empower the local community.*

Devolution of authority—transferring political authority and responsibility to a local region or community—has the potential to create space for greater community-based decision making, therefore empowering individual members as well as groups.[2] If carried out appropriately, it will, by definition, allow the community to create a decision-making structure that "relies on the collaboration of a diverse set of stakeholders operating at different levels, often in networks, from local use to municipalities, regional and national organizations."[3]

Several researchers have identified that this shift in power needs to attend to marginalized and resource-dependent groups if it is to be done equitably.[4] This shift will inherently redefine the hierarchical relationships involved in the transfer of authority[5] and so should be carried out thoughtfully. Overall, post-devolution relationships may very well include that of greater legislative influence,[6] the addition of new institutions to manage decisions at different levels,[7] and a true sharing of responsibility between government officials and community groups.[8]

and Empower—requires sharing power and authority. This approach, also referred to as "devolution of authority," is described in more depth in the Research Corner.

Empowering people requires those in leadership roles to be more inclusive, more collaborative, and open to the ideas of others. This way of working with community members will take additional effort and time. It is also essential to include those in the community who are disempowered or frequently marginalized. However, if done through a sincere and thoughtful process, we and other researchers have found that this will both enhance the quality of governance and empower community members.[1] By sharing authority and engaging others in the work of the community, you are also building teams and sharing responsibility with them to achieve the goals and actions needed for a future healthier community.

Ask a friend how they describe their best boss. It is likely they will use words such as: open to other's ideas, collaborative, offers encouragement rather than criticism, does not micromanage but gives you autonomy to problem-solve your way, respects you, and is empowering. If you are in a formal or informal leadership role in your community, model the "best boss" approach and I predict you will gain respect and be more effective in your role.

Tale of Two Bike Paths

Swansea, Massachusetts. The first community meeting for the future bike path was about to convene. The public notice had been placed in the newspaper, the agenda was set and the meeting room was ready. As the recently hired town engineer, just out of graduate school, I had developed the proposed route for the bike path. Two people arrived to the advertised meeting. That was it. A young married couple who admitted that they wanted an evening away from the kids. Bike path? Well, perhaps a good idea. My two citizens did not return to participate in a second meeting. So, I marched ahead with designing the future bike path (including plan views and cross-sections) seeking state and federal grant support as well as support from the town board. Forty years later…there is still no bike path in this town, at least not located where I had designed it! However, it was a lesson learned. Top-down decision making without involving and empowering community members frequently fails.

Nearly two decades after Swansea, I was in Keene, New Hampshire, where there were no bike paths either. The city planner showed me a failed effort from one year earlier—an expert-developed plan of pathways. When he asked me if I might be interested in helping with a bike path effort for the city, I said yes, but that I would be taking a different approach from their previous attempt (and from my previous approach in Swansea).

A friend and colleague, Delia Clark, who is an environmental educator, and I had just established a nonprofit institute[9] at Antioch University New England with a mission of "engaging people in the process of creating environmentally healthy, culturally rich, and economically strong schools and communities through leadership training, environmental education, and applied research." We had learned much from a previous effort in developing a recycling program Hartford, Vermont, (see Chapter 3: "Vermont's First Un-Shopping Center") and were committed to approaching this new challenge through a process of engaging and empowering community members. We also had an opportunity to involve environmental studies graduate students in this effort.[10]

Our approach seemed radical to many, but the city was open to trying out this atypical community-planning and decision-making effort. Over the next three months, we and our students worked hard to encourage many citizens, city councilors, the mayor, and some city staff members to attend an evening forum at the recreation center. When about 50 people arrived, we shared that they had an opportunity to develop a master plan for the future bike and non-motorized pathways for the city. The goals included developing a new pathways system where youth and adults had an opportunity to travel safely across the city. We also recognized that there was no funding currently available.

We had printed a number of blank maps of the city that showed the existing roads, streams, and major infrastructure. We divided people into a number of small groups, each provided with a map and colored markers and given the charge to discuss and lay out a master plan for pathways. An hour later, all the small groups posted their efforts and shared how they came to their proposed plan of pathways. Yes, the maps were a bit messy, but each group agreed on their approach. There was a considerable number of common paths on all the maps. We held a second meeting a few weeks later and nearly all the participants returned. They returned because they had ownership of the process, enjoyed meeting new community members who shared common values, and wanted to see how their work would be represented in the final plan.

We taped a large map on the wall that combined all the ideas. After sharing and discussing this map, all the participants were given stickers (small dots) to place on their top five routes. Within a half hour, a pattern quickly emerged. We then discussed and agree upon priorities—Phase 1, Phase 2, etc.—recognizing that no ideas were discarded but that we needed to start and then proceed on routes that were most important to the group as a whole. Everyone in the room reached consensus, with no disagreements, on how to phase in all of the proposed routes. This process also helped developed a strong advocacy group of citizens committed and ready to work towards making their shared pathways plan a reality.

But what about the money needed to pay for this? The city was able to secure 80 percent federal funding, in part due to a process that included many community members, the city council's timely unanimous adoption of this plan, and the commitment by the participants in this planning process to raise the required 20 percent match. Within one year, a new nonprofit, "Pathways for Keene," was formed, the 20 percent match was secured, and design was soon underway. Over the last 25 years, with leadership from Pathways for Keene and other community groups, many new routes have grown that include three major bridges, spanning streams, and highways. This has allowed the pathways system in Keene to connect to all major areas of the city with safe passage for youth and adults. This approach was effective in enhancing the quality of the community in part by the city council and city staff empowering and trusting community members and supporting their efforts.

The Case Studies

The following two case studies focus on the importance of allowing community members to have direct input into the goals and implementation of the development of their communities. In Northern Ghana local village members, including girls and women, were empowered to develop school programs and small businesses. Residents of local villages and towns in each of the Baltic countries (Estonia, Latvia, and Lithuania) worked together to create their first community foundations to address locally identified needs.

 CASE STUDY   Community-Led Sustainable Development in Northern Ghana

by Heather Heckel

Prologue

Each time I visit rural Northern Ghana, I am struck by the volume of broken international aid "projects"—the abandoned wells and water purification tanks, the disconnected rainwater catchments, the large agriculture training center with a caved-in roof, never connected piles of irrigation hoses being used as chicken nests, an empty health clinic that never opened, and the primary schools without desks or teachers.

This case describes an alternative model, focused on community-led development and emphasizing empowerment processes (F) over project creation. The collaboration between a community-based organization, Capacity Rural International (CRI) and the US-based NGO Engage Globally (Engage) illustrates several best practices for empowerment in rural, low-income settings. This ongoing effort demonstrates that communities can lead their own development, with financial and capacity-building support.

Introduction and General Overview

Capacity Rural International works in six rural villages in Ghana's Northern Region. Most villagers are subsistence farmers who face water scarcity, changing rainfall patterns, and high population growth. These communities face many development challenges including lack of clean water, no sanitation, low literacy, limited access to electricity, and increasing emigration to urban areas. Most girls spend hours daily collecting water and firewood. Like many rural communities, there are also diverse strengths including a strong cultural heritage, social capital, resilience capacity, and shared community knowledge.

Goals, Approaches, Challenges, and Outcomes

In 2008, Walisu Alhassan, a local tour guide, felt that rising tourism and economic opportunities in the regional capital of Tamale, could be used to benefit smaller communities. Raised in two rural villages, Walisu highly values local culture and social capital. Thus, he began his efforts by meeting with traditional chiefs and councils, to discuss development priorities.

Recognizing that these conversations involved only older men, Walisu also met with women from the villages and helped to strengthen and expand an informal women's group. He then met with older youth to discuss what would be needed to reduce urban emigration and to empower them to remain in their communities. Building on this broad consultation, the community groups agreed upon the following goals:

- establish a formal community-based NGO
- expand educational opportunities for village youth
- increase economic opportunities, especially for women

Approaches

Capacity Rural International believes that sustainable change occurs when local leaders empower communities to pursue self-identified goals. Projects are intersectional and long-term, as illustrated by the vocational training seamstress program. After three women graduated from vocational training, the community built a shop, creating the first woman-owned business in their village. The graduates, now co-owners, sew uniforms for the 120 students enrolled in CRI's two early childhood education centers. They also are training new seamstress students in the vocational program. One of the shop's co-owners shared the value of empowering community members to help each other, stating:

> We are proud to share these great skills on dress making to these young ones who want to earn a better living in the future so that they can also become responsible in their homes and the society at large. We want them one day to also be self-employed and manage their own shops in the future and this will make us very proud.[11]

Mentoring between older and younger students is also encouraged. The process is institutionalized by hiring students who complete high

Figure 7.1. Fatawu showing a younger student how to use a camera on a youth club field trip.

Credit: Kaila Drayton

school as community educators and through a youth club focused on service and mentoring. Fatawu, pictured above, is a program graduate and teacher in the early childhood center. He shared that, "my family, my community see the difference from other students who don't participate in the program...giving me a role in the program is a plus to everyone in our community."

Strategies employed include:

- Collective goal setting with traditional leaders, the women's group, and potential project participants to ensure shared expectations.
- Using local volunteers for project implementation, such as construction of both early childhood centers.
- Piloting all projects before significant investment of time or financing. This allows adjustments to projects when something is not working. For example, in a tree planting pilot project, six of ten trees died from lack of water. In the scaled-up project, a local student was hired to care for the trees.
- Respecting local culture and integrating it into programming. Both early childhood centers teach a bilingual, place-based curriculum.
- Making relationships and social capital a priority. For example, before a student receives a scholarship to attend school, CRI staff meet with families to discuss the commitment. Annual meetings are also held with teachers and students.
- Hiring all employees from the local region; most were born in the villages. There is an emphasis on staff capacity building through trainings conducted by Ghanaians.
- Collaborating with a small US NGO, Engage Globally, to provide funding and capacity-building support.

Challenges
Working with people living below the global poverty line can be challenging due to barriers of geography and distance, literacy, time availability, and cultural differences. Overcoming these barriers requires a long-term commitment and multisectoral approach.

Working with rural communities with low resources and high vulnerabilities requires sustained external funding, such as that provided by Engage. Additionally, in this case, program coordination initially depended on one leader, until others completed educational and training programs.

Community-led change is difficult to measure as assessment, especially collection of data, takes skills, time, and funding. Some outcomes, such as empowerment, are not easily quantified. Finally, the number of people reached is limited and scaling-up takes time, as is now seen by neighboring villages requesting to participate in CRI's programs.

Outcomes

In partnership with Engage, Capacity Rural International is achieving several of its original goals, including:

- school enrollment for 120 early childhood learners and 35 secondary school students
- comprehensive student support with food, clothing, health, sports, and mentoring
- vocational training for 15 young adults, annually
- establishment of small businesses, so far employing 14 local residents, including eight women
- piloting of agriculture, literacy, and health programs for women

Community empowerment and participation outcomes include:

- increased academic and professional skills of young adults, many of whom are now serving as mentors and leaders in their villages
- enhanced economic opportunities—as Fuseina, a seamstress shop co-owner, shared: "This business has been very helpful to us and our family. We make a good living from the income especially when we have a large order of uniforms to sew and we also make good money from our day-to-day customers who come to place orders for their dresses. Through this business we are now able to have all the basic needs for our children. We are married and we support

our families financially if our husbands don't have money for medical needs."[12]

- expansion of participation in the women's group to five villages and 80 members
- creation of the first parent-teacher association in the region, which offers women another participation and leadership opportunity

Reflections on Principle F: Delegate and Empower

A number of community building principles are embodied by CRI's work. First, this is a model for how to empower low-income subsistence farming communities to manage their own sustainable development (F). By valuing community strengths and engaging in extensive relationship building, strengths are emphasized rather than gaps in development.

Figure 7.2. Student being presented with a new school uniform sewn by graduates of the vocational program. Observing are two traditional leaders, the student's mother, and a teacher.

A key strategy is including a broad range of community members in an ongoing participatory decision-making process (A-J). This process leads to practice with civic engagement and opportunities for positive community building experiences, such as when families and chiefs attend ceremonies at the early childhood education centers, as pictured below (B).

As capacity increases through local employment, trainings, and community meetings, this enhances the ability of the community to collaborate with external partners, such as Engage Globally (B). Ultimately, empowerment of the community, in this case, is an enabling condition for sustainable development (K).

Core lessons include:

- Community-led development requires participatory decision making by a wide range of community members. This may involve the intentional

Credit: Walisu Alhassan, Capacity Rural International

creation of women's and youth groups to complement traditional decision-making structures (A).

- Local project management increases efficient use of resources and uses local knowledge (goats eat trees) to avoid problems and to adjust project designs (trees need more water), increasing the likelihood of positive outcomes (I).
- Designing projects that utilize community volunteers, create local employment, and facilitate mentoring can significantly increase both economic opportunities and personal empowerment (F).
- Outcomes may be difficult to quantify or assess in terms of traditional quantitative data-based monitoring and evaluation.
- This community-driven process requires a long-term external partner.

CASE STUDY

Climate Change and the Minnehaha Creek Watershed: Where Will All the Water Go? Minnesota, USA

by James Gruber and Leslie Yetka

Prologue

This is a story of how an urban area came together to figure out what to do with all that rain. Climate change was already affecting this south-central region of Minnesota and needed to be addressed. The Minnehaha Creek Watershed District was a key local partner in this multistakeholder process.[13] Rather than hiring experts to design and build additional "grey" (concrete) infrastructure, the watershed district worked with local governments,[14] NGOs, universities,[15] and others to engage a wide range of stakeholders in coming together and developing an integrated, comprehensive approach. Outcomes included changes in land use and planning approaches, promoting low-impact development with less impervious areas, encouraging rain gardens, enhancing storm water retention through "green" infrastructure, addressing educational needs, and developing strategies for sustainable financing of new stormwater systems through impact fees on impervious surfaces. It was hoped that this participatory process would not only help solve the current problems but also create partnerships and expand local knowledge to ensure that climate change adaptation and resilience would continue to address on-going needs.

Introduction and General Overview

When we were asked to help plan and co-lead this public participation and planning process[16] in the Minneapolis region of Minnesota, we jumped at the opportunity. While climate change is a worldwide problem that requires a worldwide solution, local communities have an important role and responsibility to address its effects now. In this case study we will share how the public participation and decision-making process was a key element in helping to create a climate change adaptation plan for a neighborhood in the cities of Minneapolis and Victoria (A-B-F-J). The locally assembled public process team, working closely with the science team, planned and implemented a collaborative stakeholder-driven planning process that engaged a wide range of constituency groups (B-D-E). This two-year process resulted in specific and prioritized adaptation strategies for addressing the growing stormwater-intensive flooding events.

Goals, Approaches, Challenges, and Outcomes
Goals

Our overarching goal with the Minnehaha Creek Watershed Stormwater Adaptation project was to increase resilience, adaptive capacity, and social capital by engaging the public with current climate change science and accessible local data and fostering collaboration and trust among agencies and the general public (B-E-I).

Approach

Long-term environmental, economic, and social sustainability can only be reached by empowering individuals and communities to understand the root causes of local problems and to participate in creating solutions.[17]

Credit: Diane Desotelle, City of Duluth

Figure 7.3. Duluth Flood June 2012, Vermilion Street.

The team developed an overall approach that was founded on the assumption that the quality of outcomes would be enhanced by incorporating social values, interests, and concerns of all those affected, including the best available knowledge and science, into the decision-making process (E). It was further recognized that any recommended actions or solutions, no matter how brilliant, are of little value if the process is not recognized as legitimate (G). The team was therefore dedicated to having this process be fair and well-facilitated and ensuring that it followed due process. Finally, the team recognized the need to raise awareness of the current climate change situation, build networks and partners, and develop a shared understanding of both the challenges that needed to be addressed and opportunities on how to move forward in addressing them (B-D).

The specific approach involved the following distinct phases:

- *Advisory Committee.* Few societal changes can be accomplished without a broad group of partners. We identified, engaged, and formalized an inclusive Advisory Committee to aid in engaging a broad range of stakeholders, as well as providing guidance on how to direct the engagement process itself. This Advisory Committee also provided an opportunity to build leadership capacity within the various groups the committee represented (B-I).

- *Outreach and Convening Stakeholders.* In order to get a broad cross-section of stakeholders, we reached out to representatives from various levels of government (local, regional, state, federal), NGOs, academia and education organizations, nonprofits, and community associations. For ongoing public outreach, we established several communication channels, including a dedicated website and a project newsletter, as well as a series of public forums (A-B-D).

- *First Forum.* During the first forum an update on the current and historic precipitation patterns in our region was shared. Participants then assessed the situation based on their personal knowledge and initial information and data collected by the science team (E). We had crafted guiding questions for discussions that allowed stakeholders to express diverse perspectives, reflect, and gain an understanding of underlying causes of local flooding. The participants then framed an overall vision and developed broad objectives (B-E-H). Four areas were prioritized: 1) education approaches, 2) land use and planning, 3) stormwater infrastructure and low-impact development, and 4) sustainable funding for stormwater systems. Working groups were developed to address each area.

- *Working Groups.* Each working group met several times (B). They identified barriers to progress on climate change adaptation and identified potential strategies and tools for implementation. These potential strategies were then vetted using an impact vs. feasibility grid.[18] Ideally, we wanted to identify the strategy with the highest feasibility of being implemented, along with the greatest impact.

- *Second Forum.* The final phase of the engagement process convened stakeholders to develop specific action plans in order to form a framework for community adaptation planning. Because these action plans were based on the prior work of the working groups and the priorities identified by the stakeholders themselves, they served to increase the legitimacy and relevance of the actions proposed (D).

Credit: James Gruber

Figure 7.4. Participants at the first forum assessing the current situation.

Challenges

Throughout the public participation process multiple challenges had to be addressed. Often scientists and experts are used to providing information, but are less accustomed to listening to alternative ideas or approaches proposed by citizens (E-I). There was also the challenge of shifting local leaders' current focus on inadequate short-term fixes to more long-term and sustainable ones. Finally, as with any collaborative stakeholder process, it can be difficult to get a broad diversity of participants with diverse backgrounds and viewpoints to actually participate. This may require multiple forms of communication as well as person-to-person invitations (D).

Outcomes

The stakeholder outreach process provided an opportunity for broad stakeholder input to develop a community adaptation framework that was locally relevant and grounded in scientific data (A-B-E). The public participation process allowed for co-leadership and co-creation of priorities and implementation strategies (I). One participant reflected, "Comments from diverse stakeholders, not just technical professionals, is important." A specific set of prioritized actions, each with an implementation framework, was agreed to by the participants and was embraced by local government and other officials participating in this initiative (J). Linkages between groups were strengthened (B). By raising awareness and building broad involvement, critical land-use policies and prevention actions are more likely to receive the necessary political support, so that they can compete with the plethora of other demands that local communities are facing every day.

Reflections on Principle F: Delegate and Empower

It was not easy to engage some local or regional government officials who considered themselves experts and who already thought they knew what was needed. However, by involving these officials in community forums and working groups, we believe that they perceived their informal authority grew by working with others and that this would make it easier to accomplish their goals. For example, the city council would be more willing to heed their advice. We have observed over the years that by engaging and empowering community members to "be at the table," better decisions are made. The more empowered people are in a process of change, the more willing they will be to embrace critically needed community change.

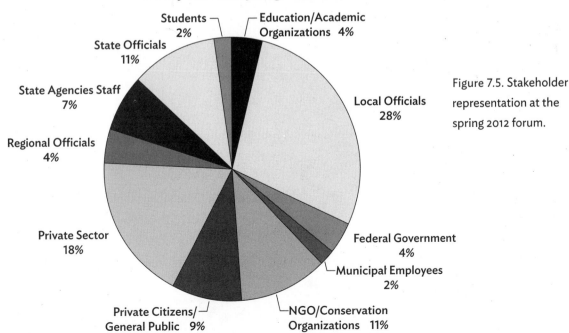

Participants at Spring Forum

Figure 7.5. Stakeholder representation at the spring 2012 forum.

Principle F—Delegate and Empower

Do (Or Consider Doing)

✓ Encourage all those in leading meetings and forums to practice active listening, perhaps by holding a training workshop.

✓ Design all community or public meetings so that they welcome ideas and input, are not intimidating to visitors, and record what community members say.

✓ Hold community events on a recurring basis, for example, to celebrate local accomplishments, vision for the future, and engage in current problem solving.

✓ Ensure that those not usually present can participate. This may require childcare at the event or offering rides to the homebound and senior citizens.

✓ Involve community members in new initiatives before data gathering or technical and policy experts develop plans or solutions.

✓ Include citizens or community members in all strategic planning activities.

✓ Create Community Teams and Advisory Groups, as needed, with clear charges for how they function including the identification of their members, roles, responsibilities, and timelines.

Don't (Or Think Twice)

✗ Don't justify top-down solutions only because they are the most efficient approach, since it is likely they will be neither the most efficient nor the most effective in the longer term.

✗ Don't pretend you are open to new approaches to solving a problem if you have already committed to an approach and you are actually trying to sell your idea.

✗ Don't assume that young people with ideas that you don't fully understand are not worth considering as part of an overall plan.

CHAPTER 8

Earn Trust

Work to Earn Public Trust and Legitimacy

> *Whoever is careless with the truth in small matters cannot be trusted with important matters.*
>
> — ALBERT EINSTEIN

Building Trust Is Integral to All Community Work

An effective and healthy community needs to set trust building as integral to all of its work and actions. Trust in community leaders (formal and informal) is directly linked to their credibility and to the respect that they have earned. While earning this trust may take a significant amount of time and effort, it can be lost in a mere moment of poor judgment. It is common knowledge that, in the eyes of community members, the legitimacy of an organization or an initiative is built upon public trust. According to studies (see the Research Corner), participatory approaches and transparency in activities including decision making, as well as the actions of stakeholders and partners, are critical for building and maintaining the legitimacy of an organization.

Ask yourself, "What are the characteristics or actions of individuals in my community who have earned my trust?" Your list might include such attributes as: honesty, sincerity, open mindedness, high integrity, that their words and actions match, they admit mistakes,

EARN TRUST

G

Work to Earn
Public Trust and Legitimacy

Five Characteristics

1. *Work must be viewed by the community as legitimate to build community trust.*
2. *Local leaders are integral to efforts in establishing trust and credibility.*
3. *Support by local elected officials can build trust and legitimacy.*
4. *Participatory approaches to problem solving and decision making are critical for building legitimacy.*
5. *Transparency in activities, including decision making, supports the building of trust.*

An organization needs to be trusted by its community in order to be considered legitimate[1] and to produce a lasting, positive impact. Therefore, building public trust and transparent participatory functions[2,3,4] should be foundational to any organization's work.[5] Influential local leaders will oftentimes play a role in establishing trust and credibility.[6]

Recent research shared by a panel on "Building Trust and Public Integrity"[7] highlighted three findings to achieve this goal: 1) give citizens the tools and the space they need to be powerful including access to information, 2) lock in open government for the long haul that includes institutionalizing laws to prevent rolling back open government reforms, and 3) build bridges, not walls where governments and citizens successfully work in partnerships. Other research[8] has identified that building community trust includes: 1) *Contractual Trust* where promises are kept and expectations are clear; 2) *Communication Trust* where community members are provided timely information; 3) *Competency Trust* relating to the ability of people to do their job and; 4) *Caring* and believing others are acting in the best interest of the community members.

keep promises, are fair, etc. This list is long and difficult for most of us to fully achieve. However, if community leaders or a group of citizens working together wish to truly earn the trust of others, a commitment to embracing these norms is essential. Earning that trust could be considered an ongoing work in progress and, when we do not meet these standards or norms, I suggest admitting mistakes or shortcomings, and then going back to work. I have found that community members will know when you are striving to live up to these values.

There is no one way to earn a community's trust; nevertheless, it is absolutely foundational in all efforts to create meaningful change. I will share a short story of how earning legitimacy and the trust of community members can be achieved by how you approach your work.

A Recycling "Pyramid Scheme": Neighbors Talking with Neighbors

I had doubts that we, as town officials in Vermont, had enough trust and support from the residents to effectively launch a successful major town-wide curbside recycling program. Penalties, fines, and governmental edicts are common approaches, but not how we wanted to proceed. I was fully aware that some residents did not have any interest in this change and some were hostile to the concept of recycling. We knew we needed a different approach to implement this program.

During a meeting with the volunteers of our solid waste recycling committee, we came upon the approach of "neighbors talking with neighbors" rather than government officials sending out notices. This would be accomplished by creating a recycling "pyramid scheme," starting with gathering together eight highly respected community members to serve on the Citizen Leadership Council. The individuals we chose were long-term residents whom we believed were trusted, had high credibility, and were respected by their neighbors. Our hope was that their support for the new curbside recycling program could influence their neighbors' acceptance. Each Council member's job was to endorse the program and to recruit five Regional Leaders. Each of the five Regional Leader's job was to support the program and to recruit five Block Leaders. And each of the Block Leaders recruited five Canvassers! Each Canvasser was to visit approximately ten neighbors the week before the recycling program started.

Two months later we held workshops for the hundreds of volunteer canvassers on how to describe the new recycling program to their neighbors and provided them a simple flyer to hand out or hang on their door. The week before the start date, this networking approach resulted in somewhere close to 5,000 visits of neighbors talking with neighbors. I was told by numerous people that this was a positive experience for these volunteers. That same week the town highway department dropped off the bright blue recycling bins.

The first week of curbside recycling was amazing! The streets were lined with blue bins with 80–90 percent participation rates. What surprised me even more were a few people who put out their bin with little or nothing in it. I am assuming the neighbors talking with neighbors approach created peer pressure to participate! The trust, credibility, and respect of the Leadership Council and the network of volunteers permeated the entire community's effort to implement change. Soon half of our solid waste was being recycled. This also lowered the solid waste management costs to the community. As an unanticipated side benefit, local town officials also earned trust and credibility for working with community members rather than telling them what to do.

Essentials for Building Trust in a Community

After reviewing my own experiences and research shared from others,[9,10,11] the following appear to be the most commonly shared elements for building trust for those in leadership roles.

- *Honesty* of those in leadership roles. This includes admitting mistakes when they occur, and not being loose with the truth, even in minor matters.
- *Respect* given by leaders that is genuine and includes respecting the inputs of *all* community members, even if it is sometimes difficult to hear. This includes assuming that others are acting in the best interest of the community, unless proven otherwise.

- *Openness* that includes effective communication with others, embracing transparency in the work of community leaders, and broad sharing of critical information in a timely manner.
- *Accountability* of the actions of those with authority. There is some system of evaluation and feedback for the action of community leaders.
- *Competency* of those in leadership and managerial roles.
- *Involving others* including minority groups and those typically marginalized in problem solving. Community leaders are open to their ideas and assistance in developing and implementing new policies and programs.

The Case Studies

The following two case studies are from Randolph, New Hampshire, and from the Olympic Peninsula of Washington state. In these cases, a small group of community members were able to build trust between disparate groups that helped contribute to preserving the culture and economic vitality of their town or tribe as well as the health of the local ecology.

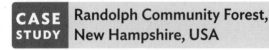

CASE STUDY Randolph Community Forest, New Hampshire, USA

by James S. Gruber

Prologue

The transformative changes that were achieved in the town of Randolph, impacting not just the current residents but many future generations, would not have been possible without the community-wide and regional public trust and legitimacy that was earned by the leadership team. They earned this trust through how they worked with all members of this local community and their regional partners. This included their full commitment to inclusion, participatory approaches to problem solving and decision making, embracing transparency, and truly listening to the hopes, dreams, and concerns of the public and partners involved in the project.

Introduction

One day during a long New Hampshire winter I came upon an incredible success story of a local community. I was undertaking an international research study, based upon information I had acquired from attending a World Bank Foundation workshop in Washington on successful local community-based natural resource management programs. These 300-plus programs, originating from every corner of the world, provided the initial information for the 12 Organizational Principles that are the foundation of this book. That day, during a call to colleague with the Quebec-Labrador Foundation Atlantic Center for the Environment, she asked me, "Have you heard about Randolph, New Hampshire?" Somewhat embarrassed to not know about this work in a nearby community, I placed a phone call to David Willcox, one of Randolph's community leaders and town moderator. I immediately became engulfed with a fire hydrant of information. This town, through a community-led effort, acquired and established a community forest that was one third the land area of the town without any tax payer monies (especially important in the "Live Free or Die" anti-tax state of New Hampshire). That spring I headed to the small town, nestled in the White Mountains. A state police officer, an environmentalist, and an international development consultant (known locally as the "gang of three") met with me. Their story was inspiring, reflecting what can be accomplished by a small rural community.

General Overview

Prior to my spring visit with the gang of three, I reviewed a plethora of information online and that was mailed to me. I also conducted an online survey of other Randolph residents to gain a broader understanding of their community efforts.

I read that this mountainous, forested region has a history of logging that goes back over a hundred years. Primarily spruce and fir were cut and hauled during the winter on sled to the railhead for transporting to sawmills. By the mid-1940s and early 1950s the Brown Company had logging camps in the area that were able to harvest hardwoods such as sugar maple, beech, and yellow birch.[12] The region's current economy includes timber harvesting, maple sugaring, and a growing recreational and summer tourism (including hunting, fishing, hiking, and climbing). Current wildlife in this boreal woodland region includes bear, deer, moose, and foxes. Randolph, a town founded in 1824, has a year-round population of under 400 residents with a larger seasonal population. It is located adjacent to the White Mountains National Forest.

By the 1990s, the Randolph community no longer could assume that the intact forest, that was the historic foundation of this town for the past hundred years, would continue into the future. Community members concluded that if they did not take action the new private owners (a multinational corporation that had little affiliation with this region) were likely to subdivide and sell off large tracts of this forest. These subdivisions would likely be converted into developments and other uses that would forever alter the historic ecological, sociological, and economic roots of the community. In fact, only a few years after the establishment of the Randolph Community Forest, other lands owned in New England by this same multinational corporation were sold off to a company known for forest liquidation.

Today, through the creative and dedicated leadership of local residents who were committed to protecting the quality of life of their community for future generations, Randolph and its Community Forest are thriving. This innovative effort has been recognized by numerous

Figure 8.1. Randolph Community Forest property, Rollo Fall.

Credit: Jenn Barton Scarinza

organizations in the US including the Trust for Public Land, the Northern Forest Center, and the Quebec-Labrador Foundation's Atlantic Center for the Environment. This community forest contains over 10,000 acres in the towns of Randolph and Jefferson.[13]

Goals, Approach, and Challenges

During my meeting that warm spring day in Randolph, John Scarinza (the state police officer), Walter Graff (the environmentalist), and David Willcox (the international urban development consultant) shared with me that the community's overall goal was "to protect the quality of life of their community for future generations by acquiring, then protecting and sustainably managing, this forest land." They emphasized that this land had been facing potential, perhaps imminent, development.

Their overall approach to achieve this goal was by:

- shifting from pulpwood extraction towards a new emphasis on sustainable long-term hardwoods and potential green-certified saw log production
- supporting appropriate outdoor recreation such as hunting, fishing, hiking, and skiing

Figure 8.2. Trail building crew at Rollo Fall.

Credit: Jenn Barton Scarinza

- promoting ecological protection that included wildlife habitat management and the protection of fragile plant life

This gang of three all stressed that there were two immediate challenges that any community leader needed to face if they were considering actions to preserve this intact forest for the future generations. They had to "convince the town that the land was under threat" while at the same time "convincing people we could do it." They also recognized that this "takes courage and to some degree a high amount of risk." Although this was a high order, they shared that there were also many other technical and organizational challenges such as the required negotiations with the US Forest Service, raising significant private and grant funds for acquisition, negotiating agreements to transfer development rights, and creating a community-based organizational structure.

These three committed volunteers, with no formal authority, from different types of careers and political perspectives, collaboratively led the community to establish the Randolph Community Forest. I proposed to them that they brainstorm all the critical steps of their approach and they agreed. I will provide a summary of each of their steps along with a few quotes from them and the dozen other residents that were interviewed.

Outline of Process Used for Planning, Development, and Initial Implementation of the Randolph Community Forest

Step 1: Evaluation of Opportunities and Threats Through Processes of Engagement

Their approach to this traditional strategic planning step was what resonated most with me. They emphasized the need to "build a broad base of project supporters by listening—really listening—to the concerns of the public and partners involved in the project." (A-D) Then they initiated community dialogue and outreach to neighboring towns, state officials, elected representatives (state and federal), and federal agencies (e.g., Forest Legacy Program) (A-B). They worked to understand what potential resources might be available including financial, community leadership (political and business), and social capital (for example, members of the Randolph Mountain Club) (B-C-J-K). They shared that they needed to "take time to understand what we are trying to protect and why" by assessing the potential threats of *not* taking action (e.g., fragmentation of timberland, loss of public access, loss of traditional public use, and new housing development resulting in increases in the cost of community services) (E).

Step 2: Articulating a Vision

They approached this challenge not from a problem-solving mindset but by being driven by a shared, inclusive vision. They thought that this approach would "lay out a broad enough vision to…appeal to as many groups as possible, so everyone can have a certain amount of buy-in into the success of the project" (A-B-G-I-J-L). The resulting shared vision reflected the priorities of the three main stakeholder groups: environmental conservation, traditional hunting and fishing opportunities, and sustainable economic return from forest products.

Step 3: Seizing the Opportunities — Failure Is Not an Option

The leadership team stated that achieving a bold shared vision requires finding and then seizing opportunities. They needed good luck, reflecting that "good luck has been defined as the intersection of hard work and opportunity; I think (the community members) had both and it worked out great." They went on to assert that an ambitious idea "can be accomplished if a network of committed individuals and organizations pushes the project forward with failure not an option." (A-B-I) To identify opportunities, the team met with numerous potential partners (typically over food, in a home, in groups of six to eight individuals at a time). Potential partners included NGOs, the Forest Service, politicians, state government, local citizens, and many others. They reiterated that "partnerships are a very valuable asset and the more on board, the better." (A-B-G-I) They stressed the importance of having political, social, and cultural diversity on their core leadership team so that they could more easily "bring together a variety of people and organizations with very differing viewpoints." (A-B-C-G)

Step 4: Formulating a Plan of Action

Their plan of action was framed by three formal guiding principles that all had "wide, deep and strong support" from the community (A-C-K-L). These were: 1) no new local tax money or burden on the local tax payer; 2) land use to support education, traditional recreation, working forest, public access, and wildlife habitat; and 3) future management under the town's planning board. They stress that "it was possible that resource protection and a sustainable management plan could have been achieved with rancor," (B-C-J) but that was not acceptable since building public trust and legitimacy was core to their approach (G). Also important for moving forward was achieving small, incremental steps including interim agreements with provisional commitments to keep this effort on track.

Step 5: Telling the Story

Telling their story to fundraising organizations, community members, and potential partners was foundational to their approach in building confidence, gaining partners, and asking for support (B-D). They emphasized, "Believe in what you are doing; however, you must listen and be flexible." The leadership team also shared that their "key to success was the insistence on public meetings, bringing in the neighboring towns, providing provision for groups who had specific interests...to have a say in future management." (A-B-D-G) These public meetings also allowed them to "emphasize both how this will maintain the current [desirable] character of the community" along with the concern that "a do-nothing option will [adversely] change the community's character." (D)

Step 6: Raising the Money

They asserted that core to successful community fundraising are networking, a clear articulation of the community's needs by community members, and the trust and credibility of those requesting the funding. To raise funds for this type of major effort "it is critical to have someone local who is well respected and willing to stand up and make the case as to why this is so important to the community." (G) They smiled and shared, "Expect lots of no's, turn downs," and "Don't get discouraged." An old tenet they shared was: "Money follows good projects," and "If it's the right thing to do, then do it." (B-G)

Step 7: Negotiating the Easements and Agreements

It was clear to me that the leadership gang of three had built broad respect within Randolph and with many other stakeholders. The public trust and legitimacy that they commanded was instrumental in their role of negotiating numerous agreements (G). Remember, they had no formal role or authority and were unpaid volunteers, but through the first six steps built what can be referred to as a "strong authorizing environment." They had the credibility to take the lead in developing first drafts through a number of working sessions with different groups. For example, one session was held on timber cutting and logging and another on how the new community forest could support the local economy and preserve critical ecosystems (F-I-J). They also negotiated with the US Forest Service and drafted special state legislation. They noted that it was essential to maintain the momentum. One resident noted that what is needed for this critical negotiation to be successful is to "have a small, dedicated group of the right people with the right skills." (F-G-I)

Step 8: Closing the Deal

Annual and Special Town Meetings in New Hampshire are where many good ideas end in the dustbin. This was not the case for the proposed Randolph Community Forest that would include one third of all the land within the town boundaries. The process prior to the vote at a Special Town Meeting was transparent, inclusive, and responsive to the wide range of social values and political perspectives of the community members (A-B-C-D). Votes on the ordinance, management

Credit Jenn Barton Scarinza

Figure 8.3. Taking tree sample data in maple tapping area.

system, and the revolving fund all passed. This allowed for the completion of the purchases, writing of interim management agreements, creation of the new Forest Commission, and the development of a Forest Stewardship Plan. And all these next steps were undertaken through a collaborative participatory approach. The Randolph Community Forest was born.

Outcomes

The Randolph Community Forest, which is 10,000 acres in size, was established nearly 20 years ago. The community's dreams and hopes have come to fruition. Their Stewardship Plan (2014 to 2023)[14] describes their future priorities as to: "...manage the Community Forest sustainably and to earn profits from timber harvesting to cover the management costs of the Community Forest" and supports the "...protection and improvement of the Community Forest's biodiversity and adaptation to the changing environment; the enhancement of traditional outdoor recreational opportunities; the encouragement and support of research and educational activities related to the flora and

It was very important to lay out early on that this land would be a "working forest" in the traditional sense of cutting forest products which would contribute to the local economy, while maintaining an unbroken forest landscape that was open for public access.

— A Community Member

fauna existing within the Town; and the conservation of ecologically important tracts of land within or near the Town."

Reflections on Principle G: Earn Trust

This case study illustrates nearly all 12 principles, some to a greater extent than others. Here, I will only discuss how Principle G: Earn Trust can be illustrated by this case.

Principle G: Earn Trust notes that to gain this type of trust and legitimacy, the work of the leaders must be viewed by the community as legitimate. It also stresses the importance of participatory approaches to problem solving and decision making along with supporting transparency throughout a change process.

The leadership for this major initiative came from three local residents who were committed to protecting the quality of life of their community for future generations. They were neither paid nor held any formal authority to lead this challenge. This leadership team valued all members of their community and actively sought their input, guidance, and involvement. They emphasized how they represented the full range of social values within their community. They joked that the three of them included the right, the left, and the center in political perspectives. Core to their approach was seeking to listen—really listen—to all points of views and to seek inclusive approaches that represented the full spectrum of views within their community. They grew their credibility through how they worked to build a broadly shared vision that reflected the priorities of all stakeholder groups. As a result, these individuals were highly respected by the other members of the community.

My interview with 12 other community residents frequently raised the importance of engaging and involving all community members in this potential community forest idea from the visioning to the development of implementation agreements. Respecting and valuing this leadership team came out in nearly every interview.

It is also interesting how the three leadership team individuals described their roles and what they worked to achieve. First, they stressed

Key to success was the insistence on public meetings, bringing in the neighboring towns, providing provision for groups who had specific interests...to have a say in future management.

— A LOCAL RESIDENT

the importance of helping the community members recognize a serious problem they needed to face: the forest land was under threat and the do-nothing option would likely result in serious loss to their community's quality of life. Second, they said their job was to provide encouragement and convince community members that they had the ability and courage to face this problem and protect this land by establishing a community-based forest. These primary roles of the leadership team are consistent with the principles of practicing adaptive transformative leadership.

Adaptive transformative leadership, developed by Heifetz and Linsky in 2002,[15] refers to leadership that works to help society face challenges or problems and then supports them in seeking and implementing their solutions. This seems to capture the approach of this leadership team. Rather than a top-down, expert-driven approach, their participatory and collaborative approach worked to engage and empower community members and also raised the trust of community members. And this trust was critical. Without the broad and deep public trust and legitimacy that this team earned, I doubt if this initiative would have been successful.

CASE STUDY | Restoring the Strong People: The Lower Elwha Klallam Tribe and the Elwha River

by K. Whitney Mauer

Prologue

Over 100 years ago, an indigenous community of the Olympic Peninsula of Washington State, the Lower Elwha Klallam Tribe (Klallam Tribe) lost much of their land and their way of life when dams were constructed that blocked the Elwha River's flow and decimated the salmon population and the ecosystem. Over more than 30 years, the tribe, environmental organizations, and state and federal agencies have worked to restore the ecosystem through a change process founded on building trust and working through collaborative partnerships. Now the river flows free and its ecosystem is being restored.

Introduction and General Overview

The first dam was constructed on the Elwha River in 1910, and the second in 1926. At no time during the construction or the operation of the dams were the members of the Lower Elwha Klallam Tribe consulted or included in the decision making about the dams, the river, or the use of surrounding natural resources. The dams resulted in the decimation of the fish populations on which Klallam economic well-being was founded. In addition, the Klallam lost home places, their creation site was submerged, and their cultural practices and livelihoods were harmed.

In 1976, the license to operate the Glines Canyon dam expired. Seizing on this opportunity, the tribe filed a petition in 1986 with the Federal Energy Regulatory Commission to shut down the dams and restore the Elwha River. Klallam elders testified to the Senate Committee on Natural Resources, bearing witness to devastating effects that the decline in salmon had on the cultural and economic conditions of the community.[16] The activism of the Klallam people and the coalition of environmental groups led to the passage of the Elwha River Ecosystem and Fisheries Restoration Act in 1992. It took another two decades of planning, environmental assessment, and funding appeals to finally remove the dams from the river. Throughout that time, the Klallam people have persistently and resolutely advocated for a restoration plan and process that meaningfully includes Klallam input, promotes equitable access to resources, and strengthens Klallam economic systems (C). They have partnered with state and federal agencies to monitor the river, listen to community members' needs and hopes, and adapt programming for natural resources, economics, and cultural heritage to further support the renewal and regeneration of the river and its people (A-B-C-E-G-I). In the summer of 2014, the Lower Elwha Klallam Tribe celebrated the last blast of Glines Canyon dam that freed the Elwha River.

In consultation with the Tribal Council, I visited their reservation several times between 2015 and 2017. My interview assistant, tribal member Patricia Elofson, and I conducted a series of group interviews in which community members described their experiences of

Credit: Whitney Mauer

Figure 8.4. The Elwha River winding through a former lake bed after the removal of Glines Canyon Dam.

the ecosystem restoration and its role in community recovery and revitalization.

Goals, Challenges, Approaches, and Outcomes
Goals

Bring back the fish. Tribal staff and members stated one common goal time and again: restoring the salmon populations in the Elwha river. As a salmon people, the Klallam regard fish as integral to their cultural and economic needs. Interviewees talked about a longing for conditions that the generations who lived on the pre-dam river had known, with one elder describing the ideal restored river as "so thick with fish you can walk across their backs." The Lower Elwha Klallam Tribe's goals for the Elwha River restoration include:

- restoring local salmon populations
- revitalizing salmon traditions
- acquiring and accessing ancestral lands in the restoration project area
- strengthening economic development prospects such as commercial and subsistence fishing

Challenges

As the Elwha River flows from its headwaters in the Olympic Mountains, it passes through Olympic National Park, private lands, and finally reaches the Lower Elwha Klallam Tribe Reservation where it meets the Strait of Juan de Fuca. This patchwork of land ownership created through Klallam land takings, posed a significant challenge for restoration management. Maintaining a connection to land while also protecting oral traditions and narratives, healing practices, and family roles and responsibilities is a part of building resilience in Indigenous communities.[17] For the Lower Elwha Klallam, the presence and operation of dams along their ancestral land of Elwha River has impeded their community resilience.

Approach

Tribal members and leaders recognized that the restoration would only be successful from their perspective if they played a significant role in restoration planning. Collaborative work has been a vital component of the dam removal and restoration process (A-B). The Tribal Council and staff worked to build relationships with restoration partners and involve tribal members in many aspects of the planning and implementation (A-B-F-J). For example, as the tribe and their partners continue scientific monitoring, Tribal Council and staff provide updates on fishing and beach access to community members through tribal newsletters, council meetings, and other public information sessions (D-E). Additionally, council-approved community research, such as the interviews we conducted, provides opportunities for community members to share their perspectives and ideas (A-H).

Tribal leaders have emphasized Klallam empowerment in restoration decision making and research that integrates scientific knowledge with local Klallam knowledge (F-E). Toward these ends tribal fisheries staff talked with tribal members and collected stories of historic fishing sites that they used to determine the placement of log jams downstream of the dam removal (G). Log jams in historic fishing sites can promote fish recovery and ecosystem health, help shape the flow of the river through the reservation, and promote revitalization of culturally important fishing sites.

Attention is paid to ensuring that feedback loops are used to further build the trust necessary for cooperation to continue (G-H). For example, in our interviews, the tribe's Natural Resource staff explained that they recognized the fishing moratorium placed a significant burden on the tribal members who need fish for subsistence. Because of this, the staff provides fish to the community when there is an abundance of hatchery fish. From our elder interviews we learned that some of the elders had adapted to the dammed river by smoking pink salmon, a fish that is typically less desirable as a food source because of its small size. In light of our conversation, the staff made the provision of hatchery pink salmon to elders one of its priorities.

As the restoration continues, Tribal Council and staff work closely with the National Park Service (NPS) and other federal and state agencies to remove remnants of the dams from the river, restore fish habitat, and reintroduce key fish species to the river (B). The tribe and partners, including state and federal agencies[18] work together to manage the scientific monitoring of the river, estuary, and marine ecosystems with a close eye on fish populations (E).

Outcomes

Today, the Lower Elwha Klallam Tribe, National Park Service, and the state of Washington are co-managers of the fish in the Elwha River. Built on trust, this partnership (as well as the ones described earlier) allow for a more comprehensive understanding of the ongoing impacts of dam removal than any one group would be able to assess on their own. Such collaborative work has gone beyond the restoration itself to include a partnership between the tribe, the National Park Service, NatureBridge,[19] and Western Carolina University to provide a science education program that integrates science and tradition into a hands-on learning experience for Klallam youth (A-B).

The Lower Elwha Klallam community's response to the unleashed river include hope and concern. They described a rapidly healing river and sightings of more "flying, swimming, and walking animals," specifically more fish in the river, elk, eagles, crab, and bear. The most striking change at the reservation is the emergence of a large sandy beach, which replaced the pebbles and rocks near reservation homes. Tribal members are now accessing and enjoying this new resource with their families and friends. Despite positive changes, reservation residents were also concerned about other changes that may accompany the emergence of places to explore. Their concerns were about children's safety around the water, potential conflicts over beach space and use, and increased visitor access to the river, beach, and reservation. As visitor access increases, residents want to protect their privacy and safety, and maintain the integrity of Klallam places, customs, and autonomy.

Still, there was a strong sense of hope for the future, a sense of wonder and discovery at the changes, and momentum for utilizing the restoration to strengthen the Lower Elwha Klallam community. As one tribal elder said to me,

> Here we are and here we still are. I try to look forward…I'm proud that all of these things that have been accomplished. That our children are grasping hold of educations (*sic*) and being able to be challenged in so many areas and going in those directions and being able to be a part of that. So, I keep praying, Lord, make it good for them. Because these are our territories.

His quote echoes sentiments I heard from other tribal members: a cautious optimism for a restoration that is about more than the environment. The restoration embodies a renewal of the multigenerational, collective identity of the Strong People that is deeply tied to the landscape.

Reflections on Principle G: Earn Trust

It takes courage to trust. Tribal leaders realized that for the restoration of the river and salmon population to be successful, they would need to cooperate with many partners. An essential step in this collaborative process was that they "had to build trust." Since ecological restoration

Figure 8.5. A Lower Elwha Klallam Tribe member walks to the beach from her backyard.

necessitates monitoring and adapting to ecological and social changes, this trust building would be a long-term process rather than a singular event. Tribal leaders recognized that, despite the success of their petition to remove the dams, members' hopes and joys for the renewed river were still tinged with a sense of worry and loss that have been shaped by a history of resource decision making outside of Klallam control. Therefore, they focused not only on working collaboratively and building trust with external partners but also on working to build trust with other members of the tribe.

Listening and responding to concerns has been a successful approach in re-establishing trust with leaders and, even, outsiders. By using community input to plan and adapt natural resource, economic, and cultural programming in response to ongoing changes, restoration partners can support and enhance opportunities for the Strong People to thrive.

A member of the tribe's Natural Resource staff stated, when discussing the building of relationships with restoration partners that included the National Park Service, "The relationship between the Park and the Tribe was shaky at first. We had to build trust and that has taken time…. And it's great right now I would say. There's a lot of trust."

Principle G—Earn Trust

Do (Or Consider Doing)

- ✓ Ensure that your words are aligned with your actions, all the time. Since trust and credibility are directly linked, growing one will grow the other.
- ✓ Work to build legitimacy though participatory approaches to problem solving with community members. This will build both your legitimacy and the trust of community members.
- ✓ Encourage participation by trusted community leaders.
- ✓ If you make a mistake, admit it, and then move on.
- ✓ Share (or attribute to others) the credit when things go well. As Harry S. Truman said, "It is amazing what you can accomplish if you do not care who gets the credit."

Don't (Or Think Twice)

- ✗ Don't be loose with the truth, even in minor matters. Take heed of Albert Einstein's wisdom: "Whoever is careless with the truth in small matters cannot be trusted with important matters."
- ✗ If you don't know the answer to a question, don't fake it. Sometimes saying, "I don't know," actually can enhance credibility.
- ✗ When efforts do not work out, don't try to hide the situation and don't point fingers.

CHAPTER 9

Embrace Feedback

*Improve Effectiveness Through
Monitoring, Feedback, and Accountability Systems*

> *Examine what is said and not who speaks.*
>
> — AFRICAN PROVERB

Monitoring and Feedback: Using Nature as a Guide

Nature and its dynamic ecological systems can be used as a model for how healthy local communities function. Nature provides a continuous flow of information and communication with dynamic feedback loops in the air, the water, and the soil. An ecosystem establishes a dynamic interdependence between a myriad of plants and animals that balances competition and cooperation, a process also referred to as symbiosis. This is an interdependent system that can respond to unanticipated changes, such as floods, droughts, and diseases, *and recover*! The health and vitality of a human community and the effectiveness of its organizational systems are similarly dependent on a continuous flow of information and communication with dynamic feedback loops. Without these, there will be inadequate accountability and critical changes that are urgently needed may be avoided or seriously delayed.

EMBRACE FEEDBACK

Improve Effectiveness Through Monitoring, Feedback, and Accountability Systems

Five Characteristics

1. *Tight feedback loops are supported by openness, transparency, monitoring, mutual accountability, collaboration, and power sharing between the stakeholders and partners.*

2. *Effective feedback systems, including feedback from social networks, allow for opportunities to learn from mistakes, uncertainty, and crises.*

3. *Local appointed or elected representatives of communities must themselves be accountable to their constituents if community-based conservation is to be responsive to the community.*

4. *The performance of those who make decisions should be periodically reviewed by those who are affected by the decisions.*

5. *The social and technical capacity for monitoring, evaluating, responding, and enforcement is necessary for effective and dynamic systems.*

Dynamic feedback and accountability systems will strengthen the efforts of any organization. Such systems are critical in building organizational capacity to grow and to serve its community.[1] There are many forms of feedback. However, numerous researchers claim that the following are primary: monitoring and evaluation,[2] learning from mistakes, uncertainty, and crisis,[3] and feedback from social networks.[4] Accountability is imperative for all organizational structures and activities that are meant to be community-driven and -focused.[5] In short, technical structures to receive and respond to public feedback are integral to community-based initiatives.[6] This includes a commitment to social responsibility and a method of enforcement.

Seeking Feedback: How Do I Get People to Respond?

Today, it is harder than ever to solicit significant feedback from your community members. Recently when I was about to complete a purchase at a local village market, the phone rang. The owner mumbled as he was about to examine the caller ID on his phone, "Is this another fake call?" There are so many robocalls and bots permeating our computers and social media sites that today we are hesitant to respond to surveys or answer a call from community leaders we do not know. If you need broad and useful feedback from your community on a new initiative, a proposed project, future planning for land use and development, or how to respond to climate change, I can offer a few suggestions for you to consider that have worked for me and my colleagues. I will share an example.

A few years ago, Keene, a small city in New Hampshire, needed comprehensive input from its community members on their preferences for future improvements to the historic downtown and adjoining areas. This downtown, the heart of the city, includes senior, single-family, and college student housing. It also includes a wide mix of retail, commercial, and entertainment establishments and some government buildings. There are small parks and green spaces in this region. Even though it was essential to solicit input from a wide range of participants and stakeholders, there was a very limited budget to collect this feedback.

Our approach, that provided valuable and specific feedback from individuals representing this wide range of stakeholder groups, was to partner with other trusted organizations in the city. We used an online survey instrument, in this case, Survey Monkey. In order to reach all of these groups, we asked trusted leaders such as a college president, a vice-president of a large insurance business, the president of the Chamber of Commerce, the director of a local land conservation NGO and others, to distribute our survey to their members. They did this by providing a survey link through their organizational mailing list, list-serve, or within their newsletter, along with their personal endorsement of completing this survey. They were not asked to share their emails or other internal lists with us, so it did not violate their organizational confidential policies for their students, employees, or members. For those who were not online savvy, such as seniors, hard copies of the survey for pen and pencil completion were provided to the library and the senior center. We employed local graduate students to lead this community service effort with work-study financial support. The result—thousands of completed surveys that provided extremely valuable ideas, preferences, and data to guide the city's planning effort.

Feedback and Accountability of Local Leaders

All of us will probably agree that local appointed or elected leaders of our communities must themselves be accountable and responsive to its members. A regular local election is one form of accountability of elected representatives, if all are allowed (and encouraged) to vote. Fortunately, democracy is still strong in many parts of the world, though it is now being challenged. Those in leadership roles who take actions to limit feedback and accountability are the greatest threat to democratic processes and the future health and vitality of a community. I suggest that prior to electing new leaders of a small or large community, you ask for their specific approaches and commitment to community feedback and specifically how they would be held accountable to those who will be affected by their decisions.

Non-elected formal leaders of NGOs, agencies, and businesses, also need to have effective systems of feedback from the employees and those that they serve. This needs to be done without fear of potential retribution or adverse consequences.

The Town Report Cards

A bright green report card was sitting on every seat at the annual Town Meeting, waiting to be completed by the residents. It asked them to assess the quality of last year's work for each of the town departments, including the town manager's office. The Fire Department of this Vermont community received, on average, the highest grade, an "A." Other departments did not do as well. In addition to a grade (from A to F), we asked for ideas on how we could do better for the coming year.

Simple, perhaps atypical, but this provided valuable feedback on how we were serving our community. The community members thanked us for asking!

I have found that a leading indicator of positive community culture is how hard the leaders of the community work to gain input from their community members. This input can be on how effective they are, on critical decision making, and/or on planning and visioning their future. Refer to Principle A: Involve Everyone, and Principle F: Empower People, for more ideas on seeking community feedback. It is also critical to share the results of these information-gathering efforts (refer to Principle D: Be Transparent).

The Case Studies

The first case study looks at an innovative, successful business in New Hampshire that promotes feedback as a critical part of management and product design. The second case study discusses a fishing community in Turkey, which has been sustainably managing its inshore fishery through effective feedback loops.

 CASE STUDY Healing Products and Healthy Business: The W. S. Badger Story, Gilsum, New Hampshire, USA

by Bill Whyte

Prologue

Our mission statement provides a context for how we, the founders, go about the work we do: we focus on running a business that is "fair, fun and profitable, where money is a fuel, not a goal, and where our vision for a healthier world finds expression through the way we treat each other and the people we serve." This is the "healthy business" part of our mission.

I think the two-pronged approach of healing products and healthy business provides a rich ground for community development. And clearly, all of the growth and good we've done over the last two decades has been supported by a rigorous multidirectional flow of feedback.

Our mission along with principles like "generosity," "individual responsibility in a team concept," "fun is good," and "supporting organic and sustainable agriculture through our purchasing practices" are written concepts that we have taken to heart and use on a daily basis to inform our conversation and decision-making process.

Introduction and General Overview

The W.S. Badger Company was born in the back room of our home in Gilsum, New Hampshire, in 1995. We started our business by making and selling one herbal balm, with the modest goal of earning enough money to support our young family. I was a carpenter by day, balm maker by night and on weekends I drove around New England selling our balms. My wife and daughters helped pack and ship from our dining room table.

Presently, from our custom-built facility in Gilsum, we manufacture and market a hundred plant and mineral-based herbal products, including highly rated natural sunscreens, and products for healthy hair and skin. We have a committed staff of over 90 and sell our products worldwide. One of our company's principles is to embody "a personal and caring approach to communications." Giving and receiving feedback can be stressful and challenging (H). Yet giving and receiving constructive feedback has enhanced every aspect of the Badger business. Feedback improves productivity and quality. It has directed us to refine formulas, reduce waste, identify problems, and capitalize on opportunities we might have missed. Feedback is the spark for creativity and innovation.

In this case study, we'd like to shed some light on the way we've embodied Principle H: Embrace Feedback and how openness to critique and new ideas has helped to fuel and sustain Badger's growth.

Goals, Approaches, Challenges, and Outcomes

We began as a family working together to create something good and that pattern has stayed with us and shaped our growth for over two decades. Currently, I am a member of our eight-person, consensus decision-making leadership group. Two of my daughters serve as

CEO (Collaborative Executive Officers) and my wife Katie is COO (Collaborative Operations Officer). With a focus on continuing to cultivate community, good communication, and family values within our company, my wife and daughters use their positions as COO and CEO, respectively, and as consultants and volunteers, to bring healthy community to other business groups and organizations in the region (A-B-D).

Some unique aspects of Badger Business and its family-centered pattern include:
- a subsidized childcare center for Badger staff children
- fair pay at a living wage
- free, local, and organic lunch to our full staff, every work day
- Badger company-funded volunteer hours for staff
- Babies at Work program
- extended maternity and paternity leave
- profit sharing
- work flexibility when health or family issues require a staffer's time

Figure 9.1. Iris, Badger's director of sales, and Bill at a tabletop trade show 2012.

How We Finance Community and Change

Rather than issue dividends, all earnings have been retained to the operating budget since the company was formed. Unlike many businesses, we don't try to maximize profit for the owners. Instead, from our annual income, in addition to adequate profit, we allocate funds to support internal wellness programs and charitable giving. The Badger mission statement says, "Money is a fuel not a goal." Our goal is to make great products, to run a healthy business, and to make a difference. Toward this end, Badger has become a B Corporation.[7]

We have a policy that the highest paid person in the company can receive no more than five times the lowest salary. This enables us to pay a living wage. Valued compensation in lieu of higher pay, especially among executive-level persons who could be making more money elsewhere, includes the sane work schedule, work-life balance, and understanding and flexibility when needed. At every level of the organization, feeling valued, appreciated, and heard fuels engagement and cooperation (H-G).

Metrics

We've had surveys conducted by others, and we've run our own internal, anonymous surveys to assess things like engagement and job satisfaction (E-H). These are extremely high. The survey results are verified by our ability to attract and keep skilled staff. Basically, in a state where finding skilled help can be daunting, we have no problem. And it is rare for someone to leave Badger. Many of our staff are highly qualified by way of experience or advanced degrees. Sometimes they leave when positions become available in their area of expertise, but most Badgers stay.

Feedback Guides Product Development

In our second full year, when customers asked us to make some lip balms, we didn't want to, but acquiesced, and our sales doubled. Our customers wanted balms for babies. Balms for sore muscles. We really knew very little about that kind of business, so we were hungry for advice and feedback and always willing to entertain a good idea or make a needed change (I-H).

From the Point of View of the Community

To this point, I've described all this in the first person—as if I did it all! In reality, in a climate of openness, where feedback is honored and embraced, members of the Badger community rise to the occasion (A-B-D-H). Over the years, we've convened twice yearly for company retreats at the direction of my wife and co-founder Katie Schwerin. The biggest concern at these retreats has always been growth. The fear that we would become "corporate."

Systems for Accountability and Monitoring

As we developed an organized corporate culture, we grew organically and respectfully. Directors, managers, and team leaders receive no special privileges. No status offices. No reserved parking places. When something we try works, we do more of it. When something works poorly, we fix it, transform it, or abandon it (E). One principle is: "Individual responsibility in a team concept." Accountability and monitoring are natural parts of the communication system when the environment supports openness, honesty, integrity and a striving for excellence (D-G-H). Think of it as an internal, organic family system.

We have conducted trainings for team leaders as well as for all staff, emphasizing communication skills that lead to good listening, with an emphasis on what's going well as opposed to focusing on things that are not working (H). The idea is to do more of the good stuff and overwhelm the bad. We teach using terms like, "I wish," and "How to," to frame feedback. We learn to paraphrase to ensure understanding and to let the other know they have been heard and understood (I).

Reflections on Principle H: Embrace Feedback

Badger has never put the bottom line and finances as our primary organizing factor. We put people first. I personally don't use the term "employee." That term defines a person as someone the "owner" has

Figure 9.2. Badgers
wearing flannel, 2015.

Credit: Kelli Strickland

hired to work for money. In contrast, we are team members. Human
beings working together to get the work done.

There is a world of difference between coming to work for money
versus coming to work to be with your friends in a community, striving
for excellence, and making others happy in the process. You still need
and deserve the money, and you're super happy to earn it, but community and honest work feed the soul.

Badger has cultivated an environment of honesty and openness.
We value, ask for, and respond to feedback. Although the various Badgers have different roles and different levels of pay, on a human level
we know that each of us is respected and valued. We thrive on good
communication. We also thrive on kindness and generosity rippling
outward. This means feedback is not delivered; it is offered with the
health of the whole in mind.

We expect excellence. People give their best willingly. When there
is a performance problem, we do alignment building. We set agreed-
upon goals. We check back in on a known schedule and we do our best

to make things right for all concerned. And clearly, it is so much easier to do when accountability and high performance is self-motivated and willingly accepted as the norm and as the right thing to do.

Team leaders, managers, and directors know that they are in service to their team members (I). The CEO position is in service to and responsible for the health of the whole. And I use the world "health" as a specific, definable, technical business term.

Badger is clearly an ecosystem. Individuals grow healthier within it. And the whole of the system is therefore stronger. It's not that we never have problems with individuals or that the whole is always perfect. What is true is that Badger is a fun, positive, nourishing place to work. We enjoy and honor our role as a B Corp and as change makers.

It is also true that like a diverse ecosystem, we are resilient. Change happens. The unexpected happens. So, resilience comes from having a group that is engaged and open to change. We are a learning system, so that whatever goes wrong, we accept it, examine it, learn from it, and then we pull together to change, adapt, clean up, remedy, and excel.

CASE STUDY | The Conservation and Sustainable Management of an Inshore Fishery in Alanya, Turkey

by Tanju (TK) Kiriscioglu

Prologue

The city of Alanya[8] is located in the eastern part of the Antalya Province in Turkey on a peninsula between the Mediterranean Sea to the south and the Taurus Mountains[9] to the north. It is one of the most popular tourist destinations[10] in Turkey, especially due to its ancient historic sites, pleasant climate, tourism infrastructure, and picturesque shoreline replete with pristine beaches.

Alanya's inshore fishery played an important role in the growth of Alanya's tourism industry. (Inshore fisheries are those within six miles of the shoreline.) However, this achievement didn't come easy. After the Second World War, Turkey experienced several economic disruptions, one of the most serious taking place in the late 1970s.

Dire economic conditions forced the fishermen of Alanya to fish faster than their fishery could replenish itself, which resulted in additional hardship for the fishermen and the local community.[11] Realizing the predicament, the fishermen of Alanya worked together, creating an ingenious system that ensured the integrity and productivity of their fishery, which ended up playing a pivotal role in the development of economic stability and environmental sustainability in the area.

Introduction

Eastern Mediterranean pirates, cedar trees, Cleopatra, tourism, and an inshore fishery. And the silver-cheeked toadfish.[12] One may wonder what these have to do with each other. Yet, history has woven such a unique story around them. Located on a peninsula at the foothills of the majestic Taurus Mountains in southern Turkey, the city of Alanya has always been an important center of civilization. Due to its strategic location on the Eastern Mediterranean Sea and its proximity to Cyprus, the Levant, and the Fertile Crescent, it has been a stronghold for many empires.

Traditionally, the Taurus Mountains provided the cedar timber which people in the region used for homebuilding, as well as boat- and shipbuilding. For fishermen, boats made of sturdy cedar have always been indispensable.[13] Early in the first century, when the ravages of the rogue pirates in the region increased demand, overharvesting resulted in regional declines.[14] Interestingly, Alanya (then Coracesium) was the main refuge for the Eastern Mediterranean pirates while they plundered and ravaged the seas and the land.[15,16] The period of piracy in the region ended with the Battle of Coracesium (67 BCE).[17] When Marcus Antonius assigned a cedar forest near Coracesium to Queen Cleopatra of Egypt to have her fleets built[18] they took a trip to Coracesium, to a place now known as Cleopatra Beach.[19] Because so many tourists come to visit the area, Cleopatra Beach is the foundation of Alanya's economy.

Equally important for Alanya's economy is its inshore fishery. And locals know this very well because their collective memory has not forgotten the difficult years in the 70s when the fishery gave signals of stress. While those days are over, the people of Alanya have a new problem now, the silver-cheeked toadfish, what some of the seasoned fishermen refer to as the new pirates,[20] an invasive species that is known for damaging the nets, and then "looting" the catch. But the fishermen of Alanya are prepared for their new challenge. They believe that when they work together, they can solve any problem.

General Overview and Initial Presenting Situation

The fishery of Alanya is a small-scale system where currently 94 local fishermen operate two- or three-person fishing boats[21] (Figure 9.3), catching mostly bullet tuna, swordfish, red seabream, red mullet, and white grouper.[22] For several decades, Alanya's fishermen have been harvesting marine resources in a sustainable manner, providing seafood not only for the residents, but also for tourists, for whom savoring Mediterranean cuisine prepared with fresh local seafood is equally important during their visit. And for the people of Alanya, managing

Credit: Can Yeniley

Figure 9.3. The main harbor in Alanya with co-op fishermen's boats in the forefront, and the co-op building in the background.

their inshore fishery in a sustainable manner is essential because the health of their inshore fishery ensures the vitality of the tourism industry that continues to be one of the driving forces behind the local economy.[23] Therefore, the relationship between the tourists that come to visit Alanya and the inshore fishery that provides seafood is not really noticeable, yet still significant.

However, Alanya's fishery was not always in the same condition that it is today. Things were bleak in the 70s when Turkish policies of import substitution resulted in low economic growth, inflation, unemployment, trade deficit, and political violence.[24,25] The residents of Alanya, like the rest of the nation, were hit hard. The fishermen of Alanya, in an attempt to make ends meet, increased their fish landings. In a fishery where production was limited, unrestrained harvesting led to conflict among fishermen.[26] This was a time when the fishermen of Alanya were in serious trouble because for most of them fishing was their only livelihood.[27] For many fishermen in Alanya, fishing is still the only source of income that they rely on (Figure 9.4).

The early 70s were the "dark ages" for Alanya's inshore fishery.[28] Heavy competition for the best fishing spots resulted in severe conflicts, hostility, and violence between different fishing groups.[29] Unrestrained competition also increased production costs, straining the fishermen financially.[30] Alanya's inshore fishery and the tourism industry that depended on it were about to collapse.

Goals, Approaches, and Challenges

During the mid-70s, the main goal for the people of Alanya became the management of their inshore fishery in a sustainable manner which would not only

Figure 9.4. A fisherman repairing his fishing gear during the off-season.

Credit: Can Yeniley

conserve valuable resources but would also preserve the livelihoods of fishermen and the local people who work in the tourism industry (C). To be able to manage an inshore fishery that size, a substantial information and knowledge system must be in place that would foster and support learning (E-D). After all, a well-designed communication system would disseminate much-needed knowledge efficiently (D).

The vice-chair of the local fishermen co-operative (S.S. Alanya Su Ürünleri Kooperatifi) explained[31] how during the 70s the fishermen of Alanya realized the urgency to restore trust in their community (G), so this was their second goal. They knew they had grown apart from each other, and wondered how this could possibly have happened in a fishery where the fishermen had no conflicts before.

As a community, they decided to work together and involve every stakeholder to be part of the solution (J-B-A). They asked the local government to acknowledge their rights in the decision-making process, and empower them to manage their inshore fishery (F). The community leaders and the fishermen co-op agreed that a solid sense of ownership of the common pool resource would ensure solidarity and

Credit: Can Yeniley

Figure 9.5. Inside the fishermen's cooperative building in Alanya where the past is preserved on the wall.

long-term commitment among the stakeholders. The officials understood that they had to be accountable to all who were involved and that feedback in the new system would be central (I-H-B-L). As a community they knew it was in their best interest to protect their inshore fishery and minimize adverse impacts, especially at a time when there were plans to expand tourism and improve the local economy (C). In the beginning they did not know how to come up with strategies that would make the management of their fishery possible in a way that would be fair to all, without negatively impacting their livelihoods (C).

Outcomes

The first thing the fishermen of Alanya did was to establish trust within their community. To do that, they met regularly at their cooperative building and talked about their plan and different ways to improve it. They included everybody who was willing to participate in their work—in both the public and private sector. Then they worked on their social networks. It was imperative to strengthen their social capital to facilitate collaborative partnerships, which in turn would create an environment conducive to managing their fishery efficiently and sustainably. They very actively supported research: ecologist Fikret Berkes and Nobel Laureate Elinor Ostrom were among those who at one point were part of their program.

During their meetings they improved their knowledge base and awareness, and also promoted openness and transparency. To ensure equity, they clearly defined the boundaries of the system, and regulated access to their fishery. Nowadays, to be able to commercially fish there, one does not need to be a member of the cooperative, but it is mandatory to get a new license every year and also follow all the rules of the inshore fishery as laid out by the cooperative.

After several months of trial and error efforts, getting feedback from all who were involved, dealing with the unknown in the face of uncertainty, and constantly reviewing, evaluating, revising their strategy, and adapting, the members of the fishing cooperative came up with a system that reduced competition and costs, and ensured the inshore fishery's viability and sustainability.[32] Constant monitoring and efficacious feedback loops built into their system allowed them to learn from their mistakes and adjust to new circumstances. To implement a plan that they had never seen before gave rise to potential conflicts, but theirs was a participatory decision-making process in which they resolved their problems before things got out of hand.

Every year, based on the rules made by the participating cooperative members, before the beginning of each fishing season in September, a list of eligible (licensed) fishers and best fishing spots are reviewed and prepared openly by the members of the fishing community.[33] While identifying productive fishing spots, plenty of space is allowed between them for optimal production capabilities. A copy of the list of these yearly fishing locations is kept at the mayor's office and the local gendarme station. Eligible members draw lots to determine their initial fishing spots on the opening day of the fishing season. Every fishing day thereafter, the fishers move eastward to the next fishing spot, and this arrangement continues until the end of January when the fishermen change direction and start moving westward to the next fishing site until May. This gives everyone the same chance to catch the available stocks of fish that migrate from east to west from September to January, and then from west to east from January to May.[34] This unique fishing arrangement has eliminated the conflict between fishermen and continues to sustain the fishery's stocks.

The conflicts of the 70s are over, but the fishermen of Alanya now have the silver-cheeked toadfish to deal with. When the fishing nets get damaged by the toadfish[35] dolphins come over and usually eat the entire catch.[36] By changing the time and duration of fishing, the fishermen of Alanya aim to disrupt the feeding patterns of the silver-cheeked toadfish. They also constantly monitor their nets and lines and don't leave them unattended for too long, decreasing the exposure time of their fishing gear to predators. By getting feedback from the rest of the community, they evaluate progress, and adapt to changing conditions. Nobody knows what the future holds, but Alanya's inshore fishermen for the time being appear to have the invading "pirates" under control.

Reflections on Principle H: Embrace Feedback

The case study of Alanya's inshore fishery illustrates all 12 Guiding Principles. I will focus below on how Principle H: Embrace Feedback is illustrated by this case study.

Alanya's inshore fishery together with the community that depends on it is a dynamic human-nature system. After the economic hardship of the 70s, establishing accountability was essential for the system's conservation and successful management. Effective feedback loops provided openness and transparency, and also restored trust in the system, allowing opportunities for the stakeholders and officials to learn from mistakes. During the 70s, the fishermen of Alanya used their inshore fishery as if it had unlimited production capacity. The communication between fishermen was minimal, nobody appeared to be caring for the declining harvest, and nobody emphasized the importance of effective collaboration. The local and regional governments lacked leadership and their agencies failed to manage the commons. This was the time when the community banded together and established a holistic view to manage their marine resources. I believe that for a dynamic human-nature system to succeed, the channels for providing social feedback have to remain open. This is also the only way for the people to be evaluated and be held accountable for their actions. The fishermen, local officials, as well as the residents of Alanya, know that their inshore fishery is their bread and butter, and the local economy very much depends on it. Overall, the Alanya inshore fishery is a success story where local people have found a way to conserve and manage their renewable common-pool resource in a sustainable manner as they continue to thrive as a community.

Garrett Hardin's essay "The Tragedy of the Commons" described how a scarce resource like "the commons," accessible to all, is susceptible to overexploitation and eventual collapse.[37] Many commons have collapsed. The fishery of Alanya is not one of these. In 2009, the Nobel committee awarded Elinor Ostrom the Nobel Prize in Economic Sciences for her work on the commons, including Alanya's fishery.[38] Ostrom showed that Hardin's tragedy is "not inevitable,"[39] and that efficient management of shared resources is possible. The locally-managed inshore fishery in Alanya is an exercise in social reconstruction,[40] and it is by no means a perfect system. It constantly rebuilds itself and undergoes changes to ensure its sustainability and integrity.

Based on current estimates, small-scale fisheries contribute to 70 percent of the fish landings in the world.[41] It is essential to increase conservation efforts in inshore fisheries, so they can be better managed. These small-scale fisheries provide income for millions and food to billions of people, contributing significantly to local and national economies.[42] Alanya's inshore fishery can be a model for other small-scale fisheries as their sustainable management is central to the vitality of resilient communities, as well as indispensable for successful adaptation to climate change.

Principle H—Embrace Feedback

Do (Or Consider Doing)

☑ Develop tight and effective feedback systems for community leaders and ensure they are open to all members of the community.

☑ Recognize that feedback systems should be designed for leaders and community members to learn from experiences, including mistakes.

☑ Review the performance of those in leadership roles through soliciting feedback from community members, not just board members.

☑ Develop needed technical capacity and systems for monitoring activities and programs.

☑ Share as much data as possible that is collected from feedback systems. (This may not apply to confidential information on personnel or related types of issues.)

Don't (Or Think Twice)

☒ Don't assume that feedback from a survey that is only completed by a few individuals or sectors of a community represents the views of the community as a whole.

☒ Don't value feedback from "the elite" or "the connected" higher than from others, especially those most affected by a decision or program.

☒ Don't assume feedback data is always correct. Carefully examine the process of data collection and the sources of all data.

CHAPTER 10

Practice Leadership

*Practice Adaptive Leadership
and Co-Management*

> *Exercising leadership is the art of mobilizing
> a group of people to do adaptive work for the greater good.*
>
> — RONALD HEIFETZ

Critical Leadership Actions

When I use the unmodified term "leadership" it will refer to the *verb*,
not the *noun*—the *actions* not the *authority role*. The act of practicing leadership is not limited to or reserved for those who have been
elected or appointed to a leadership role. The formal role is actually an
authority role that is critical to the health of a community but not the
same as actually practicing community leadership. So, what are these
leadership actions that I am referring to under this principle?

The two critical leadership actions include:

1. *engaging your community members* and
2. *mobilizing their understanding and willingness to address the challenges, problems, and needs of their community.*

When I say "engaging and mobilizing community members," I refer to
a process that embraces and draws upon all of the other 11 principles

PRACTICE LEADERSHIP

I

Practice Adaptive Leadership and Co-Management

Five Characteristics

1. *A robust social-ecological organization is designed and structured to be a learning organization that supports adaptive capacity.*

2. *A learning organization and an optimum management system are resilient to changes or perturbation, with an ability to cope with external shocks and rapid change.*

3. *Adaptive co-management and adaptive leadership are dynamic and focused on processes rather than static structures.*

4. *Adaptive co-management approaches include roles for local government, local community members, NGOs, and private institutions and undertake decision making that includes people affected by the outcomes as well as those who are knowledgeable of the issues.*

5. *An effective co-management approach engages, trains, and mobilizes community members in the work of the organization.*

There has recently been a shift from assessing or evaluating local community organizations through a static structural view to incorporating a dynamic perspective, including issues of organizational resilience for complexity and change.[3] Within the description of the above characteristics, the terms "adaptive," "resilience," "co-management," and "learning organization" occur frequently. These are all terms used to describe adaptive leadership and adaptive co-management. Adaptive leadership[4] refers to a type of leadership that can help community members face, rather than avoid, the tough realities and conflicts that are inherent in the work of community organizations. It focuses primarily on learning how to address social change or adaptation, rather than solving purely technical problems.[5]

Co-management (short-hand for "cooperative management") relies on "the collaboration of a diverse set of stakeholders operating at different levels, often in networks, from local users, to municipalities, to regional and national organizations."[6] An integrating term, adaptive co-management combines the dynamic learning characteristics of adaptive leadership with the collaborative networks inherent in co-management. Adaptive co-management is consistent with the strategies and tools of learning organizations as described by Peter Senge in *The Fifth Discipline*.[7] Learning organizations are best able to cope with external shocks[8] since they encourage institutional and organizational diversity[9] and an entrepreneurial culture.[10] Adaptive co-management and learning organizations are dynamic and support processes, rather than attempting to define pre-planned static structures[11] and are often integral to healthy communities.

described in this book, from Principle A: Involve Everyone, to Principle L: Resolve Conflict. Such engagement builds awareness, commitment to work together, and ownership of their community's challenges.

Two recent examples of young people practicing these types of leadership actions are:

- Malala Yousafzai of Pakistan, who as a young teenager, worked towards supporting girls who were fighting poverty, war, child marriage, and gender discrimination to go to school.[1] Her efforts have made a major difference in increasing the education of young girls around the world.
- Greta Thunberg,[2] a teenage Swedish girl, who started a school strike for the climate by skipping school and sitting outside the Swedish parliament to protest for the right of future generations to live in a healthy world. With little initial support, but with determination and positive action, she was able to wake up her community, her country, and the world to the urgency of addressing climate change.

This type of leadership is very different from the effort of individuals in formal authority roles who, all too often, work to convince citizens or community members through a public relations type of sales campaign in order to gain support for an idea, which in reality has already been decided. Critical leadership actions do not focus on developing followers but on broadening and sharing leadership with all community members. A person in an authority role who convinces everyone to follow them is not practicing my definition of leadership, although many may refer to this individual as a "leader" since he/she has dedicated followers. Even if the formal leader is effective in achieving useful objectives in a short period of time, this approach may leave the community weaker, and the needed changes are often short-lived. These ideas are effectively discussed by David Mathews of the Kettering Foundation,[12] a foundation focused on the question: "What does it take to make democracy work as it should?"

Adaptive leadership and adaptive co-management are two common terms used in connection with this type of leadership. They both focus on engaging community members to understand and appreciate the strengths as well as the challenges of their community and then support community members in their efforts to address these challenges. Listening skills are essential in practicing this form of leadership. Adaptive leadership actions need to be inclusive of people affected by and knowledgeable about the issues and then actively involve them in the critical work of the community. The focus is on growing engagement and shared leadership, not followership.

Addressing complex community problems or challenges frequently requires practicing adaptive leadership. These complex problems or challenges are sometime referred to as "wicked" problems since they are difficult to define.[13] Wicked problems may include a combination of social, cultural, economic, environmental, and technical elements. Comments by Ron Heifetz[14] note that adaptive leadership work becomes necessary in "communities when people have tough challenges to tackle, when they have to change their ways in order to thrive or survive, when continuing to operate according to current structures, procedures, and processes no longer will suffice." He further emphasizes that "adaptive work generates resistance in people because adaptation requires us to let go of certain elements of our past ways of working or living, which means to experience loss…" I will share a short example of this type of change and loss below.

Stewarding Change Is Difficult: Rats and Family Bonding

The new recycling center was about to open as the old town dump had finally closed. A friend and neighbor who also served as a state senator was preparing his remarks for the dedication of the new Community Center for Waste Management and Recycling. He thanked me for my role in cleaning up the dump and getting rid of the rats. But then he paused and said, "This may sound odd, but it has been hard on my family." He went on to say, "You see, my grandfather had bonding time with my dad at this dump shooting rats. I had bonding time with my sons here shooting rats. This had become a family tradition. Again, this may sound odd, but it is hard to no longer be able to continue this tradition since there are no more rats!"

Change is difficult. Even supporting the change and knowing it is desired and needed does not always make it easier. Adaptive leadership focuses on the challenges of stewarding change that the community embraces, yet that will not be easy.

The Case Studies

The two following case studies demonstrate the role of adaptive leadership in a collaborative conservation success in the Apuseni Mountain region of Romania and in an effective on-going inner-city urban recovery effort in South Bend, Indiana.

CASE STUDY   **Local Community Collaboration in the Apuseni Mountains, Huedin, Romania**

by Paul Markowitz and James Gruber

Prologue

The Sustainable Rural Development initiative in the Apuseni Region of Romania[15] is an excellent example of the benefits of adaptive leadership. The initiative to bring about effective environmental change and sustainable economic development was led by Clubul Ecologic Transylvania (CET),[16] an environmental NGO founded by young adults to lead hiking and nature expeditions in the Apuseni Mountains, and a regional council of mayors and town leaders called the Association for Rural Development of Huedin (ARDH).[17] This region faced a range of economic, environmental, and social issues characterized by high unemployment rates, low levels of economic activity, and declining population due to the exodus of young people to urban areas. These conditions in the region had been heavily affected by the former communist regime's emphasis on large, centralized industrial development that resulted in the loss of traditional ways of living and suspicion of leaders. Therefore, these two groups realized that they not only needed to solve these problems but also to develop new and more inclusive approaches to solving them collaboratively. Their successful efforts demonstrated how a co-management approach of local government,

NGOs, and private institutions working together with communities in shared decision making can bring about effective and positive change.

Introduction and General Overview

The Apuseni Mountain Region of Transylvania is located in the north-western corner of Romania. During our visits, we quickly discovered that the region is quite spectacular. There are panoramic views of rolling hills—some in pasture, some wooded—with free-roaming semi-wild herds of horses. Settlements are small, and connected by narrow, poorly maintained, unpaved roads. The population is a mix of cultures including Romanians, Hungarians, and some Roma. Carnivores such as the lynx, wolves, and brown bears still survive in this region and there are natural and cultural tourist attractions to visit, such as waterfalls, lakes, caves, and historic villages. These exceptional ecological resources were juxtaposed with major logging equipment extracting timber from numerous areas. Streams along these clear-cut areas were grey with silt, and the narrow dirt roads were heavily rutted by the logging trucks and skidders (including rainbow puddles from leaking hydraulic logging equipment). The current economy of this region consists of limited agriculture and animal husbandry, rural tourism, timber harvesting, and some light industry. Agricultural produce was primarily consumed locally, while raw forest products were quickly exported, leading to the loss of potential income from value-added local processing into secondary and tertiary products. This was a region in transition.

Challenges, Goals, Approaches, and Outcomes
Challenges
The protection of the natural resources in the Apuseni Region and the future economic and social vitality of the communities in this region faced a number of immediate challenges. These included:

- *Economic pressures.* Residents faced economic pressures that had led to clear cutting, selling off timber, and overgrazing.
- *Skepticism of sustainable development.* CET and ARDH had to convince the local landowners and residents that sustainable develop-

ment and ecotourism were viable alternatives to exploitation of the natural resources.

- *Lack of environmental enforcement.* The Romanian national and regional governments lacked the necessary resources and capability to enforce environmental protections in the region.
- *Lack of community involvement.* Residents and property owners were not actively engaged in developing a sustainable plan for the region.

Goals

As a result, the leadership team, including CET, ARDH, and local mayors, agreed on the following overall approach:

- actively engage the community in setting priorities and implementing actions on a regional basis (A-F-I-J)
- enhance residents' economic livelihoods through the promotion of rural tourism (C)
- raise environmental awareness and promote stewardship of local natural resources (C)

Credit: CET

Figure 10.1. Community cleanup effort in Apuseni by local residents and CET members.

Approaches

Prior to this change process, CET worked effectively with the mayors over the course of six years to build a trusting relationship and initiate progress on environmental protections and economic development (B-G-K). The leadership of CET and ARDH realized that a critical missing component of their work was the active involvement and support of more community members (A-B-I). CET invited the Institute for Sustainable Communities (ISC)[18] to bring its model of community engagement to their efforts (B). Drawing upon the social capital and trust that had been established and the experience and knowledge of ISC, the region was able to broaden the involvement and support of community members (A-B-G). These groups, working together, undertook the following steps:

- Raised public awareness and support for the project, and organized a community forum that included representatives from each commune (village) (A-B-D).
- Prepared a community profile that assessed local environmental, economic, and social conditions in the region for use during the community forum (E-I).
- Trained community members to facilitate small group sessions for the community forum (J).
- Organized a day-long community forum to create a community vision and identify opportunities for local improvement. They used a range of approaches to encourage residents to attend, including organizing a poster contest for school children on a vision for the region (A-B).
- Convened a community forum with over 120 residents participating. Through small and large group sessions, participants developed a vision, identified key community needs, and selected priority projects. Local residents organized themselves into project task forces (A-B-D-F-G-I-J).
- Implementation plans were developed by the task forces that further defined project goals, determined action steps, set timelines, and assigned roles and responsibilities (F-J-I). They also identified

key individuals necessary to implement actions and solicited their participation on the task force (A-B).

- Work on selected projects, which were relatively visible and inexpensive, was led by volunteers who relied on local resources to the greatest extent possible (B).
- Held a celebration a year later that was attended by the residents who came back together to evaluate results and lessons learned and chart their next steps (H-F).

Outcomes

The community members constructed a tourism shelter and information facility and prepared and distributed regional promotional materials including a tourism map. Besides these physical changes, other types of changes were of far greater significance. One resident stated, "The greatest achievement of this effort was the creation of a local group of concerned citizens to advocate for community improve-

Credit: CET

Figure 10.2. Community members installing tourist information kiosk in Apuseni.

ments." Community members also noted how this initiative raised their awareness of the importance of empowering more individuals in each village to take responsibility; the need to place greater emphasis on developing public awareness; and the value of maintaining communication with other local residents.

The underlying goal of building a sense of community and local social capital seemed to have been achieved. In a series of interviews four years later,[19] participants said that the biggest results were:

- more people were engaged and volunteering
- positive results were achieved
- the community became stronger
- implementation efforts reflected priorities of citizens
- people recognized that there are tangible community benefits from the protection of nature

Reflections on Principle I: Practice Leadership

This positive community effort in the Apuseni Region offers a wealth of information about how communities can address environmental and economic issues at the local level while building social capital. Some key reflections on the role of practicing adaptive leadership and co-management include:

Build leadership capacity in the community. Effective, adaptive leadership is the single most significant factor in determining whether a community project will be successful. Adaptive leaders involve people in creating their own solutions and decisions are made through an open, participatory dialogue. These local officials welcomed public involvement, supported open and transparent processes, and were respectful and deferential to the citizen task forces that emerged from the public process. They understood that their economies were inextricably linked and that there was inherent value in working together. They understood that exploiting local natural resources would lead to only short-term economic benefits and were open to alternative economic models that supported sustainable development and ecotourism.

Build trust between civic groups and local government officials. Prior to the start of this project, CET had established a strong working relationship with the local mayors. They encouraged the mayors to join forces and form a regional association to promote development in the region. A strong level of trust was developed and provided the foundation for the successful implementation of this change effort. CET viewed themselves as a resource to help local officials and residents meet their goals, rather than experts to solve local problems. When the director of CET[20] was asked to describe his definition of successful project, he stated: "It is successful when they don't need us anymore… they know how to do it."

Focus on short-term doable projects. This approach offers numerous advantages. First, local residents can see for themselves the real results and that the priorities they helped establish were implemented. These small successes build collective confidence that their participation can make a real difference. Second, it provides a strong foundation for residents to move forward in addressing more difficult issues such as tourism and environmental quality on a deeper and more systemic level.

CASE STUDY Inner City Urban Recovery, South Bend, Indiana, USA

by P. Ambord, S. Salas, and J. Kenjio

Prologue

The problem of vacant and abandoned properties is a prominent challenge facing US cities, especially those that were industrial centers throughout the 19th and early 20th centuries. These cities, primarily located in midwestern states like Michigan and Ohio, have found this problem compounded by severe population decline and exclusive housing practices. This case study explores the approach to urban vacancy in South Bend, Indiana, adopted by Mayor Pete Buttigieg in collaboration with several other community stakeholders. After learning about the momentum that this community-driven initiative gained for the mayor and his community through a media outlet, *Meet the Press*, we were very excited to explore their story. This case study presents an admirable model of adaptive leadership and co-management.

Introduction

The city of South Bend, Indiana, like many other midwestern cities, faces the dire problem of vacant and abandoned properties.[21] Several significant factors have contributed to this situation in South Bend, including population decline, loss of manufacturing, the national housing crisis, and property value reassessments.[22] Between 1960 and 2010 alone, South Bend lost 23.6 percent of its population. In 2011, *Newsweek* proclaimed South Bend a "dying city."[23]

As in the Baltimore case study (Chapter 4), the city of South Bend has taken a holistic approach to the problem of urban vacancy. Under the leadership of Mayor Buttigieg, the city convened a task force with the dual purpose of assessing the extent of the vacancy problem and exploring potential elements of a comprehensive solution.

General Overview

In 2012 Mayor Buttigieg brought together city and county officials, private sector practitioners, and neighborhood advocates to create the Vacant and Abandoned Properties Task Force. They began collecting data and engaging affected neighborhoods in order to create a more sophisticated view of their property problem than had been compiled before. The task force's data collection and analysis put South Bend in a much better position to design appropriate policy, make recommendations, and develop interventions. In 2013, Mayor Buttigieg initiated a revitalization project ("1,000 Houses in 1,000 Days") while also implementing a number of the Task Force Report recommendations.

Goals, Approaches, and Challenges

The main goal of the task force was to address the negative influence that vacant and abandoned properties had on the community. Their work was guided by three principles: "First, good decisions require a full understanding of the relevant information. Second, the success of any governmental intervention must be measured by the outcomes achieved more than by the outputs produced. Third, the communities most affected by the problem of vacant and abandoned properties must be engaged in shaping and implementing the responses."[24]

Members of the task force met often and divided into subcommittees with special tasks while writing the report (I-E). They considered community engagement central to their approach to vacancy and abandonment in South Bend, supplementing their task force meetings with three public community hearings in the three neighborhoods most impacted by the issue (J-B). The first two community sessions were dedicated solely to collecting feedback about how residents were impacted by vacancy and abandonment in their own neighborhoods. These meetings not only helped to illustrate the scope of the problem, but also encouraged those attending to suggest potential solutions (D-H-I). The final community forum gave the task force the opportunity to present their initial findings and recommendations to the public and receive feedback (A-D-H-J).

In their final report, the task force recommended that the city approach the problem through four dimensions: data-driven decision making, code enforcement, land banks and tax sales, and resources and reuse. The first point—data-driven decision making—defined the overall efforts of the task force. That is, the problem of vacancy and abandonment required a deep dive into existing conditions. This included an analysis of neighborhood market conditions and market indicators which was essential for developing a formula for how the city determined which properties could be repaired, when they should do so, and how.[25] (E)

At the same time, 2013 was the beginning of Buttigieg's 1,000 Houses in 1,000 Days initiative, which implemented additional task force recommendations. Its goal, as implied, was to address 1,000 vacant and abandoned homes in 1,000 days through repair, demolition, deconstruction, and renovation. A recurring technical challenge for the group was the redundancy and inefficiency of existing processes around building laws, codes, and enforcement. Based on these experiences, the city revised and upgraded the necessary policies and codes to make them more efficient and transparent (K-I).

Another challenge of this project was equity. Due to its grassroots origins, South Bend residents have mostly supported the task force's aims.[26] But, in all, there have been ambivalent responses and impacts. For example, aspects of the 1,000 Houses in 1,000 Days initiative may have added financial pressures to affected communities of color. The project's associated code enforcement costs made it difficult for those families who intended to fix up vacant and abandoned houses, once they had the means, to keep those houses. This resulted in property loss among these communities.[27] In response to this challenging situation, residents stood up and spoke out about their concerns.

Referring to the way the code enforcement policy was applied, Mayor Buttigieg has said, "I'm not sure we got that completely right…"[28] As a result of the community's continued participation and the mayor's willingness to listen, significant improvements have been achieved. Lawsuits for unpaid code enforcement fees are slowly being dropped and major city funding was directed towards home repairs. Community members requested $300,000 in home repair grants. Buttigieg answered with $650,000.[29] The project was not perfect but the way the mayor responded to community voices has supported the building of greater social cohesion and community trust.

Outcomes

In 2013 there were 1,572 vacant and abandoned properties in South Bend. Since then, 91 percent of the properties have been addressed through demolition, reparations, or deconstruction.[30] The City has also pursued several task force recommendations with a focused effort in improving internal processes and directly addressing abandoned properties. Some specific outcomes have included:

- improved relationship with the local county related to understanding city goals and activities
- targeted city resources for housing development

- ongoing consideration of vacant lot reuse and activation
- added city resources to assist existing homeowners in preventing properties from falling into abandoned status

Additionally, the 1,000 Houses in 1,000 Days project successfully reached its goal as well as identifying many valuable lessons, such as: reliable data is often elusive but critical for program implementation; and cooperative partnerships between the local government, private interests, and residents are essential for large-scale changes. The program's focus groups also gathered resident input, which allowed the city to identify future goals for neighborhood development.

When asked about the effects of the project activities on their neighborhood, one community member shared, "Cottage Grove was [changed from] a street where a house had no chance of selling on the open market, to a street thriving with new families and a demand for housing. Out of the 1,000 homes almost half were restored; which is

Credit: City of South Bend

Figure 10.3. The community works to repair homes through Rebuilding Together.

a positive." Looking forward, another community member explained, "Smart strategies and tactics are in the works and I am optimistic that our best days as a city are ahead of us. There is an ecosystem of competent, caring, and committed talent finding their purpose here and building a better city of tomorrow by our collective good work today."

Reflections on Principle I and this Case Study

South Bend's recent urban redevelopment efforts make it clear that involving and partnering with the communities most affected by vacancy and abandonment was critical. These partnerships contributed to developing local adaptive capacities and implementing appropriate policies. This approach, led by the task force, set the stage for effective co-management of neighborhood investments. For example, their 2013 report specifically recommended city-organized code enforcement training sessions for the public as well as city support for local neighborhood associations.

In our opinion, South Bend's approach thus far has the potential to be replicated by other communities. With that said, it is also important to keep in mind that each community will have its own unique set of challenges to work through. These may include local and state laws, the local housing market, scale, etc. We were told by former task force members, "Challenges like abandoned properties have a number of intertwined issues that caused the problem over many years. Rarely is there one simple solution or an overnight fix."[31] This initiative reveals the city's impressive ability to adapt methods and processes as community needs evolve.

Principle I—Practice Leadership

Do (Or Consider Doing)

✓ Work to engage, train, and mobilize community members in the work of the community.

✓ Pay attention not only to what the community wants or needs, but also to the process by which those goals can be achieved in order to ensure that it helps strengthen shared community leadership.

✓ Help communities recognize some of the barriers that impede their progress.

✓ If you are a formal leader, have listening sessions or hold one-on-one meetings (or ask the formal leaders to do so). Share overall what you (or they) heard, focusing on trends and themes without violating confidentiality.

✓ Look for and identify strengths as well as clarifying the challenges and problems.

✓ Focus on building resiliency rather than fixing one specific problem.

Don't (Or Think Twice)

✗ Even if serving in a formal leadership role, never assume that you know what is best for your community.

✗ Don't let hubris become your Achilles heel. That is, watch your personal status needs.

✗ Even when requested to make all of the key decisions as a leader or expert do not do so until you have engaged others in dialogue. Ideally, seek consensus whenever possible.

✗ Don't let the desire for success become part of the avoidance of real challenges and problems that your community is facing.

✗ Don't underestimate what a small group of dedicated individuals can accomplish if given the support that they need.

CHAPTER 11

Decide Together

Enable and Support
Participatory Decision-Making Processes

> *Tell me, I'll forget. Show me, I'll remember.*
> *Involve me, I'll understand.*
>
> — ANCIENT CHINESE PROVERB

Moving from Them to Us

"Why should I want to encourage and support a participatory decision-making process in my community?" "Didn't we elect and hire leaders to make decisions for us?" I have heard these and similar questions and I trust that I am not alone. It is my experience that a well-structured and inclusive participatory problem-solving process that has effectively involved a broad cross-section of a community will result in better decisions and in more community support as well as ownership of these decisions. This has also been found true by many others.[1] Including community members in important and critical decisions in this manner will likely transform the divisive "us" vs. "them" conversations into a community "we" dialogue, which is an indicator of a healthy community. Clearly not all decisions need to be or should be made through a participatory process, but decisions that will have significant impact on the future should be undertaken with this power sharing approach.

DECIDE TOGETHER

Enable and Support Participatory Decision-Making Processes

Five Characteristics

1. *Effective participatory problem solving and decision making is enabled by a well-structured and facilitated dialogue involving resource users, practitioners, community members, policymakers and, potentially, social or natural scientists.*

2. *Decision making is informed by analysis of key information about environmental and human-environmental systems including life aspirations of local people.*

3. *It is vital to create a shared holistic vision and plan that anticipate probable environmental, social, and economic outcomes.*

4. *The policy creation process should include a wide range of key expert and non-expert constituencies and community groups at the table.*

5. *Participatory problem solving should provide opportunities for the sharing of knowledge and collaborative learning about social-ecological systems.*

Participatory problem solving and decision making are at the heart of effective and healthy communities. These participatory processes need to be accessible and inclusive of a representative population of the community,[2] which may be composed of policymakers, nonprofit groups, the private sector, and the general public.[3] A well-structured process will center collaboration and information-sharing[4] and include dialogue on local socio-ecological and economic systems, quality of life, and community visions for the future.[5] In decision making, all stakeholders—including the experts, general community members, and the most directly affected groups—need to be present and activated.

Research shows that participatory decision making has "improved quality of the decisions, improved legitimacy of the responsible organization, and improved capacity of the community for future assessment and decision making."[6] Many practitioners claim that in creating participatory decision-making processes it is advantageous to develop a shared comprehensive plan. Such a plan should illustrate the community's interrelated environmental, economic, and social goals, as well as outline locally relevant strategies.[7]

Common Characteristics and
Challenges of Deciding Together

There are many approaches to designing and conducting participatory decision-making processes (and entire books written on the subject). Chapter 14: A Toolbox of Leadership Strategies will lay out some ideas and approaches that we have found to be effective. Some of the most important characteristics of an effective participatory decision-making approach usually include:

- commitment by the formal community leaders to this process
- transparency of the entire process
- opportunities for all voices to be heard
- representation of the full cross-section of the community
- priorities and/or preferences of all participants being heard (and formally recorded)

In many cases, the process should be facilitated by an impartial external individual or group.

It is extremely helpful that the community has a strong social foundation before undertaking a major challenge or addressing a significant problem with a participatory decision-making process. Key elements of a strong social foundation include shared norms, common interests, mutual respect, trust in others, and a general belief in the community. Some communities may not be ready for conducting a participatory decision-making process because they do not have a strong enough foundation. Approaches for strengthening this foundation are discussed under Principle K in Chapter 12. You are also encouraged to be prepared for future conflicts that may arise and to plan for how to work towards resolution of these conflicts. See Principle L: Resolve Conflicts in Chapter 13.

Chase's Mill: A Community Recovering
Its Village Gathering Place

A 1767 water-powered mill, restored in 1919, was now empty, the roof was leaking, the windows broken. Up until the late 1980s youth had learned woodworking skills, and people had gathered in the upstairs meeting room for weddings, Quaker meetings, and memorial services. Sometimes a neighbor would chisel out a timber frame for their home or build a burial box for a deceased family member. And neighbors frequently celebrated and debated the issues of the day. What could be done to restore this historic and cultural center?

In 2013 residents of Mill Hollow and surrounding areas in New Hampshire came together to save the Mill. Commitment, labor, time, and financial contributions came from hundreds of friends of the Mill, many of whom had learned woodworking there or attended gatherings. Once restored, Chase's Mill would once again be a center for community learning, celebrations, and gatherings. But how to decide what would be appropriate for future community events and programs? How could the rebirth of the Mill serve all community members—the young, students, families, seniors, and those with certain limitations?

The leaders of the nonprofit Mill Hollow Heritage Association, founded in 2012, are committed to engage the broader community in all important decisions. They want all voices to be heard. They have organized forums, inviting a very wide range of community members, to develop ideas for future use of the spaces. The participants at the forums developed a wide range of programs in five areas: history and culture, arts and crafts, technology and science, ecology and

Figure 11.1. Chase's Mill and volunteers.

Credit: Robert Brown (*left*); Juliana Stevens (*right*)

sustainability, and woodworking and carpentry. Each of the proposed programs were prioritized with all participants and then further developed. The Association is also committed to partnering with local schools and education centers, local businesses, and other organizations to share programs and activities. In 2020, after seven years and countless hours of community efforts, the Mill was fully restored, including the water-powered woodworking machines, and Chase's Mill is once again a welcoming historic and community center for learning, celebrations, and gatherings.

This type of inclusive "decide together" process takes time, dialogue, and patience in seeking the right decisions. However, it's been found repeatedly to improve the quality of the decision making and builds the strength of the community. To reiterate the African proverb: "If you want to go fast, go alone. If you want to go far, go together." This also applies to decision making.

The Case Studies

This chapter's first case study presents an innovative inner-city Boston school for underprivileged children which is governed by a democratic participatory process that includes students and members of the surrounding community. The second shares how local communities in Southern Ecuador, working with their local government leaders, residents, and a local university, were able to protect a major Ecuadorian wetlands region in the southern high Andes.

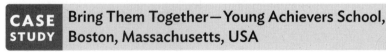

CASE STUDY Bring Them Together—Young Achievers School, Boston, Massachusetts, USA

by Bo Hoppin

Prologue

The mission of the Young Achievers Science and Mathematics Pilot School is to create an exceptional teaching and learning environment in which science and mathematics concepts are explored through new technologies and made central to teacher and student inquiry.

The school was one of the initial five Pilot Schools founded in 1995 by a passionate group of black and Latino community leaders, parents, and teachers from the Roxbury, Dorchester, and Mattapan neighborhoods of Boston. The founders envisioned a kindergarten through eighth grade (K-8) school where all children would be known and cared for during an extended learning day. Today, the school is governed by a democratic participatory process that relies on active partnerships with families, students, community members, and community institutions.

Introduction and General Overview

The school has worked to push students, parents, and community members to the front of the decision-making process. It has challenged staff to engage in extensive committee work that lasts well into many evenings. Community partners are invited to support the school's academic achievement goals by thoughtfully connecting their work to the curriculum. The school's leadership embraces local, district, and state institutions as strategically integrated partners working to fulfill the school's mission. The outcome is a sophisticated, complex K-8 school serving over 600 students.

The notion that a public school can break free from the reins of a centralized education system to create a participatory system is ambitious. Urban public schools are under intense pressure to succeed academically, which really means higher test scores. This inherently pushes schools toward centralized decision making and away from engaging the community. The Pilot School system in Boston, Massachusetts, was created with the unique vision of bringing community participation back to the schools. The pilot system has thrived in placing community at the center of a school's decision making; however, it struggles with the larger district to meet the formal requirements of school accountability.

All was going well...and then, in 2014, came the call from our school principal, a local icon known for being one tough cookie. I felt dread walking into a meeting of school leadership, teachers, and parents

Credit: Bo Hoppin

Figure 11.2. Young Achievers 5th grade students launch the row boats they built with the Community Boat Building program on nearby Jamaica Pond.

urgently called by our school principal—I knew before I arrived that she was going to ask us to enter into a high stakes bet that would require intense commitment and most likely result in a big goose egg.

Young Achievers was just emerging from five years of dramatic transitions as requested by Boston school leaders. To its credit, the school's staff embraced these transitions as opportunities. Five years into school and program restructuring we were finally getting our traction.

Now, a powerhouse principal was going to ask us to enter into yet another monstrous transition by applying for an Expanded Learning Time grant. She explained that this opportunity "was our first chance at substantial funding to realize the founder's vision for an extended school day that addressed our student's academic needs." She asked each of the nine meeting participants to share their thoughts (H-I). I expressed my dread and raised my hand as "yes" when the straw poll was called. So did everybody else. It is a credit to her leadership, knowing when to push and when to listen.

Goals and Approaches

The Massachusetts Department of Elementary and Secondary Education Expanded Learning Time grant program is a large state-run program that supports schools to extend their school day beyond the conventional 6.5 hours. Their goals are to provide teachers with more time for collaborative planning and to enrich the school day for students by leveraging the power of community partners (A-B-J). The fiscal resources they offer schools are substantial, in our case over $400,000 per year.

I attended the grant program's information session with a continued sense of dread. I had been to too many of these and the drill was always the same. A stuffy hotel conference room, peppermints, and power point presentations about accountability through data-driven decision making. Or, "Get your damn test scores up!"

This program communicated a new and refreshing message: "Let's get kids engaged in an expanded school day through leveraging the power of community partners."

The program asked schools to form leadership teams comprised of teachers, administrators, parents, and community partners to define how *they* would meet the goal of extending the school day for a total of 30 additional days of education. The state facilitated connecting new applicants to successful Expanded Learning Time schools (B-D). Most importantly, it let each grant applicant define their path through a model of support rather than prescription (I-K-F).

The Expanded Learning Time grant application process emphasized innovative approaches for engaging students and community partners in a meaningful extended school day. In just one year, Young Achievers had contracted with 17 local nonprofits. Students were more physically active at Sportsmen's Tennis Club. They were challenged to defend their opinions through the Debate League. They applied math skills through building rowboats with Boston Family Boat Building and learned ecological processes while planting a school garden with Green City Growers. Local elders tutored reading for our younger students through Generations Inc. A program called Keys to Literacy mentored our newest teachers. An entire community of nonprofits, local leaders, and citizens made learning come alive for some of Boston's most vulnerable students. So what do the outcomes look like when partners participate in decision making?

The nearby Boston Nature Center (BNC) served as one of our closest partners. Our 4th and 5th graders visited the site every other week for three hours. Their teachers stayed back at school for focused and facilitated curriculum planning. The students worked with BNC's naturalists to expand their understanding of local ecology and scientific processes. On a bitter, cold January morning, under bright blue skies with the landscape covered by a recent dusting of snow, school unfolded as a magical journey.

Outcomes

Alder says "Hey, look at that, it's a rabbit track, no wait, maybe it's a deer." Darnell: "It is definitely deer, see how the two half circles are close together." Tristan chimes in, "But look, there are two big prints in front and two little prints in back, that is a rabbit." In unison "NO WAY," and

Credit: Bo Hoppin

Figure 11.3. Young Achievers students on a tracking expedition at Boston Nature Center.

one says, "It's both deer and rabbit out here, and look at all the prints, they are all over the place!" A little farther down the trail we come across another print, they run back and grab the identification card out of my hands. All three are now gathered around this new print, struggling to also look at the tracking identification card. "What is it? Can't be rabbit, there are too many sections. Wait, I count 2, 5, 8 sections on that print. WOW! That is a coyote! Here in the city? Can't be!" Kim, the BNC naturalist, asks them how we could have found this print if there was no coyote here in the city. They quickly discard the idea that someone must have come out here and put that print in the snow. They decide it is indeed a coyote, and it must be followed.

The three boys track their coyote down a hill and onto a small frozen pond. They decide the coyote was chasing a rabbit, with ample evidence to validate their reasoning. They have sticks in their hands, which started out as guns for hunting, but became pointers to show each other characteristics of the tracks. The pointers morph into clubs to explore how the ice of this small pond could be cracked, leading to all sorts of inquiries about why they are standing on ice that is cracking, but they are not falling into the water.

The opportunity for Alder, Darnell, and Tristan to make their discoveries is how budding scientists are created. They explore, ask interesting questions, and experience the joy of being in charge of their own learning. Leveraging the resources and expertise of community partners allowed their inquiry to come alive.

Reflection on Principle J: Decide Together

The essence of Principle J is getting people to listen to each other and build together. Open and collaborative relationships can foster more creative learning opportunities for the community, and outcomes for students like Darnell, Alder, and Tristan can be stronger.

The activists who founded Young Achievers envisioned a more impactful schooling experience for their kids. They viewed a science- and math-themed school as a strategy for engaging kids in growing toward a meaningful career. For many of the neighborhood kids a passion for science and math equaled a career path out of poverty.

Fortunately, the Massachusetts Department of Elementary and Secondary Education recognizes that many of our most vulnerable schools and students need additional class time to meet academic standards. They also recognize that there are resources within each community that can be used to enrich school practices, and effectively replace "drill-and-kill" tactics. These acknowledgements, in addition to appropriate state grant programs and tireless engagement from school staff and the community, have helped to create a Young Achievers that lives up to the vision of its founders. What started as a sense of dread for making a school more complicated morphed into optimism about the power of partnership.

 Wetlands Conservation and Sustainable Livelihoods in the Ecuadorian Andes, Ecuador

by Fausto Lopez, Ramiro Morocho, Diana Astudillo, and Sandra Pinel

Adapted and Edited by James Gruber

Prologue

High in the Southern Andes of Ecuador is a major wetland that provides critical water resources to adjacent local communities on the Pacific and the Amazon sides of the continental divide. Visitors to this remote region are amazed by the verdant green hills and mountains and the pristine lagoons and peatlands. The undisturbed ecology, the vulnerable and endangered species that inhabit this region, and the exceptional water resources all directly impact the livelihoods and culture of residents including the Saraguro, Shuar, and Mestiza people who have lived in this wetland region for generations.

A local university, Universidad Técnica Particular de Loja (UTPL), recognized these ecological values, potential threats from mining and other development, and the importance of future conservation planning. UTPL has been collaboratively working with local communities

Figure 11.4. Wetland
region on the continental
divide in the high
Southern Andes.

Credit: UTPL

for over ten years to find a shared approach that will protect and preserve this critical wetland, and support the livelihoods, social health, and vitality of these communities. Recently all of the local communities were able to reach a consensus by agreeing to protect this wetland region through the international Ramsar Convention program.

Introduction

This case study is about a regional community in southern Ecuador that is made up of overlapping communities that historically have not always communicated well or have at best had different perspectives on how to best serve their members. It includes the Indigenous communities of Saraguro, Shuar, and Mestiza people and the more recently arrived Nabón people; three local governments; supportive NGOs; the local Universidad Técnica Particular de Loja (UPTL). Also participating in this effort are international partners (University of Iowa and Antioch University New England). Starting in 2010, UTPL has been active in assisting these local communities and conducting studies on the natural-ecological systems of this wetland region as well as social and cultural research within the region. UTPL also provided assistance for community development and environmental education through several NGOs. Their research is published and available in a number of journal articles.[8] The research team and their partners completed a milestone event in 2015 by designing and convening a community-based process that included two regional participatory workshops with the local people, local government officials, and other stakeholders. This event provided a forum for sharing the outcomes of previous years of social and ecological research as well as an opportunity to seek a shared vision and to create potential action steps for moving the community forward. This case study will focus on this milestone event and subsequent actions in the years that followed.

General Overview

Protection of this major Ecuadorian wetlands region in the southern high Andes is a significant concern for many groups who live here. This region, a prospective protected forest, is considered by the International Union for Conservation of Nature (IUCN) as a Category-6 Landscape: protected area with sustainable use of natural resources. These are critical ecological regions that are occupied by rural, typically Indigenous, communities.

To enhance societal outcomes from this research, the research team at UTPL decided to include regional residents and leaders in gathering data and in decision making throughout this multiyear process (A-B-E). They conducted a range of research efforts that examined both the social, cultural, and ecological conditions in the field during a five-year period prior to convening these multistakeholder workshops.[9] This allowed the UTPL project team members and their partners to build relationships with members of the three indigenous communities as well as with leaders of local governments, state institutions,[10] and NGOs in this region. This process strengthened the enabling conditions and the public trust and legitimacy of UTPL prior to the workshops (K-G). The project team also decided to draw upon prior research and published principles of effective Community-Based Natural Resource Management[11] to both guide the participatory research process and to assess the process during the final workshops (A-E-H).

Goals, Approaches, and Challenges

The primary goal of this regional effort was to find consensus on how to conserve this critical wetland region in a manner that would also support the local social and livelihood needs of the Indigenous people and local towns. This required a broad understanding of the ecological systems by the community members, including how to protect the endangered species and maintain the quantity and quality of water from this wetland that is central to supporting the social and economic vitality of the region (D).

The second goal was to build bridging social capital and trust between the different Indigenous and local government groups. The term "bridging social capital" refers to the growth of interpersonal relationships between individuals and groups that do not frequently associate. This building of social capital and trust started years before the workshops (B-G-K).

Figure 11.5. Loja, a local community in the Southern Andes watershed region.

Credit: UTPL

The third goal was to determine if there was a broad enough understanding, sufficient support, and commitment to future cooperation to seek to have this critical wetland region designated under the 1971 Ramsar Wetland Convention and Treaty (D-F-L). Two regional workshops were designed and held based upon best practices of collaborative multistakeholder processes[12] (A-B-J) to help achieve these three goals. These were held in the Yacuambi region (eastern side of the Andes) and in the Oña-Saraguro region (western side of the Andes).

Approach and Challenges

There were some challenges to the hoped-for success of these workshops. Two early concerns were the differences between the three tribal cultures and the history of the exclusion of Indigenous groups and local communities from centrally planned projects for the region. The five years of UTPL participatory research and outreach had done much to lower those barriers and build trust between groups. The techniques that were found most effective for gathering local knowledge and information (and reaching consensus with stakeholders across our region) were participatory workshops and sharing technical information on the ecological and social impacts of wetlands through presentations and talks. These presentations needed to be accessible to lay persons, by being clear and by avoiding technical and scientific jargon. It is critical to transform technical lectures into simple language for people to understand.

Leaders of this research and decision-making process also had to face the challenge of bringing people together, sometimes from significant distances from the wetlands, with limited transportation options and financial resources. The decision to hold the two workshops on either side of the mountain made it possible for more people to attend.

These two multistakeholder workshops, held in May 2015, focused on the feasibility of community-based and collaborative management for the future of the Saraguro-Oña-Yacuambi Wetlands. The workshop process was designed to share the natural science and social science research completed by UTPL over that previous five years and to seek a shared vision and approach as to how to move forward on preserving and protecting this major páramo (alpine tundra) wetland region (A-B-D-F-J). The workshops were structured to provide an opportunity for local government leaders, along with national and other stakeholders, to contribute ideas and resources to the conservation of this critical wetland region. A primary objective of this workshop process was to ensure that the ecological concerns and the priorities of the local communities were well reflected in the future plan (C). It was recognized that different cultural communities might define conservation goals differently (C). UTPL and their partners wanted to ensure that all voices were heard and that any plan to move forward reflected and respected this diversity of perspectives (A-C-E). The workshops also offered an opportunity to conduct an assessment of this community-based research project based upon published principles for successful community-based natural resource management efforts.[13] (H)

Both workshops were well attended and resulted in shared visions, prioritization of the concerns and problems of the region, and a framework of a strategic plan to move forward (A-D-F-J-L). This was done through small groups, report-outs, and discussions all designed to ensure that participants had a clear voice in prioritizing issues that were developed (F-J-K).

Figure 11.6. Small group working session at workshop.

Credit: James Gruber

Despite the success of this effort, recent involvement by an Ecuadorian government ministry has delayed the implementation process due to a previous mining concession near this region. Nonetheless, due to the broad support and trust earned thought the years of engagement of local stakeholders that included discussions, local workshops, consensus building, and broad sharing of this proposed conservation proposal over a number of years, it is now likely that the Ministry will provide final formal approval in the very near future.

Outcomes

There are four shared overall outcomes from the two workshops that are based upon written feedback and follow-up discussions with the workshop coordinators. These are:

- a clear growth in social capital and trust between and among the stakeholders
- broad support for moving towards a Ramsar Wetlands designation without conflicts between stakeholders involved in this major initiative
- the recognition of remaining questions and concerns about how it would all work and ideas on developing a future management plan of this wetland's region
- an increased level of awareness and commitment to work together, across both the western and eastern sides of the Andes

Another outcome of the workshops included assessing future management approaches. The strongest and broadest support was that "all three municipalities and its Parroquias (sub-regions) should conserve the (wetlands) area." The least support was for "the Ministerio de Ambiente (National Environment Ministry) to be responsible for the (wetlands) area." Local communities were ready to step up to work together to manage and protect this critical natural resource (F-I-L).

Perhaps the most significant outcome of the workshops was that there were virtually no disagreements or concerns raised about moving towards a Ramsar Wetlands designation (J). As noted above, there

Figure 11.7. Local community members placing priority dots on a generated list of concerns and/or problems that needed to be addressed to conserve and manage this critical wetland region. Location of workshops: Yacuambi (Zamora Chinchipe) and Oña (Azuay), Ecuador.

Credit: James Gruber

were a number of unsolved questions about logistics in implementing this conservation initiative, including the process for developing a management plan (I). However, equally important, there was an increased level of awareness and commitment to work together, across both the western and eastern sides of the Andes (A-B-C). The positive energy was at times palpable among the participants.

The final outcomes from the workshops included conducting an assessment of the leadership approach that UTPL had adopted over five years ago when they initiated this effort (H). Three of the 12 Guiding Principles were assessed by all participants. These were: Principle B: Work Together (*Build Social Capital and Collaborative Partnerships*); Principle E: Support Research (*Promote Research and Information Development*); and Principle J: Decide Together (*Enable and Support Participatory Decision-Making Processes*). All participants rated the five key characteristics associated with each of these three principles on a scale from −3 (least important) to +3 (most important). The preponderance of rankings was positive with an average ranking for each of these three Principles of +2.47 or higher. It was clear that the approach stewarded by UTPL resonated with nearly all stakeholders and was instrumental in growing trust, knowledge, understanding, and support for moving together to conserve this wetland region through a collaborative approach (B-E-J).

Reflections on Principle J: Decide Together

This case study illustrates nearly all 12 Guiding Principles. However, we will only focus below on how Principle J: Decide Together is illustrated. Building a common base of shared information and promoting decisions based upon a broad base of knowledge directly linked to this wetland region was the foundation of the approach. Leading a change process requires building a broad understanding of the critical issues and why change is needed. This required time and persistence for the local Indigenous communities, municipalities, as well as the staff of the Ministry to understand why protecting this wetland is important to them today and for their future. This participatory process has enhanced the legitimacy of governance solutions to this wetland regional conservation effort, increased positive connections and relationships across this region, and reduced future regulatory costs associated with long-term conservation and management. Ideally, establishing an ongoing role for community members will enhance knowledge, ownership, and commitment to the long-term stewardship of this critical wetlands resource.

It should be noted that the final two workshops were carefully designed and led by experienced facilitators with experience in large-group decision-making processes. Workshop agendas were designed to encourage involvement of local stakeholders in giving feedback, sharing their ideas, and setting their priorities.

In conclusion, we hope that this participatory, community-based planning process may be a model for other wetland conservation initiatives. Conserving critical ecological resources through a collaborative decision making with all community members is a foundation for building a healthy, vibrant, and sustainable community. It is hoped that the broad ownership, knowledge, and social capital that has grown within and between local communities during the past years will continue into the future.

Principle J—Decide Together

Do (Or Consider Doing)

✓ Undertake participatory, well-structured decision-making processes that include opportunities for dialogue among all participants and allow for all voices to be heard.

✓ Establish ground rules (or norms) at the beginning, so that dominant or powerful individuals do not push out others.

✓ Seek a fully representative cross-section of your community to be included in the process.

✓ Create opportunities for all involved to gain a more holistic understanding of the issues being discussed. This may mean sharing technical data, social or cultural information, environmental and economic information, and the views of those not usually represented.

✓ Ensure that all people can share their own priorities and preferences. Then design a process for the larger group to vote on these priorities and focus on those that have the most votes. (Specific options are discussed in Chapter 14.)

✓ Involve community members in creating action plans and in participating in their implementation.

Don't (Or Think Twice)

✗ Don't assume that all participants have a similar level of knowledge or understanding.

✗ Don't just send off email announcements and invitations and assume you will have participation from a broad cross-section of your community. Working through existing community groups and some one-on-one invitations will probably be needed.

✗ Don't assume that this can be done in a short time frame.

✗ Don't assume that the experts' advice is right for any particular community.

✗ Don't shy away from allowing disagreements; sometimes they lead to creative solutions.

CHAPTER 12

PRINCIPLE

K

Strengthen the Foundation

Strengthen Enabling Conditions

> *The loftier the building,*
> *the deeper must the foundation be laid.*
>
> — THOMAS À KEMPIS

A Strong Social Foundation

Communities, like buildings, cannot stand without a strong foundation. As a civil engineer, I am well acquainted with structural failure from an underdesigned and underconstructed *structural* foundation. Initially it may look fine, but eventually cracks start to form and, in the end, the structure will not withstand the wear of time and use. Communities need *social* foundations that include shared norms, common interests, mutual respect, trust in each other, a belief in their community, and confidence in their ability to succeed. This social foundation may also include an awareness and understanding of the challenges that a community is facing, without the feeling of hopelessness in the face of these challenges. Similar to the reinforcing steel in a concrete foundation, I believe that positive *community norms* provide the structural support that holds a community's social foundation together.

STRENGTHEN THE FOUNDATION

K

Strengthen Enabling Conditions

Five Characteristics

1. *Community has common interests, shared norms, and a relatively healthy local social structure in which divisions are not too serious or disruptive of cooperation.*

2. *The community and its resource systems have clearly defined boundaries.*

3. *While the public is unsatisfied with the status quo, it is not feeling hopeless.*

4. *Citizens and stakeholders are willing to participate due to a high sense of community and/or dependency on the local natural resources.*

5. *There is adequate support and investment of financial and other resources to support transitional costs.*

Research shows that community norms strongly influence what community members value, their beliefs, and what actions they take.[5] It is essential to improve preconditions that strengthen the local foundation prior to undertaking a new effort or initiative. This strengthening can reduce challenges and increase the likelihood of success. One precondition is that the community is culturally and/or socially united, or at least is able to work together despite some division. Communities that have a homogenous social structure,[6] common interests, shared norms,[7] and a history of cooper-

ation[8] are more likely to be able to work together in a multistakeholder, consensus building manner. Other preconditions that indicate a willingness by individuals to participate in local community initiatives and decision-making processes are that community members: 1) value their community, 2) rely on local (human and natural) resources,[9] and 3) are currently dissatisfied with the status quo but do not feel hopeless.[10] Clearly defined boundaries[11] and standards that govern and manage community systems are also an important pre- or early condition for enhancing the likelihood of future success. If most of these indicators of a strong foundation are present, it signals that the community is ready to begin the change process that will enhance their future health and vitality.

However, it is often the case that some of these enabling conditions are inadequate or too weak to take on a challenging initiative. If this is indeed the case, the initial work of the community needs to focus on strengthening their social foundation, which includes forming positive social norms. A booklet titled "An Introduction to Positive Community Norms"[12] provides sound ideas on how to grow and promote positive community norms. Other areas that may need to be addressed may include resolving conflicts and securing adequate resources to undertake the initial steps for moving forward.

Community Norms—Or, What Is Normal?

Initially, when reviewing the factors that healthy and resilient local communities reported as most important, I was surprised by their emphasis on shared community core values, beliefs, and attitudes. Years later, I see that norms are truly essential in understanding a community's strengths, weaknesses, and ability to move from surviving to thriving. Community norms are defined as "those values, beliefs, attitudes, and behaviors shared by most people in a group."[1] They are also defined as "what is considered normal social behavior in a particular group or social unit."[2] Norms strongly determine what most people value, believe, and take action on—in short, "the way we do things around here."[3] I have observed that when shared norms are embedded in a community it enhances their ability to recover more quickly from natural, environmental, economic, or social hardship. Acquiring reinforcing steel for a structural foundation is easy; strengthening a community's social foundation, however, requires time, effort, patience, and a commitment to grow positive social norms. Many of the case studies in this book report on specific steps that communities have taken to build their social foundation.

An example of the transformative power of changing norms can be observed in the impact of the book *Silent Spring* by Rachel Carson, published in 1962. Her work changed local and national norms across the US and in many other countries. It challenged the belief that "humans could obtain mastery over nature by chemicals" while it also "warned of the dangers to all natural systems from the misuse of chemical pesticides such as DDT and questioned the scope and direction of modern science."[4] Her efforts encouraged people to critically question the unbridled use of chemicals to kill insects and improve agriculture (a social norm propagated by the chemical industry), and helped to build a new social norm of valuing and protecting our ecological systems. This change in beliefs and assumptions has contributed to the health and wellness of communities throughout the world.

Building a Stronger Social Foundation for Your Community

So, what steps do you to take to understand your community's social foundation? And how do you promote positive social change that can build an even stronger foundation?

It is important to recognize that what you perceive, or what others in authority roles assume to be the community's core values, may be inaccurate. These views may be outdated and not include views of the younger generation, members of minority groups, newcomers, and others who are less involved. That is why community gatherings can be an essential tool for listening and seeking to understand community values, past experiences, and visions for the future. These gatherings are most effective when they are inclusive and representative of the community as a whole. This may not be possible in one community gathering, so sometimes multiple events are needed. It is critical that we consider and include all different perspectives, values, beliefs, and worldviews, as well as community hopes and dreams for the future. Try not to ask, "What are your biggest problems," but instead, "What do you value most in your community?" Answers may range from "potluck gatherings," "safe bike paths for our children," "clean rivers," "having local college students feel welcome," "a carbon-free town," to "all are welcome here." These statements begin to reveal the social networks, shared activities, and values that bring and hold the community together. If these are weak and/or conflicting (which is fairly common) then a process of dialogue and seeking areas of agreement can build an appreciation of each other and greater tolerance for different views. Sometimes, working together on a small project can serve as a catalyst to building this type of social foundation.

Many of the case studies and short stories in this book share their approaches to bringing community members together as an opportunity to build relationships and trust. Examples of these include: community gardening, cleaning and painting places of worship, working on community energy conservation, building a greenhouse for a school, starting a recycling center, and cleaning up neighborhoods.

Also, don't forget to include the youth! Their creativity and imagination, frequently expressed through artwork, can inspire a community, particularly when the art focuses on an issue that is being discussed. For example, the Lithuanian students at a Community Foundation planning forum presented their drawings of the future for their community. In another instance, the artwork at a community recycling center was a collage of a rainforest and its creatures, which represented what the children in that community wanted to protect by recycling their waste. Chapter 14 will share more ideas on how to apply this and the other principles through a wide range of approaches for engaging community members.

Growing Social Foundations:
Kinshasa, Democratic Republic of the Congo

A few years ago, I was asked to visit two communities within greater Kinshasa, the capital city of the Democratic Republic of the Congo (DRC), to speak with their leadership. The DRC is one of the poorest countries in the world, and Kinshasa, a city with an infrastructure built for about two million, had rapidly swelled to over ten million without substantive changes to their infrastructure. As a civil engineer, I saw wide-scale infrastructure failure with an increase in diseases due to the massive amounts of solid waste clogging the drainage systems. Waste was being dumped on open land and vendors were selling goods and wares on tops of piles of waste. The city water was unsafe for drinking or even for brushing your teeth.

One of the two communities, a religious community, had already built a neighborhood hospital and was starting to build a school. Now it was facing the challenge of managing urban solid waste that posed a negative impact to their health. Virtually all open land in the city of Kinshasa was strewn with waste. This religious community[13] took on the tasks of clearing away massive amounts of dumped solid waste in order to expose soil that could support food crops. Locally grown food was being successfully grown by these families. Unfortunately, because

Credit: James Gruber

Figure 12.1. Challenging
conditions in Kinshasa,
DRC.

the gardens were located in a city with severe food scarcity, they needed
to be guarded 24 hours a day. This is an example of the critical linkage
between conservation, pollution abatement, and critical support for
the needs of local families. I was humbled by the dedication, creative
problem solving, and the strength of this religious community to work
collaboratively with so few resources.

The other community I visited was a women's cooperative[14] that
was working to plan and build a new, safe, and healthy neighborhood
outside the main city on undeveloped land. They were a strong organization, dedicated to developing an environmentally healthy and socially safe community, without corruption, for all their members. I was
amazed to see the level of participation by its members in creating the
neighborhood vision and plans. They had laid out the land for home
sites, a school, and a hospital, as well as constructed the initial buildings. The social foundation appeared wide and deep as they tirelessly
worked together for a better future.

Credit: James Gruber

Figure 12.2. Joyful children and youth of Ou Allons Nous-Oan, Kinshasa, DRC.

Both of the of these communities had very limited financial resources, but each were still able to craft a shared vision and make substantive progress toward realizing that vision. I believe that their successes to date were directly linked to their strong social foundations and shared norms.

The Case Studies

The next case study is an engaging story of a rural church community in Norwich, Vermont, that attributes their transformation from surviving to thriving to the strengthening of their social foundation, including building self-confidence and trust. Then there is a brief case-in-point about an outdoor program in North Carolina that demonstrates the effectiveness of a well-designed program in strengthening community and shifting norms. The last case study from the Baltic countries (Estonia, Latvia, and Lithuania) in Eastern Europe shares how citizens engaged in creating a local Community Foundation can strengthen the social, environmental, and economic foundation of their community.

CASE STUDY   Getting Unstuck: A Congregation Moving From Surviving to Thriving, Norwich, Vermont, USA

by Patience Stoddard

Prologue

Over the course of five years, a congregation in trouble (losing both members and vitality) not only achieved its long-term vision of having its own sanctuary for Sunday services, but also became a more trusting and joyful community committed to contributing to the wider community. The initial steps taken to set achievable goals and to focus on improving communication and building trust were the keys to the successful outcome. While this case study is about a faith community, many of the approaches and steps taken could be useful in a variety of organizational and community contexts.

Introduction and Presenting Situation

For about 20 years, early each Sunday morning the staff and a few members would go to the Meetinghouse (a 150-year-old farmhouse) to pack hymnals, flowers, and educational supplies into boxes and carry them into cars, in order to move them to a large windowless room of a local elementary school for the Sunday service. After the service, this whole hectic process was repeated in reverse. Twice the congregation had begun a process to design and raise money to buy or build a larger gathering space, but both efforts had failed. Since the Meetinghouse was too small for most Sunday services or larger community gatherings, they continued to need to rent space for both. While renting space had originally been seen as temporary, it had become a permanent way of life. The community was tired and shrinking in numbers and in confidence. When I met them, they were trying something new— meeting on Sunday afternoons at a church across the river. Despite this effort to change time and venue, the membership was continuing to shrink and leaders were becoming increasingly discouraged about the future.

Several transitions in leadership were also putting stress on the community. Their prior minister had left the congregation with many of their mutual hopes for growth and a new building unsatisfied. A temporary interim minister had to leave prematurely due to illness. Just before her unanticipated departure, long-term conflicts had come to a head and led to a controversial board decision regarding a behavioral covenant. This decision resulted in significant turmoil, the departure of several members, and schisms within the community. When they hired me to serve as a part-time temporary minister, I soon realized that if it did not make some significant changes, this congregation might not survive.

Goals, Approaches, Challenges, and Outcomes

Before working with congregational leaders and staff to develop any concrete goals, my first job was to listen and begin to understand this community's hopes and challenges. To begin this process, I asked 15 active leaders to meet with me individually to share their thoughts and experiences. I began the meeting by asking about two or three things the congregation did well. (B-J-I).[15] It is my experience that beginning with assessing strengths is an effective and nonthreatening way to begin a successful change process. In terms of strengths there seemed to be agreement that the members genuinely cared about each other and the congregation had a cadre of experienced and skilled leaders. Many also cited the quality and popularity of their lay-led summer services held in the backyard or library of the Meetinghouse, often adding, "because we feel at home." This was my first clue that their Sunday homelessness had taken a toll. Moreover, their appreciation of their tradition of lay-led summer services suggested that in some ways they could trust one another's wisdom (G-K).

I then asked each of them the following three questions:

1. How would you characterize your relationship with past professional and lay leaders and assess their effectiveness?
2. What was your experience of and opinion about the leadership's handling of the conflict that led to the loss of members?
3. How important to the lasting success of this congregation is having your own space for Sunday services and ceremonial occasions?

The answers to the first two questions varied, but it became clear that there were divisions in the community and a need to rebuild trust in lay and professional leadership. They also seemed hungry for effective leadership that could help them move forward. The answer to the third question was surprisingly unanimous. "If we can't come together to fulfill our vision of our own building, we will probably not survive," stated one person bluntly.

From these interviews and my own observations, I realized that this community was not ready to start a new building plan or even to try to increase membership in the short term. I concluded that before they could achieve their vision, they needed to be more confident in their community and more trusting of one another (G). To accomplish this, congregational leaders, staff, and I set the following five initial goals:

1. raise morale by focusing on assets rather than deficits and creating opportunities to successfully reach short-term, achievable goals (B-G)
2. support and broaden lay leadership and encourage open communication and dialogue (D)
3. diminish the number of committees (they'd had 17 committees for a congregation of 60 people) and simplify organizational structure, ensuring that form would follow function (F)
4. more fully understand what had and hadn't worked in past building efforts, and develop an alternate path to that goal (H)
5. find ways to discuss differences and resolve conflicts while maintaining relationship (L)

Here are some of the actions taken to address these specific goals.

Goal 1. Focus on Assets and Set Achievable Goals
A few early decisions helped us begin to establish and strengthen enabling conditions. The first decision was to no longer rent space and return to their Meetinghouse for Sunday services. By focusing most of their energy on what they wanted in the future (a new building or site),

they had ceased to appreciate and take care of their current asset—the Meetinghouse/farmhouse, an ideal location and seven-acre property with a nature trail which served the wider community (C). Before planning for the future, there was a need to attend to the present. The Meetinghouse had fallen into disrepair—the paint was peeling, the handicapped ramp was broken, and the gardens were overgrown with weeds. The second decision was to have an all-hands-on-deck work weekend to rebuild a ramp, paint the interior, pull up the weeds, and begin work to refurbish the nature path (C-B). That day 80 percent of the membership showed up, including children as young as 8 and elders as old as 90 (A). Not only was much work accomplished, but people were laughing and singing; and new attendees quickly felt a part of the community. Several years later, when members were asked to reflect on what had helped the congregation turn around, many spoke of the work weekend as a turning point. "We stopped talking about what to do, and started doing something."

Another example of assessing and building on strengths was in the area of social justice and outreach. Many members expressed disappointment with the lack of social justice work and community service being done by the congregation. Before creating a committee or deciding where to put their efforts, I suggested that they begin with a task force to assess what members of the community were already doing (B-D-E-I). The task force set about interviewing all members. The result astounded everyone. The task force created a map showing the 132 different organizations and causes that were being actively supported by members of this small community. These organizations included the local homeless shelter, the Family Center for at-risk children and their parents, a free medical and dental clinic, an interfaith environmental organization. They were also providing educational tuition for several youth who belonged to their sister congregation in Northern India. It was a few more years before a Social Action Committee was formed, but the visible tribute to individual efforts encouraged more involvement and better coordination much earlier.

Goals 2 and 3. Broaden Leadership, Encourage Communication,
and Simplify Organizational Structure

We also invited a skilled facilitator to lead an all-day vision-to-action workshop (see Chapter 14).[16] Seventy five percent of active members attended the workshop. Every voice and idea mattered and was re-corded (A-B). The workshop included an opportunity to look together at the recent and past history of the congregation and to discuss ac-complishments and failures, which allowed for an open discussion of rifts that had developed as well as sharing in a nondivisive way their appreciation and disappointment with former leaders (D). They also created a detailed map of the wished-for future with a procedure for voting on priorities (J).

By the end of the day several specific action groups were formed to address the priorities, each with a minimum of three members. These task forces focused on a number of areas of congregational life from the newsletter to an all-congregation team approach to welcoming and hospitality (A-F). All the task forces were successful at setting new goals and making needed changes, though a few first needed to be modified along the way (H). Their success led to more flexible ways to manage and organize the congregation. Many formerly monthly committees

Figure 12.3. Vision-to-Action forum.

Credit: James Gruber

were replaced by task forces, short-term working groups, and teams which set their own schedule and were open to all (F).

Goal 4. Assess What Did Or Didn't Work in Past Building Efforts and Develop an Alternate Path to Adequate Space

One task force focused on assessing two prior building committees to learn from what had worked well and better understand what hadn't been fruitful (H). It was also tasked with researching a variety of affordable buildings—size, materials, and estimated cost—which could meet the needs of a small but growing congregation (E). A few members of former building committees were involved in this process as well as some newcomers to the congregation. At its annual meeting nine months later, the congregation voted unanimously to create a steering committee of trusted members to evaluate architects, contractors, and designs for a new affordable building. There were several all-congregation meetings at various steps in the building process where all voices were heard and dissenting views were sought and respected. Much to my surprise all the decisions along the way (to choose a design, mount a capital campaign, and begin breaking ground) were discussed, voted on, and approved unanimously by all community members. One and a half years later we were all singing "We Are Building a New Way" and celebrating the first service in our new sanctuary.

Goal 5. Find Ways to Discuss Differences and Resolve Conflicts While Maintaining Relationship

This goal took the longest time to be fully achieved. Perhaps this was in part related to the congregation's history. A prior congregation with some of the same members had had divisive conflict over the Vietnam War and the resulting rifts led to its demise. Whatever the reasons, this community, like many others, was afraid of conflict. When people got upset, they simply left. Changing this pattern was a multistep process that had begun with the interviews of leaders and the vision-to-action workshop and continued throughout the transparent and frequently reviewed building process.

For a while after moving into their new building everyone just basked in the atmosphere of unity and accomplishment. However, eventually, tension rose around putting up a Black Lives Matter sign in front of the church.

The board and staff were in full agreement from the outset. However, it was decided that the issue should be brought to the entire congregation for discussion and a vote (F-H-J). Much to our surprise, individuals voiced a range of concerns. The leadership thought that postponing this decision might be an opportunity to practice having difficult conversations. (It also allowed time for more education on racism and white privilege.) This year-long process included two multiweek discussion groups, several worship services, and three congregation-wide discussions. When finally put to a vote the issue was decided unanimously (with a couple of abstentions). The many open and accepting conversations throughout this process served to reduce the fear of conflict that had haunted this congregation for more than a decade (L).

Reflection on Principle K: Strengthening Enabling Conditions

I believe that the key to the transformation of this community was the strengthening of enabling conditions. The community already had committed and skilled leaders and a desire to serve the greater community, but had lacked self-confidence and a secure trust in one another. Because they had set goals and failed before, they were hesitant to try again. While clear about what they wanted, they were unsure of what the next step should be and of how to handle the inevitable disagreements which go with making changes.

Somewhat ironically, the determination to slow down—and even take a few steps back before moving forward—proved essential to accomplishing long-held goals and aspirations. Now when you drive up to this faith community's home, there are rainbow and Black Lives Matter banners, flourishing gardens, and solar panels up on the roof. The once dark and empty, but now renovated farmhouse is ablaze with activity. When a recent newcomer was asked what she first noticed, she

Credit: James Gruber

Figure 12.4. Celebration at the close of a Sunday service.

mentioned, "The friendly, joyful energy is palpable. I knew right away that I wanted to be a part of this community."

CASE IN POINT | **Connecting Underrepresented Families to Their Local Environment, North Carolina, USA**

by Megan Ennes and M. Gail Jones[17]

There are many barriers to engaging in the outdoors for families from underrepresented groups. Some of these barriers are physical (e.g., lack of transportation[18]) and others are cultural (e.g., traditional lack of participation).[19] Museums and other science centers have a unique opportunity to engage communities with their local environment and the out-of-doors.

To help connect members of our community who do not traditionally engage in the outdoors, we developed a year-long family science program.[20] The program took place at an eco-station owned by our museum partner. The space is free to the public and offers a variety of educational programming set in the outdoor classroom and on the grounds. The family program sought to offset many of the barriers to participation that underrepresented communities encounter, such as cost, location, lack of awareness, and safety.[21] The program was based on research and included elements that have been shown to encourage family engagement, such as free programming, transportation to the program site, meals, and free materials. To address safety concerns, parents were encouraged to participate with their children and many safety guidelines were implemented.

The program was designed to build community by requiring that families participate together ("family" was defined by the participants themselves). Additionally, we built community by sharing communal meals that also helped to address food security issues. To help the families connect with the outdoors, we brought in scientists from the local community to engage the families in activities such as bird banding, tree identification, and using camera traps. The families participated in hands-on activities such as assisting with the banding and releasing of birds.

By the end of the year, the families reported that they had changed the way they interacted with the environment. Some parents said they had begun visiting the eco-station outside of the program. Others said they had shared the name and location of the eco-station so others in their community could take advantage of the resource. Additionally, parents who said they had not previously engaged in the out-of-doors reported hanging bird feeders while others had begun planting gardens.

The parts of the model that we felt were vital to the program's success included the shared meals, inclusion of the entire family, and community mentors who represented the demographics of our participants. One major lesson that we learned is that while we attempted to offset the major barriers to outdoor participation, we missed an important one: appropriate winter clothing. After our first cold weather event, our museum partners began bringing additional outerwear families could borrow. Addressing this enabling condition made a major difference in the comfort and engagement of our families.

Museums and other science centers can engage typically under-represented communities in the outdoors by creating safe, communal opportunities for families to explore the outdoors together. Once the families have built a connection with their local environments, they are more likely to expand their engagement because they see the value and feel more empowered to do so. Developing more programs like this one can help build greater connections between communities and their local resources, which is beneficial for both the community and its natural surroundings. It can also help build greater diversity and connections within the wider community and thereby strengthen the social foundation of that community.

CASE STUDY — Creating Local Community Foundations in the Baltic Countries: Estonia, Latvia, and Lithuania

by James S. Gruber

Prologue

After nearly 50 years of crushing German and Soviet occupation, the three Baltic countries were finally free. They started working to recover their sociocultural identity and sovereignty: language, culture, and self-rule. Communities, for the first time in many years, were allowed to elect their mayor and town council representatives. They were also working to re-establish free media, nonprofit organizations (NGOs) and the overall civic sector. This case shares how citizen engagement and empowerment to grow a local community foundation can help build the foundation for a socially, environmentally, and economically healthy community. In the Baltics, these local community foundations were formed by local citizens, coming together, in resource-poor locations. Today these community foundations provide long-term sustainable mechanisms for community support.

Introduction and General Overview

My colleagues[22] and I had the opportunity to work with local communities in Estonia, Latvia, and Lithuania as they were beginning to recover from the tyranny of the Soviet Union's years of occupation.

I became involved through the Baltic-American Partnership Fund (BAPF) program whose ten-year mission was to strengthen civil society in each of these countries. Specifically, we worked with residents and leaders in local communities[23] in each of these countries to help them create their own community foundation that could help their community not only restore their livelihoods, but thrive in the future. BAPF describes this effort and how it is linked to building social capital in the following:

> Community foundations can be a powerful tool to stimulate local philanthropy and grass roots civic engagement, even in poor, small rural areas. As one colleague in Latvia noted, the community philanthropy movement in the Baltics has broken the myth that "you have to be rich to give." The community foundations in Latvia, Lithuania, and Estonia are less about resource accumulation and donor services than they are about building social capital in their communities, although increasing local funding and achieving financial sustainability are certainly long-term goals.[24]

During the 1990s, my colleagues and I at Antioch University New England[25] worked with local communities in the US and in Eastern Europe using our Vision-to-Action Community Forums and similar participatory decision-making processes. We and the Quebec-Labrador Foundation's Atlantic Center for the Environment[26] were asked to offer this approach to local communities in each of these countries through workshops, working sessions, and forums.

Goals, Challenges, Approaches, and Outcomes
Goals
The participatory planning and community philanthropy initiative was designed to increase civic engagement at the community level by bringing together community members, representatives from local NGOs, government officials, and local business owners to identify

and discuss community values and approaches to community development (A-B-K-J-I). The overall goal of this effort was to assist local communities in each of the Baltic countries to build their capacity for civic engagement and take significant strides toward the establishment of local community foundations that could be self-directed and locally sustained. Each of the initial six communities we worked with applied to participate in this program. A secondary goal of this initiative was to provide technical and programmatic assistance, such as providing trainings on effective forms of governance for community foundations, to assist in the transition away from a central-government model of problem solving and toward a community-based model (J-F).

To approach this overall goal, it was recognized that a vital part of the process involved developing a new tradition of participatory planning and community philanthropy. This is the kind of cultural change that cannot be taught, legislated, or imposed by outside entities. It can, however, be encouraged, guided, and facilitated with help and training requested from outside.

Credit: James Gruber

Figure 12.5. Strong social and religious culture, Siauliai, Lithuania.

Challenges

Working in three different languages and three unique cultures that were recovering from years of occupation and top-down bureaucracy by the Soviets was both challenging and invigorating. Though the concept of community and individual philanthropy dates back centuries in parts of Eastern Europe, including in the Baltic region, recent political history did not include a sense of voluntary philanthropy, as we know it in the West. Periods of forced "volunteerism," a repressive political climate, and distrust of the government sector have all been barriers to the communities' exploration of formalized philanthropy programs.

Some community members voiced initial reservations and resistance, expressing doubt about the success of a public participatory planning forum. One official in Riga, Latvia, stated, "There is no tradition in Latvia of speaking publicly about issues of concern." Also, a local mayor expressed concern to us that bringing many citizens together in his town to talk and plan for the future would simply end in chaos. We assured him that this would not be the case, and we got his support. We also were aware that unless each of these communities were able to develop the skills to research and utilize the resources and expertise located within their own community, the longer-term outcomes would likely be poor (E-K).

Approaches

Each of the communities were involved in a six-phase process. These were:

- *Training in Participatory Planning.* The forum leaders in each community received detailed instruction on such topics as: how to invite community members, stakeholders, and the media to the forum; meeting with participants; forum format; logistics; and follow-up strategies (B-J).
- *Establishing a Background in Philanthropy.* Local community leaders were provided well-researched materials on philanthropy in both Eastern Europe and the United States (E-I).

- *Public Forums.* Large community forums were organized and convened in each of the communities to identify major community needs and address them in small work groups (A-D-L).
- *Community Foundation Organizational Structure and Strategic Development.* Work sessions were held on topics such as: mission and vision; community foundation structure and the roles of board, staff, and volunteers; creation of a development plan; fundraising and asset development; grantmaking and strategic partnering (J-K).
- *Study Tour.* The tour focused on exploring the structure and format of community foundation philanthropic traditions in the Czech and Slovak republics (E).
- *Evaluation Session.* Valuable feedback was solicited from all communities (H).

Numerous challenges were identified during community foundation planning sessions. Some included questions on how to:

- build a broad base of continuing community support

Credit: James Gruber

Figure 12.6. Local Lithuanian leaders and US consultant in Vilnius working on developing community foundations.

- clarify the community foundation's mission and vision
- identify the needs of target constituency groups
- build community-wide trust
- create additional linkages with other NGOs and business and government leaders
- create and build a permanent and growing base of financial capital
- disseminate to the public information about community foundations
- develop an effective procedure for making grants to begin addressing local projects and community needs

As a result of the participatory planning workshop and community forum, "Community members were able to take initiative in local problem-solving without dependence on local government.... People have been motivated to serve as volunteers and provided their knowledge and skills for free and in-kind contributions."[27]

Outcomes

This opportunity for citizens to come together, identify their aspirations for the future, along with taking initial organizing actions (probably for the first time in many years) was inspiring and energizing—for them and for us. A few community foundations were initially formed with local citizen leadership, nearly all in economically struggling towns and villages. Local governments soon realized how this engagement effort was building social capital and further engaged citizens in their town. The first foundation started in 2002.

A few comments follow from the initial Estonians, Latvians, and Lithuanians involved in creating community foundations (2002) on engaging their community members in building a stronger community and establishing a community foundation for their future:

- Latvia: "It was like Latvia had gained a second liberation."
- Estonia: "The main lesson learned: people are ready to do very much for the community if the goals are clear and the initiators are trusted and respected."

• Lithuania: "Two years ago we had no idea except a theoretical one. Community philanthropy is expanding; there are many opportunities."

Today, there are over 15 community foundations across all three Baltic countries that support a wide range of community-oriented projects, primarily with local resources. Their towns range in size from 3,700 to 177,000. Their community foundation projects range from cultural heritage initiatives, sports and recreational facilities, and a water science and playground center to academic scholarships for disadvantaged children. Funds are raised locally from citizens, local businesses, and other contributors and the citizens themselves decide, through an open process, how these funds will be used to support the health, vitality, and future of their community. These local community foundations not only grow financial capital to support local priorities, but also grow social capital and embrace citizen empowerment for a healthier community.

Reflections on Principle K: Strengthen the Foundation

Reports from communities across the three Baltic countries, written years after the initial community foundations were established, confirm that this citizen-driven approach to building civic capacity has grown support for local cultural, educational, and environmental needs. Equally as important, the process of working together continues to support the strengthening of the civic foundation of these communities.

Principle K—Strengthen the Foundation

Do (Or Consider Doing)

☑ Before undertaking a major project or initiative, allow time for assessing the strength of the community's social foundation through multiple approaches. These may include: reviewing the history through documents, holding one-on-one interviews with individuals, or holding open listening sessions.

☑ Provide a summary of what you have found from your assessment efforts while respecting individuals' confidentiality.

☑ Include a community gathering or forum where people have an opportunity together to assess past actions (successes and shortfalls) and share their hopes or vision for the future.

☑ Recognize the enabling conditions that should exist in order to begin a successful change process. Indicators of adequate enabling conditions include: 1) people value their community; 2) people have some dependence on communal resources; and 3) a significant number of community members are dissatisfied with the status quo but do not feel hopeless.

☑ Consider bringing people together to develop a statement that summarizes the community's social norms and get endorsement from most community members. Throughout the change process work to support these positive community norms.

☑ Try out some smaller community efforts to confirm that the enabling conditions are adequate to take on a larger effort or initiative. The smaller effort, if successful, could also raise enabling conditions and motivate community members to participate more actively.

Don't (Or Think Twice)

☒ Don't just listen to a few individuals who are in positions of authority. They may have a misperception of some community values, beliefs, attitudes, and behaviors.

☒ Don't accept information or data without confirming them.

☒ Don't assume that by addressing a specific problem you have gotten to the root of the problem that is damaging the social foundation. Keep asking questions.

☒ Don't get caught between two paths or two camps. Although you may be told that there are only two ways to proceed, there is almost always a third way.

☒ Since each community's journey is unique, don't try to duplicate another community's efforts. However, you can learn from them.

Resolve Conflicts

Anticipate Conflict and Work Towards Resolution and Cooperation

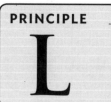

PRINCIPLE

L

> *Whenever you're in conflict with someone,*
> *there is one factor that can make the difference*
> *between damaging your relationship and deepening it.*
> *That factor is attitude.*
>
> — WILLIAM JAMES

Preventing Conflict

The best way to resolve conflicts is to work to prevent them from forming. If your community is able to practice the first 11 principles, it is far less likely that you will need to apply this last principle. If you review the numerous books on conflict resolution, you will see that most, if not all of these principles, such as working together, protecting resources and promoting fairness, being transparent, embracing feedback, and deciding together, will both help prevent and resolve conflicts. When I visited several communities around the world that were widely recognized as being success stories, I was amazed at the level of cooperation, the positive relationships, and strong social capital that I observed. "Success" is an odd term with many definitions and indicators. I use indicators of success that include ecological integrity, economic

RESOLVE CONFLICTS

L

Anticipate Conflict and Work Towards Resolution and Cooperation

Five Characteristics

1. *Difficult realities and conflicts are inherent in community social-ecological-economic systems.*
2. *Design participatory decision-making processes that promote dialogue and reduce factionalism.*
3. *Plan for and develop capacity and strategies for conflict management and resolution at the time of initiating a community social-ecological-economic initiative.*
4. *Work to transcend rivalry and competition between organizations or stakeholder groups.*
5. *Recognize the central role of institutions outside the community organization in mediating economic-environmental-social society conflicts.*

No multistakeholder, community-based initiative is without some form of conflict. Therefore, strategies for conflict management and resolution between individuals and stakeholders should be established early on.[1] The conflict may lie in disputes over control between neighboring communities, contrasting perceptions of land use between domestic and national or international agencies, or in deeply rooted angst between individuals or groups. For example, literature on participatory conservation reveals that there are oftentimes long-standing divides between local communities and governmental conservation agencies.[2] This may mean that they have a history of mistrust and antipathy. Such a divide makes working together arduous and, without proper mediation, sometimes even more damaging to the relationship.

In my own experience, I have found the following approaches to anticipating and addressing conflict to be helpful. First, it is important to recognize the role that external institutions can play in mediation and relationship building.[3] Additional approaches include promoting and facilitating meaningful dialogue in participatory decision-making processes, working to dissolve organizational rivalry,[4] actively minimizing factionalism among stakeholders,[5] and developing conflict resolution services that are accessible and inexpensive.[6] Although I hope that these approaches are helpful, there is still a need for more research and tools to support conflict resolution in community-based initiatives.[7]

security, empowerment and responsibility, and social well-being (see Chapter 1 for more discussion of community success). There appeared to be a very low level of conflict in these successful communities.

Understanding and Addressing Conflict

Conflicts can rise from many sources. When people do not feel respected or do not believe that their voice is heard, conditions are ripe for conflict. In your community there may be deep, pre-existing conflicts that impact trust, create factions or divisions, and will directly affect the ability to do future work together. Conflicts can even arise from what most people would call positive change, since change requires letting go of what may be comfortable and familiar and adjusting to a new future.

Naming or recognizing conflicts and then trying to understand where they come from is not easy, but is critical to addressing and transforming them. When people are upset or arguing about what appears to be a minor concern, frequently there are historic or underlying issues that need to be acknowledged. Active listening and recording what people say is a good step forward in showing respect, and possibly getting to these more deeply rooted challenges. Designing participatory decision-making processes that promote dialogue and share airtime will demonstrate respect and value for all participants. This approach has been shown to rebuild trust and reduce conflicts.

At the same time, it is important to recognize that some level of conflict or disagreement is healthy, particularly in decision making. Group think has been shown to contribute to poor performance of a group. Healthy disagreements are a sign of a community with a strong foundation. Even if there are historic divisions and unnamed conflicts, working on strengthening the community's foundation and mutual trust (see Chapter 12) can give people space to raise conflicting ideas or experiences and engage in productive community dialogues.

I will share an example of a conflict resolution approach that worked for one community. There are many different approaches. However, foundational to all conflict resolutions are these four steps: recognize the conflict, seek to understand the roots of the conflict, come together to develop a plan of action, and then implement the plan. This may not be easy, but avoidance of conflicts can result in far more serious consequences.

Disorderly Neighborhoods

Many residents in the older residential areas near the local college in Keene, New Hampshire, were very upset with the behavior of younger people living in rental housing. There were complaints about frequent and loud late-night parties, renters leaving "stuff" outside their houses, excessive use of alcohol, lots of cars and motorcycles, frequent police calls, and general behaviors that were making their neighborhood less enjoyable. These concerns were brought up to the city council with the request that the council consider passing a new city ordinance. On the one hand the concerns seemed valid; on the other, personal individual freedom is highly valued in New Hampshire, as one can see from the motto on every license plate: "Live Free or Die."

How can a balance be reached between protecting individual freedoms and respecting the needs of others? This growing conflict, referred to by the city council as the "Disorderly Neighborhoods" issue, needed to be addressed. But how?

The city manager[8] stopped by to speak with me at the university about an idea to bring the people together to address their concerns. He expressed his view that a new ordinance or law should be the last approach to addressing a conflict. He hoped that an effective process, with all the key parties participating, could resolve this conflict in a better way.

I agreed to create a process and convene all the key parties in an open community forum. The "Disorderly Neigborhoods" forum would be designed with the intention to help everyone better understand the root issues that were creating the conflict and to facilitate a process for all parties to both develop potential solutions and undertake actions that could resolve this conflict. Personally, I did not know if this would be possible, but I have often been surprised to see how creative people can be when you bring them together to solve what could be considered an intractable "wicked" problem.[9]

A few weeks later, the basement of the library was full. Attendees included residents of the affected neighborhoods, landlords, representatives of the local college, members of the city council, the local media, local housing officials, members of the police department, city officials, and other concerned citizens. The plan was to hold two community forums. The first was primarily to discuss and prioritize the problems and identify some initial ideas as to how to solve them. The process was fairly simple. We invited everyone to identify what they thought were the underlying issues that had created these problems. After these were recorded on multiple flip chart sheets, everyone indicated (using colored dots) what they thought were the top five issues. The issues with the most votes were combined into four categories. One category, for example, was, "How landlords interacted with their renters including clear expectations." Then participants chose the groups they wanted to work with in developing potential approaches or solutions. These needed to include not just *what* should be done but *how* this could be accomplished. By working together landlords, residents, local college officials, police officers, and others began to build better relationships and grow a greater understanding of individual perspectives and challenges in this conflict. I believe that the honest and heartfelt dialogue during this forum was just as important as the hoped-for follow-up actions and future solutions.

The first forum ended far more positively than it started. The four smaller work groups (each representing one of the overall categories) agreed to meet during the coming two weeks and then give their recommendations at the second forum. I provided all participants, including the media, with a transcript of this meeting including all of the initial ideas developed in the four smaller groups.

The second (final) forum began with reports from each of the four working groups sharing their potential ideas and approaches. There were many practical and valuable approaches that went far beyond what a local ordinance could accomplish. Together, they developed a clear, agreed-upon blueprint of actions. For example, a neighborhood association stated that they had an important role, even a responsibility, to personally welcome younger people into their neighborhood so that the newcomers could feel that they are a part of the neighborhood. Building social bridges was critical. In another example, the landlords stated that they had a responsibility to speak and work with other landlords who were not present at the forum. These and other actions were agreed to and all hoped they would resolve the current conflict. In the end, no ordinance was needed.

Working a conflict together, face-to-face, including exploring and confronting the underlying issues is, I believe, essential for developing sound, community-driven and socially acceptable solutions. This type of process allows each party to take responsibility for developing and implementing agreed-upon solutions. It also provides an opportunity to build greater trust, an essential ingredient for implementing change.

The Case Studies

The first case study tells of a regional land use and transportation planning initiative in New Hampshire that brought together various municipalities and state agencies who were able to overcome their differences and work collaboratively to manage future growth and conservation. The second illustrates the successful efforts of a rural community in Ghana to address conflicts between tribal beliefs and Western medicine and create a shared vision that led to improved health services and the preservation of biodiversity and the local forest.

Community-Driven Regional Land Use and Transportation Planning in Southern New Hampshire, USA

by James Gruber and Charlene Phillips

Prologue

Too many well-intended efforts to address growth and change in communities of all kinds fail to achieve desired results due to conflict. Carefully designed, open, and more inclusive processes of visioning, goal-setting, and implementation can loosen and untangle the Gordian knot of conflict within and across communities and lead to more successful outcomes. This was the lesson learned by the New Hampshire Department of Transportation (NH-DOT) and 26 New Hampshire towns and cities trying to effectively plan for the future impact of the doubling of the Interstate highway running through their midst.

Introduction and General Overview

Outcries were heard from city and town council meetings and environmental groups throughout New Hampshire when state and federal authorities decided to double the size of Interstate Highway 93 from four to eight lanes. Studies showed that this expansion would significantly impact growth in the adjacent 26 local communities. After much rancor, many editorials, and pressure from local groups opposing the expansion, a settlement was reached to set up a $3.5 million fund to help these cities and towns plan for this growth during the coming five years.

New Hampshire state agencies worked intensely with professional land-use planners and other highly qualified experts for nearly a year to develop a program that would assist these local communities in their efforts to effectively plan for growth. The results were not well received. The debate then focused on who would get what. Lawyers from these cities and towns started to discuss litigation in order to receive their share of the $3.5 million fund. Recognizing that a different approach was needed, the NH-DOT boldly decided to set aside their previous work and start anew with all of the 26 local communities at the table (A-B). They named this initiative the Community Technical Assistance Program (CTAP).[10] The revised approach was intended to help the communities and other stakeholders involved identify *their own* goals, the challenges to achieving these, and to galvanize the community in order to enable *them* to produce the strategies and solutions needed to turn their hopes, goals, and objectives into realities (A-B-J). Through this more open and participatory process, it was hoped that current conflicts between state and local government could be resolved and potential conflicts between adjacent communities could be avoided (L).

To accomplish this robust goal, NH-DOT decided to seek the assistance of a university-based nonprofit that specialized in developing inclusive, collaborative processes to help communities and regions find shared solutions to challenging problems. Antioch New England Institute was approached to assist in this process and accepted the opportunity (and challenge). We were also able to include many service-learning graduate students in assisting with this innovative, bottom-up effort.

Goals, Approaches, Challenges, and Outcomes

As the first step of this new approach, the head of NH-DOT Planning Division, Ansel Sanborn, proposed to establish three groups to guide the planning process. The first group would include individual representatives appointed by elected officials in each of the 26 cities and towns. The second group would be representatives from local nonprofit environmental groups, businesses, and conservation, social, health, and educational organizations. The final, third group, would include regional planning organizations as well as representatives of state agencies. These three groups would be actively involved throughout the planning and future implementation process.

The next step was to design the initial strategic planning effort that included three monthly open forums of 60 to 100 representatives of these three groups(A-B). We believed that building strong collaboration and a sense of ownership by all participants involved in this process would be foundational for a successful outcome. These forums would be open to the public and the media. As a result, the goals were deeply rooted in bringing people together to learn from each other and then incorporating the values of multiple perspectives (E). An objective of the entire process was that it would not be expert driven and that the base-level knowledge of all participants should be raised through their participation (E). There was also the open acknowledgment that there was no silver bullet or straightforward solution to the challenges these communities were facing. It was anticipated that future assistance would likely include training, education, marketing, planning tools and analysis, and specific technical assistance to provide local towns with better planning capabilities. However, the types of assistance communities could receive would not be predetermined and the process would actively involve local governments, local nonprofits, and state government agencies in this decision-making process (B).

The first kick-off forum included a visioning session, where a hundred community, local nonprofit, and government representatives were asked, "How do you want your community to look, feel, and be

Credit: James Gruber

Figure 13.1. Mind map
at first forum.

as a home, 20 years from now?" After covering a wall with responses, participants were then given five dots to place on the areas they believed were most critical. One outcome of this process was a visual mind map and a list of high priority areas that were converted into future objectives.

The second forum included confirming 15 specific objectives to frame the planning process; identifying barriers that needed to be confronted: and developing and prioritizing preferred strategies, available resources, and approaches most likely to address them. The 15 objectives are listed below.

Objectives of CTAP based on visioning mind map

- *Economic Vitality.* Provide a livable wage for all local residents, provide a solid business base, ensure an adequate supply of affordable and workforce housing, and have sustainable and balanced economic growth and tax base.
- *Business Development.* Support broad-based business development that provides local employment and living wages.
- *Agriculture.* Strengthen local farms and preserve farmland; encourage food self-sufficiency.
- *Rural Working Landscapes.* Protect and maintain lands, infrastructure, and economic systems that support local farming and forestry.
- *Environmental Protection.* Protect natural resources in conjunction with economic needs. Protect natural resources and environmental health, including groundwater and aquifers, wildlife and wildlife corridors.
- *Green Infrastructure and Open Space.* Establish and conserve an interconnected green infrastructure by preserving open space such as farmlands, productive forests, wildlife corridors, recreation areas, rivers, and other natural areas. Ensure convenient public access to open space, parks, and recreational opportunities.
- *Funding Municipal Services.* Assist local governments in establishing stable, consistent funding approaches for public infrastructure and services.

- *Delivering Municipal Services.* Ensure continuation of strong town services and schools, so municipal services such as schools, fire, and police protection are able to grow sustainability to meet projected growth, and provide for world-class public schools.
- *Regional Cooperation.* Develop and support new methods of regional cooperation to support local government delivery of public services, allocate some financial resources on a regional basis, and meet environmental quality and open space objectives.
- *Downtowns and Community Centers.* Target and support development and redevelopment in existing downtowns and community centers, reusing built infrastructure, and rehabilitating buildings of historic value. Promote walkable downtowns and villages, consistent with historic patterns in the region.
- *Vibrant Communities.* Support and encourage cultural resources (arts, music), safe neighborhoods, diverse populations in communities (in terms of age and economic class), and opportunities for parks and recreation. Foster an atmosphere wherein community members are involved in their local communities, know their neighbors, volunteer in their communities, and participate and engage in civic dialogue about local issues.
- *Transportation.* Promote safe, efficient, accessible, and diverse multimodal transportation solutions to services and goods, including bicycle and pedestrian paths, inner-city and intra-city transit options, and park and ride systems.
- *Innovative Land Use Patterns.* Ensure a mixture of different land use types that include commercial, industrial, and residential development which emphasizes compact development in town centers, encourages environmental remediation, takes into account the impacts on natural environment and resources, and limits adverse impacts on rural character.
- *Rural Character and Small Town Feel.* Maintain unique and diverse rural character and small-town New England feel with vibrant town centers and main streets, walkable neighborhoods, and historic preservation of buildings and landscape.

- *Housing.* Ensure a diversity of housing stock that is affordable for a range of income levels, renovate historic and existing structures, ensure buildings are energy efficient, and that housing decisions reflect local needs and priorities of all socioeconomic groups.

The final full forum continued to synthesize ideas, approaches, and priorities including issues around the allocation of available resources. This effort resulted in four overall themes with a work group assigned to each one. Each work group was tasked to develop specific plans and budgets for their theme (F).

- *Theme A Community Infrastructure:* 1) Funding and delivering municipal services, 2) regional cooperation, 3) housing, and 4) transportation
- *Theme B Environment Protection, Land Use, and Open Space:* 1) Environmental protection and land use, and 2) open space protection
- *Theme C Downtown/Village Centers and Community Vitality:* 1) Downtown and village centers, and 2) community vitality.
- *Theme D Local Economy:* 1) Economic vitality and business development, and 2) agriculture and working rural landscapes.

At the close of the final forum, members of a steering committee were elected by the participants (F). It included three representatives from each of the three groups (the 26 local governments, local nonprofits, and state government) and a representative of NH-DOT. This group then provided leadership to oversee the newly formed theme working groups as they undertook their work.

During all three forums, different approaches were used to encourage local community members, local nonprofit representatives, and state government leaders to engage with each other. For example, participants were assigned seats next to people with whom they were not familiar. They were asked to collaborate in brainstorming to identify shared goals and related barriers. They were given space to talk about what was important to them, both as individuals and as representatives—their historic centers, their playgrounds, their schools, their sacred spaces. Together they were able to identify the shared hopes and needs for their economy, for their conservation areas, for the layout of their neighborhoods, and beyond.

Approximately three months after the last forum, the four theme working groups completed their work and reported their efforts and recommendations including specific programs, work plans, and associated budgets (see Figure 13.2). The combined plans, their budgets

Credit: James Gruber

totaling $2 million, were unanimously approved by all participants and the first phase of planning for growth was underway (F-L).

Figure 13.2. Setting priorities.

In parallel with the forums and the efforts of the work groups, there were outreach efforts to local communities to share this planning effort. These included New Hampshire Public Radio programs, a website, news articles, newsletters, three booklets, and a local school program where the youth produced drawings of how they imagined their future community (D).

Reflections on Principle L: Resolve Conflicts

This case study brings to light critical strategies for building community and finding common ground among a diverse array of committed participants. It provides a structure for learning how to grow and move forward together, while preserving and protecting community values and character. It also illustrates that anticipating conflict and working towards collaboration and cooperation is imperative in order to create the resilience needed to meet the very complex challenges of our time and work towards building healthier communities.

Collaborative planning efforts that are transparent, include all voices, promote dialogue, and are grounded in democratic principles can help resolve conflicts by building trust, relationships, and the understanding of different perspectives and values. These efforts are not easy or accomplished quickly, but they can build a stronger community with less rivalry and factionalism and more hope for the future.

CASE STUDY	The Hunter, His Herbs, and Community Biodiversity in Fian, Ghana

by John Bosco Sumani

Prologue

The Fian community's St. Jude Herbal Centre and Garden is the product of a community effort to improve health services for the community through assuring the accessibility of healing herbs. The people of Fian rely on herbal and other forms of traditional medicine. However, after years of poor land use practices, the savannah, which contains the raw materials for herbal medicine, has become degraded. This has led to resource scarcity, competition, and conflicts among some users. This case study demonstrates that the mobilization of disparate stakeholders and community members to support a common initiative is possible provided conflicts are resolved through cooperation and collaboration.

Introduction

I discovered the inspiring story of the origin of Fian Herb Garden in 2004 when I was on an assignment under the UN Global Environment Facility (GEF). The three regional offices of the Ghana Environmental Protection Agency (EPA) in Northern Ghana were implementing the GEF-sponsored Northern Savannah Biodiversity Conservation Project (Biodiversity Project). Under that project, organizations, communities, and individuals working on issues related to sustainable natural resource management in the Northern Savannah Zone were identified and sponsored.[11] (B) I was sent to the Upper West Region because I came from that area and could understand and speak the local dialect. It was there I met, the now deceased, Mr. Banoenoma, founder and director of St. Jude Herbal Clinic (Herbal Clinic), precursor of the Centre and Garden. He told me the story of how the Herb Garden came to be:

> As a hunter, one day I was undertaking a hunting expedition, and a bush animal showed me different herbs and the diseases they treat. Since then, I have been harvesting these herbs to treat my patients. However, it got to a point the patients were so many that I had to establish a clinic called St. Jude Herbal Clinic. It also got to a point where the patients were so many and the herbs too far away and scarce due to environmental degradation and climate change. To address this difficulty, I mobilized the Fian community members and other external stakeholders to establish the Fian Herb Garden in order to domesticate and conserve the plants and shrubs that provide us with the herbs. (A-C)

This is indeed an inspiring story that led to the establishment of a biodiversity conservation initiative, a community garden, a herbal health clinic, and eventually a training center for herbalists.[12,13]

General Overview

Fian is a rural community located in the Upper West Region of Ghana. It is predominantly a farming community with a population of about 2,800.[14] In Ghana, like most West African countries, the use of traditional herbs and roots to cure diseases is very common. However, with the arrival of colonial powers, traditional medicinal practices were overshadowed by the introduction of Western medicine. In Ghana as well as in other low-income countries, Western medical systems are recognized by the government as the primary means of delivery for healthcare services. Nonetheless, there are opportunities for Indigenous medicine and modern medicine to form a symbiosis. It is under this collaborative framework that the St. Jude Herbal Clinic was established (A-B). The mission of this institution is to complement the provision of modern health services with local medicinal practices which the people trust. It should be noted that many public health researchers and policymakers are also advocating for the integration of traditional and modern medicines in addition to training herbalists in the basic principles of the biomedical sciences[15] (G).

Prior to my official visits to the Fian community in 2004, I often heard about the different diseases the director of the local clinic was treating with his herbs. My visits under the auspices of the Biodiversity Project gave me insights into the Herbal Clinic's activities. According to the director, the herb garden was established to grow plants and shrubs to produce herbs for the Clinic. Other stakeholders added that this initiative came in response to the scarcity of herbs from the wild, mainly due to indiscriminate bushfires, environmental degradation, and de-vegetation. This innovative herb garden was the first of its kind in the area because, prior to its establishment, traditional and herbal medicine practitioners were accustomed to harvesting their herbs from the wild. It was obvious that this herb garden was used as an approach to conserve the local herbal medicinal plants in order to ensure their viability, availability, and proximity to the Clinic.

Goals, Approach, and Challenges

I interviewed the director and other stakeholders (staff, trainees, and patients) of the St. Jude Herbal Clinic to understand their vision, goals, and approach to health service delivery. In response, some interviewees revealed that their goal was to provide sustainable herbal medical services to complement the original St. Jude Clinic's Western allopathic approach in order to better address the health needs of the people of Fian and other Ghanaians (C-K).

The sustainability of these healing plants in their natural habitat is adversely affected by a plethora of factors:

- *Climate Change.* These plants require adequate rainfall to grow, but the rainfall has not been that reliable over the years, the director claimed. He further said the little rainfall amount showered on the plants was also mostly dissipated through evapotranspiration fueled by the extreme heat in Northern Ghana.
- *Bushfires* also constitute a challenge to the effective delivery of sus-

tainable herbal medicinal practices. Indiscriminate bushfires often devastate trees and shrubs, including medicinal plants. The annual ritual bushfires have also negatively impacted the regenerative capacity of these medicinal plants.

- *Deforestation* through harmful human activities such as harvesting fuel wood, agricultural activities, and overgrazing are destroying the vegetative cover, some of which could be used as herbs.

The director also valued the training of aspiring herbalists as part of the process (A-F-I). To this end, a training center was created and funded through the Herbal Clinic and Garden to support research, improve local knowledge, and build trust in the community (E-B-G). This open and transparent approach to providing sustainable herbal medical services was innovative, since other local traditional medical practitioners do not share their knowledge with others outside their family lineage or, even, to all family members (J-L-G). For instance, the elders of the Duong Bone Setters Clinic (in my own village) refused to talk to me about the clinic because I do not come from the family that owns and operates it. This closed, nontrusting approach to traditional medicine is not sustainable and can often lead to conflicts in the community.

Being aware of this possibility, the leadership and management team of the Herbal Clinic and Herb Garden put in place a conflict resolution mechanism to provide a platform to settle emerging conflicts, and also to give and receive feedback from both parties (I-H). For instance, my contact at the clinic pointed to the presence of complaint channels, a dispute resolution committee, and rules and regulations aimed at addressing complaints, concerns, and disputes among stakeholders. He related how a community member's complaint that part of the Community Reserve was his father's farmland was resolved amiably using the conflict resolution mechanisms instead of resorting to the traditional authorities (i.e., landlords and chiefs) or courts.

Some stakeholders of the clinic also revealed that the prevalent high poverty levels of patients also adversely hamper the effective operations of the Herbal Clinic and the functioning of the Herb Garden. Even though over 70 percent of Ghanaians depend on traditional medicine for their healthcare needs, most of them are so poor that they can hardly afford the cost of treatment.[16,17] According to the J. Nyerengen, the Clinic's secretary, the Herbal Clinic has a policy of not turning away patients because they lack the financial muscle to pay for its herbal services. As a result, the Clinic has been using its limited resources to treat patients who cannot afford the cost of treatment, thus putting itself in a precarious financial situation (B-C). Since the Herbal Clinic is not accredited by the Ghana National Health Insurance Scheme (NHIS) to provide healthcare services, it does not qualify for cost reimbursement. This problem of noncoverage of some traditional medical services by the NHIS has also been reported in the literature.[18]

Outcomes

The Herbal Clinic and Herb Garden have made tremendous contributions to the healthcare delivery system, the training of herbalists, and the integration of livelihood activities into its operations. Here are some of the results of their exceptional work.

Improved Healthcare Delivery. A one-acre herb garden (Figure 13.4) was established to ensure readily available herbal products. Before the establishment of the garden, the staff of the Clinic and Training Centre used to travel far to harvest herbal products. An elderly woman who went through the training in herbal medicine at the time of the interview also said: "At my age, I couldn't have been able to cover considerable kilometers to look for herbs. The other day when they brought an epilepsy patient, I just went behind the director's house and brought herbs from the garden. This would not have been possible ten years ago".

The availability of herbs in the garden also has a positive impact on the patients themselves. A local teacher said: "But not for the presence of the herb garden, a snakebite patient who was brought in almost lifeless, [probably] would have died because we did not have the snakebite herbs in stock…but we just went to the garden and brought the herbs in less than eight minutes to attend to him."

Training of Herbalists. According to Mr. Banoenoma and his staff, training of herbalists is a vital component of herbal conservation initiative. To him, training of more herbalists ensured the sustainability of the herbal medical practice in the community. According to the Centre's secretary, (personal communication, July 3, 2019), the St. Jude Herbal Training Centre had trained 65 herbalists by the end of June 2019.

Biodiversity Conservation. Some of these healing herbs had become scarce or even extinct due to different forms of environmental degradation and harmful human activities. The creation of the herb garden reversed this trend to a considerable extent. For instance, the late Mr. Banoenoma revealed that: "Some years back, we used to risk our lives traveling as far as Kpare, Jolinyiri or even Samanbaw (these are communities) and yet, we could not find our herbs. Now, I can just go behind my house to harvest herbs from the Garden".

Community Forest. The staff of the Training Centre in partnership with the Fian community also established a 740-acre regeneration site (Community Forest), with plans to expand it to 1,235 acres in the future. According to my contact, local members have undertaken afforestation, reforestation, and enrichment planning within the

Credit: John Bosco

Figure 13.3. St. Jude Herbal Training Centre.

Community Forest since it was established. The reserve was not only meant to be a second source of herbal products but also to serve as a savannah biodiversity conservation strategy (see the Fian Community Reserve below).

Enhancing Local Livelihoods. Also, the Clinic and Training Centre has been mainstreaming livelihood activities into its operations. For instance, the 740-acre community reserve acts as an agroforestry project where economically valuable trees such as shea, dawadawa, and cashew are being nurtured and protected within the reserve. Fian community members also grow crops between these. Men usually mount beehives within the community biodiversity regeneration site and herb garden, and women have been trained in shea butter extraction and soapmaking as shown in Figure 13.5. These activities serve as sources of food and income for rural women.

All these efforts have improved the socioeconomic lives of the people of Fian and its environs. They have provided sources of food, nutrition, employment, and income leading to the utilization of local resources to build the local economy of Fian and its environs. For in-

Figure 13.4. Fian community reserve and herb garden.

Credit: John Bosco

Credit: John Bosco

Figure 13.5. Women grinding shea nuts.

stance, a woman herbalist said, "In addition to the gifts [money, food items, farm labor] we have been getting from our patients, we also earn income through the sale of our shea butter. It is not the best, but it is better than doing nothing."

Recognition and Financial Support. These activities have led to recognition by both local and international organizations. For example, the UN Global Environment Facility has given small grants to aspects of the project and the Nadowli District Assembly constructed a six-classroom building to provide accommodation for the Centre's patients and trainees.

Reflection on Principle L: Resolve Conflicts

My experience with this community has taught me a few lessons about approaches to conflict resolution and its impact on sustainability.

1. The dual goal of improving local health care and the conservation of local natural species was a powerful motivator to find ways to resolve conflict in this community. In my interview with Mr. Banoenoma, he said: "Health is wealth. You know [most] of us here are farmers, and if a farmer like any other worker is sick [he or

she] cannot work or may not be very productive." He further claimed that running a successful herbal clinic and garden depends on cooperation and ability to resolve conflicts in order to restore trust.

2. The willingness of local members to achieve a shared vision and to work towards a common objective helped to resolve long-standing conflicts and led to meaningful and lasting outcomes. For example, the death in 2015 of the clinic's founding director did not prevent the Herb Garden and the Herb Clinic from staying in operation. This demonstrates that the St. Jude Herbal Clinic's leadership's approach to herbal medicine delivery is sustainable and needs to be emulated by other traditional medical practitioners.

In summary, Mr. Banoenoma, together with local community stakeholders, was able to use effective conflict resolution and cooperative strategies to mobilize the people of Fian and the neighboring communities, as well as other external stakeholders, to participate in the dual vision of promoting Indigenous medicinal practices and improving overall health services. This participatory and collaborative endeavor can serve as a role model for other organizations seeking to help their communities move forward while continuing to honor local practices.

Principle L — Resolve Conflict

Do (Or Consider Doing)

- ✓ Recognize that some conflict is healthy and important in effective decision making.
- ✓ Create and agree upon norms and set clear expectations.
- ✓ Remember, even positive changes require the discomfort of letting go of "what was."
- ✓ When a conflict is raised during a decision-making session that isn't directly related to the issue on the table, acknowledge it, record it, and move on.
- ✓ Recognize that many conflicts are created when individuals do not feel respected or heard. Active listening and writing down what you hear may be the first step in giving respect to others.
- ✓ Help to resolve conflicts by moving from discussing *what* they disagree on to *why* they disagree.
- ✓ Consider hiring an impartial outside individual or group to help mediate conflicts and help parties work through their differences.
- ✓ Recognize that some misunderstandings arise because people make assumptions about people they don't know. The more people understand the values and experiences of others, the easier it is to have a productive dialogue on the issues.

Don't (Or Think Twice)

- ✗ Don't assume that what people are arguing or are upset about is the real issue. Frequently there are deeper underlying issues that need to be identified, recognized, or acknowledged.
- ✗ Don't expect to always reach 100 percent agreement because there are often valid differences of opinion as well as differing values and worldviews.
- ✗ Don't be surprised if it is the little things that cause conflicts (e.g., arguing over a small expense in an annual budget or the specific wording of a statement).
- ✗ Don't assume that all conflicts are an emergency and need immediate attention and resolution. This may result in avoiding other more important issues.
- ✗ Don't use a facilitator who is associated with one perspective in the room when leading a participatory decision-making process.

CHAPTER 14

A Toolbox of
Leadership Strategies

> *Let us put our minds together and*
> *see what life we can make for our children.*
>
> — SITTING BULL

Collaborative Leadership and Empowerment

In this final chapter I seek to provide you with a toolbox of leadership strategies for engaging and working with community members. Specifically, I present a collaborative planning approach for leading community change through a participatory decision-making process. Also included are some do's and don'ts on planning, organizing, and facilitating a community meeting, along with some specific examples of ways to enhance a community gathering or convening event. I hope you find these practical ideas helpful as you work, practicing collaborative leadership, to empower your community members to support the health and vitality of your community.

A Collaborative Planning Approach

Engaging communities to help them move from surviving to thriving requires practicing adaptive leadership. To repeat what was stated in Chapter 10: Practice Leadership, there are two critical leadership actions (1) engaging your community members and (2) mobilizing their understanding and willingness to address the challenges, problems, and needs of their community. The following collaborative planning approach lays out a ten-step process for engaging community members in response to a significant concern or need. These steps will typically require two large meetings (for Steps 1 through 6), a number of smaller working group meetings to complete Step 6, and a final large meeting for Step 7. The final three steps (8 through 10) are typically undertaken through the formal organizational decision-making processes. Figure 14.1 illustrates this process, showing how the output of each step is the input for the following step. It should be noted that the output for Step 10 is also the input for Step 1, as revisions may be needed, based on a feedback loop.

I have been able to use a version of this collaborative planning approach for climate change adaptation, recycling-waste management, water and wetlands conservation, land use and transportation plan-

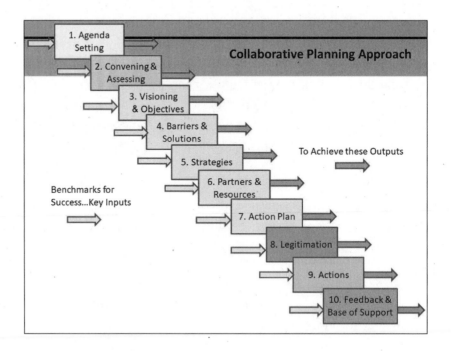

Figure 14.1.
A collaborative
planning approach.

ning, growth management, and other community planning efforts. Not all steps may be relevant or applicable to your specific situation. I will also offer specific tools for working with community members during a collaborative approach. Under each of the Steps, I describe the step, potential strategies and tools, and offer an example or two.

1. Agenda Setting: Providing a Wake-Up Call

Unfortunately, natural and human-caused disasters are the most frequent agenda-setting events. However, sometimes serious challenges or problems don't show up until information is gathered or shared. For example, lead contaminants in the water supply, pesticides or herbicides causing cancer, a local increase in drug addiction, or the growing incidents of severe flooding and droughts may pose a serious challenge or threat that may have otherwise been missed. By raising awareness of this type of silently gathering storm, community members can provide a wake-up call to others by communicating why taking action now is needed.

Strategies and Tools
One approach for raising awareness is gathering facts and information. A local university could help with this effort, for instance by testing the water supply, collecting demographic information on health problems, and writing formal reports on their findings that can be shared with elected officials and the general public. Citizen scientists could also help collect data.

Another approach could be elected or appointed leaders or citizen groups organizing and holding listening sessions on the presenting issue, such as lack of affordable housing, rapid growth problems, or neighborhood violence. Facts are important, but also making space for the faces and voices of the citizens will help raise the awareness of an issue, provide a needed wake-up call, and, hopefully, create an agenda for future action. And don't forget to seek the voices of those who are unable to attend a community event through other means, such as surveys, going door-to-door, or perhaps meeting at the senior center or the homeless shelter.

Example

The case study, "Randolph Community Forest, New Hampshire" (Chapter 8) describes how three individuals (a state police officer, an environmentalist, and an international development specialist) were able to raise concerns about the possibility that 10,000 acres could be sold off by an international paper corporation for development. If that occurred, the town would forever change its character and lose a critical ecosystem, a forest recreational area, and the economic base of a sustainably managed forest. This wake-up call (or agenda-setting effort) and the successful work that followed ensured the healthy rural character and economic future of this community.

2. Convening and Assessing: Getting Everyone into the Room

Once the community is aware of a need to take action in response to some type of agenda-setting event, it is essential to convene a broad cross-section of the community in a timely manner. An informal leadership team is extremely valuable at this time to help reach out to others. Again, seek out team members who reflect the experiential and demographic diversity of the community. The convening event should also bring together a broad range of stakeholders, typically including community leaders, social or natural scientists, engineers, policymakers, business leaders, those who are typically marginalized in society, and even those who doubt (or counter) the existence of the problem or challenge. The more diverse the group, the better the assessment, and the more ownership and participation there will be in the actions that follow. You will also need an impartial convener or facilitator who is skilled in managing large group events. A local NGO or university are two possible sources for this individual. After the convening event, it is recommended to conduct further external data gathering, as needed. This can be completed by a local NGO, university member, or consultant.

Strategies and Tools

The convening event could focus primarily on assessing the present challenges related to the issue at hand. (Note: A convening event could also be used to assess the strengths of a community using the Asset Based Community Development approach). Typical steps for assessing a challenge include:

1. Document current conditions from perspectives of community members and experts.
2. Include diverse views and perspectives in both small and large group discussions.
3. Provide an opportunity to reflect on the situation.
4. Help participants understand the underlying causes or problems.
5. After the event, collect and analyze essential data based on priorities identified at the convening.

Rather than have local leaders tell the participants what they see as the most important issues, I strongly recommend that you start by asking a few key questions that will allow everyone to participate and to create a shared understanding. For example, for one initial convening event on climate change adaptation, we posed these questions:

- In what ways have you observed or heard about land-use/development and changing weather patterns impacting this region?
- Do you think some of these impacts might reoccur?
- What are the underlying causes and/or problems?
- What do you think are the top reasons why these impacts might reoccur?

After all the participants' ideas filled multiple flip charts, we give each participant five colored sticky dots to prioritize the responses to the last question. The results were later grouped. We have found that this or similar types of processes provides both depth and breadth to understanding the issues. Following this activity, we recommend asking the question: What data/information is needed from scientists or others that will assist in making future decisions?

Examples

The "Community-Driven Land Use and Transportation Planning, New Hampshire" case study (Chapter 13) used a similar approach to find common ground among the 26 local governments participating. The case study "Mobilizing the Local Voice to Support Protected Area Governance" (Chapter 6) effectively used the Asset Based Community Development approach, a convening and assessing method, to help the local villages inventory their assets.

3. Visioning and Setting Objectives:
Articulating What the Future Should Look Like

Rather than always focusing on fixing a problem or on what is broken, I have found it to be particularly helpful to support a community in developing their own vision of what they wish their future to look like. Later they can work on how to get there. Many individuals have shared with me that they are very wary of doom and gloom as primary motivators to take action, noting that this approach will "suck the oxygen out of the room." They have further emphasized that a positive vision is critical for engaging citizens and local leaders to act.

The development of a shared vision and the articulation of objectives (based on the vision) can be achieved through a number of collaborative multistakeholder processes. To clarify a term, an "objective" is a clear outcome statement, such as: "Phase out most single-use plastics in the next 20 years." A set of agreed-upon objectives is essential for setting a shared direction for future community efforts. Important characteristics of all successful visioning and objective-setting processes are that they are transparent, open to the public, seek consensus, and include representatives of all of the key stakeholder groups.

Strategies and Tools

A vision map or graphical representation of the desired future is a common approach to setting objectives.[1] I will describe a typical visioning and objectives-setting process below. There are other approaches that also work. Here are a few steps in creating a vision map with between 20 and 200 people.

Vision Map (refer to Figure 14.2)

1. Have a skilled facilitator, train two scribes, bring colored markers, and attach to a wall a large sheet of white paper (approximately 4 feet by 20 feet).

2. In the center of the map write or attach a sheet with the overall goal of the map such as: "How we want our community to look, feel, and be 20 years from now" or "A carbon-neutral community in 20 years."

3. Go around the room and let each participant share one idea that is then mapped as either a limb or a branch off a limb or a twig off a branch. They choose what is written and where. No ideas are rejected.

4. Make sure that everyone can speak once until everyone who wishes has offered an idea. Then do a second round, etc. The process takes

Credit: James Gruber

Figure 14.2. Example of a vision map.

less than an hour for up to 200 participants (if you have two people scribing).

5. All participants are then given five sticky colored dots to place on what is most important to them. (And, yes, they could put all five on the same place!)

6. After voting is completed, I suggest that you have a break (perhaps with coffee and cookies). During the break the facilitator will work with the scribes to draw large circles around areas with lots of dots that have a similar theme. (Sometimes people request that you also add up the number of dots; while somewhat useful, this is not necessary.)

7. The facilitator gives a name to each clump in order to name 8–12 overall objectives (but with limited time, do not try to fully write out or wordsmith the objective).

8. After the break, review the named objectives.

Note: Due to the strong ownership that this procedure engenders, participants frequently request to have a group photo in front of this map!

Example

The case study "Getting Unstuck" in Norwich, Vermont" (Chapter 12) found this vision-mapping approach seminal to their ability to successfully move ahead.

4. Identify Barriers and Solutions: Recognizing Challenges and Concerns and Potential Ways to Address Them

At a typical New England town meeting, when you stand up to propose a new idea, expect to hear at least three reasons why it is a poor idea or will not work. This is natural in part because change is difficult. Recognizing and addressing real and perceived challenges or concerns—the barriers to potential community actions—is essential in order to move forward on developing effective and socially acceptable strategies. These barriers can include social, financial, political, logistical, technical, philosophical, and cultural issues.

Objective: Incorporating changes in rainfall patterns into stormwater infrastructure design	
Barriers/Challenges	**Potential Approaches to Resolve Each Barrier/Challenge**
1. Changing design standards requires predicting the future…that is impossible 2. … 3. … 4. …	• Adopt the new (pending) state rainfall standards that will reflect current rainfall patterns. • Continue to record and analyze local rainfall patterns, supported by…fees • …

Credit: James Gruber

Figure 14.3. Barriers and solutions flip chart.

Strategies and Tools

To get these challenges and concerns out on the table, I found that one of the most engaging and effective approaches at a large meeting is to break into small groups and participate in a process I call "Barriers and Solutions." I have found that this facilitated process has been one of the most effective approaches for engaging community members in problem solving, raising their understanding and knowledge level, and beginning to develop an initial list of prioritized approaches. I sketch out each step below. This process will result in each of the objectives (determined from the previous step) having a list of barriers and suggested ways to overcome them.

Barriers and Solutions (cf. Figure 14.3)

1. Write one objective on top of each flip chart sheet (refer to Step 3 above).

2. Form diverse small groups and give each group one or two of these sheets.

3. Ask each group to write up to five of the toughest or most serious barriers/challenges (refer to Step 4 above).

4. Rotate or trade the flip chart sheets among groups so that each group receives another group's list of barriers/challenges.

5. Then have each group identify specific potential approaches to resolve each of the other group's barriers/challenges. These approaches are not just *what* to do, but *how* it can be done.

6. Record all approaches on the flip chart.

7. If time permits, ask each group to also record potential resources/ organizations/partners that could help with each approach that they propose.

8. Collect and tape all flip chart sheets on the wall.

9. Ask each small group to present their potential approaches to the full assembly.

10. Each of the participants are then given five to ten colored sticky dots to place on the best approaches.

11. Votes are then counted and recorded on the flip charts. The top ten approaches are noted.

Example

The case study "Wetlands Conservation and Sustainable Livelihoods in the Ecuadorian Andes" (Chapter 11) used this approach in their workshops. This process allowed the local communities, including three Indigenous communities, to identify the potential future challenges that conservation and management of the wetlands entailed.

5. Approaches: Impact vs. Feasibility

The vetting and prioritizing process needs to consider technical and financial considerations, social and cultural values, public priorities, and issues of environmental justice. It is common knowledge that local communities frequently have a wide range of demands that exceed their limited financial and human resources. As a previous town administrator, I became acutely aware that actions on newly identified needs must compete with other current demands. If meeting a new

Credit: James Gruber

Figure 14.4. Community
feedback voting on
proposed solutions.

need can be linked with other existing programs or resources, it is far
easier to support. For example, charging for waste disposal (pay-as-
you-throw programs) can both reduce property taxes and generate
funds for a new recycling program.

Strategies and Tools

The Impact vs. Feasibility process needs to follow the Barriers and
Solutions process to help a large group focus on and prioritize what
initial actions to take. Below I sketch out each step of an Impact and
Feasibility process.

Impact vs. Feasibility (cf. Figure 14.5)

1. Draw on a flip chart the grid shown with "Feasibility" on the ver-
   tical axis and "Impact" on the horizontal axis. Then add low, medium, and high to both axes as shown.
2. Write each of the top ten approaches (along with the objective it is
   associated with) on a large sticky note.
3. In a room with all participants: 1) describe what factors to consider
   for feasibility of all approaches and 2) what factors to consider for
   rating the impact.

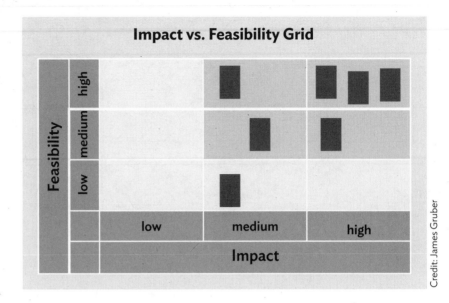

Figure 14.5. Impact vs. Feasibility grid.

a. *Feasibility* may include, but is not limited to: technical and financial considerations, social and cultural values, public priorities, environmental justice, and impacts on the disempowered.

b. *Impact* refers to the benefits of achieving the objective.

4. The facilitator vets each idea by moving each sticky note around the grid (through low, medium, and high) until there is a general consensus. Discussing feasibility and impacts as this activity is taking place could help with reaching agreement. Some sticky notes may be on a boundary between categories.

5. Read back the result in each of the grid boxes to ensure that all in the room are in agreement.

6. Clearly, focusing on those approaches in the high feasibility and high impact area (or those nearby) should be recognized as first priorities moving forward.

Example

The "Community-Driven Regional Land Use and Transportation Planning, New Hampshire" case study (Chapter 13) is an excellent example of the use of this approach. I have used this approach with numerous local community climate change adaptation efforts.

Think about Having a Dessert Bake-Off...

"This is the best public meeting I have ever attended" a senior participant told me at the close of a long public evening meeting. "Why?" I wondered. The meeting had been engaging with large and small groups and report-outs, but...what she loved was the dessert bake-off!

Rather than bringing some cookies and a few drinks, we had decided to offer $50 for the best dessert brought to the meeting. When the desserts arrived, they were each given a number and cut into small pieces. During the meeting break, we invited all the participants to choose as many desserts as they wished to taste test, and then to vote (with their three sticky dots) for the best ones. The long table was covered with desserts, each with a number and a place to vote. Most people brought their family's favorite. The competition was stiff, the desserts incredible, and the sugar-induced energy after the break, I think, enhanced the amount of work we were able to accomplish that evening. At the end of the meeting, a $50 bill was presented to the winner with great appreciation from all present for the best-fed public meeting in the history of the town. You may wish to try this.

6. Partners and Resources:
Finding the Right Partners and Critical Resources

Leveraging assistance (and potential resources) from partners has been recognized as essential for many types of change or adaptation efforts. The National Research Council[2] specifically noted the importance of "identifying opportunities for co-benefits and synergies across sectors" as a leveraging strategy. The final outcomes of this step include the identification and initial engagement of potential partners along with identifying potential sources for the types of resources that will be required.

Strategies and Tools

Once there is a list of prioritized approaches from the Impact vs. Feasibility vetting process, it is best to immediately name and form working groups, each taking on one (or two, if related) approaches. It is important to ask for initial volunteers for each of these groups, as well as setting an initial meeting date, and a convener or host before the meeting adjourns. The groups will then work separately on seeking information for the unanswered questions including: 1) potential partners, 2) types of resources needed, and 3) where these resources may be procured. Try to attract individuals who show interest, commitment, and (ideally) some knowledge related to the objective and approach(es). Additional working group members can then be recruited by the initial members. Hopefully, some of the right partners are already "in-the-room" either figuratively or actually. If participants were able to identify potential partners and resources under Step 4 and 5, then you have an initial list as a starting point for each working group. Each of the working groups should then report their findings and recommendation to a full group session. At that large meeting there will be opportunity to seek additional input into their recommendations.

Example
Core to the development and delivery of programs by Vital Communities of the Upper Valley, Vermont and New Hampshire (case study in Chapter 5) was their ability to create numerous partnerships that were able to help them both deliver programs and secure critical resources.

7. Action Plan: Formulating a Plan for Change
The old adage: "It takes a village to raise a child," also applies to raising your community (or making significant or critical changes)...the whole village is needed! The action planning session strives to have all the key stakeholders in the room when an action plan is formulated. This action plan should be grounded in analysis of data, as well as financial, political, social, cultural, and environmental considerations. Building broad-based engagement and ownership of the process, including a clear understanding and recognition of the need and types of action that may be required, is an important component in order to assure that action plans are actually acted upon. This was reiterated by a local community leader in another environmental planning process, when she said, "A policy is nothing if it doesn't rest on burning public opinion."[3]

Strategies and Tools

Action plans need to be specific in order to be useful. They should include *who* will do *what* by *when* in what way (*how*) including listing the responsible parties. All too often action plans are developed and then just sit on a shelf. By including a broad cross-section of community members in framing actions plans, broader ownership will be achieved and follow-through is more likely to occur. Figure 14.6 is an example of an Action Plan Framework. Similar action plans (although sometimes far more comprehensive) are needed for each of the top ten approaches.

Example

The Minneapolis, Minnesota, Climate Change Adaptation Planning Initiative[4] was able to develop a comprehensive framework of action plans that have guided future climate adaptation efforts in urban neighborhoods.

Figure 14.6. Example of an Action Plan framework.

Sample Action Plan: Land Use Planning and Policy

Objective: Identifying and encouraging proactive strategies for managing stormwater, including green infrastructure, low impact development, and stormwater reuse.

Project: Adapt development and zoning codes to minimize the use of structural conveyance associated with transportation by preserving natural corridors and conveyance systems.
Benefits: traffic calming, natural corridors preserved, more stable conveyance systems.

Timeline: Not identified

Responsible Parties: Met council, MN DOT, League of Minnesota Cities.

Action Items:

1. MN DOT and Met Council develops policies that require communities to preserve natural conveyance systems through design of transportation systems.
2. Develop a model ordinance that cities can adopt requiring that roads avoid or span natural drainage pathways rather than fill them in or using berms, culverts.
3. City develops/amends comprehensive plans and adopt zoning controls consistent with policy. Preserve areas prone to flooding and natural conveyance systems (includes an inventory).
4. City public works projects implement the comprehensive plan.

Credit: James Gruber

8. Legitimation and Community Leadership: Making Formal Decisions

Prior to undertaking substantive actions, there is a need for formal legitimation of the priorities and recommendations. Steps 1 through 7 can be considered an informal collaborative planning process. The formal implementation of priorities requires the involvement of those formally charged by society or the community to make policy decisions and appropriate funds, such as a city council or a nonprofit board. My experience is that when the community members actively undertake the research and planning, and are committed to a course of action, their formal leaders will embrace their efforts.

Strategies and Tools

Keeping the formal community leaders involved throughout the process is the key to their future support. This includes inviting them to work sessions. They may not support some of the initial ideas, but this can change. I have seen formal political support shift towards community-driven initiatives many times!

Example

As described in the case study "Wetlands Conservation and Sustainable Livelihoods in the Ecuadorian Andes, Ecuador" (Chapter 11) local consensus-building efforts were able to secure the critical support needed from the Environmental Ministry and build legitimation of their efforts.

9. Actions: Implementing Change

Positive actions and results build both confidence and broader support. Therefore, it is important to encourage initial action on the prioritized approaches (which balance highest impacts with greatest ease of achieving results). I strongly suggest undertaking smaller, more timely efforts first, as these have the best chance of providing positive outcomes in the short run. This type of quick win will build support and momentum for the more challenging actions to come.

Some actions contribute to other goals such as improving public health or enhancing economic competitiveness. These actions with linkages are more likely to be given a higher priority.[5]

Strategies and Tools
Community members need to attend and actively participate in the formal meetings of elected and appointed community leaders to keep these issues in the forefront.

Example
The case study "Local Community Collaboration in the Apuseni Mountains, Huedin, Romania" (Chapter 10) shares how initial actions with positive feedback generated trust and support from elected and appointed community leaders for the proposed community change initiatives.

10. Feedback and Base of Support: Embracing Community Feedback on Actions Taken

As a final stage in this change process, it is important to monitor and assess the effects of the actions taken. This will inform future planning and actions. Dynamic feedback can direct the frequently needed mid-course changes. I have found that providing timely feedback to policy-makers and the public is essential for implementing a change process in a cost-effective and socially acceptable manner. Feedback should also help maintain and build a broad base of support for the overall change effort.

Strategies and Tools
Forming a citizen- or community-member feedback advisory group is a common approach. Work with the formally appointed and elected leaders to create this group that includes a clear charge and specific expectations.

Planning, Organizing, and Facilitating a Community Meeting

There are many publications on how best to facilitate a community meeting.[6] The list below that I have developed is compiled from 25 years of trial and error. You will need to decide what works best for you. Here are our recommendations on what to do and what to avoid.

Do (Or Consider Doing)

☑ Get the word out through multiple outlets. Make sure that all community members are made aware of the meeting and feel welcome.

☑ Work to ensure that you get a broad cross-section of your community members to attend. This means making one-on-one contact with members of groups that are typically underrepresented and those who are most likely to be affected by pending future actions.

☑ Review a draft agenda with the key stakeholders to ensure that it is appropriately designed.

☑ Use an accessible space considering attendee difficulty with mobility, hearing, and other physical needs.

☑ Avoid a meeting space where speakers will be on a platform or stage above other participants and attendees.

☑ Consider providing childcare at the meeting and transportation to the meeting for those who need it.

☑ Start the meeting with developing an agreement on ground rules or meeting norms.

☑ Honor everyone's time. Have clear starting and ending times. You may need to be flexible during the meeting but be firm about the ending time.

☑ Use nametags to reduce the awkwardness of not knowing others.

☑ Structure the meeting so that there are large and small group discussions and activities. This will make the meeting more engaging and will encourage all to participate.

☑ Make sure that airtime is shared. For example, a potential meeting norm is that everyone has an opportunity to speak once on an issue before anyone speaks a second time.

☑ Provide snacks and something to drink.

☑ If there are follow-up activities, make sure to confirm *who* will be doing *what* and *when…* *prior to adjourning!*

Don't (Or Think Twice)

☒ Don't expect than an email blast will get people to attend a community meeting. It usually doesn't.

☒ Don't allow experts or individuals in roles of authority to give long speeches or presentations at the beginning of the meeting. If they are needed, keep them short and succinct.

☒ Don't invite everyone to fully introduce themselves. This may take up too much of the meeting time.

☒ Don't try to resolve conflicts during the meeting. Acknowledge the conflict and continue with the agenda.

☒ Don't use technical jargon or acronyms unless each are clarified.

Example

The Elwha River Ecosystem partners are currently embracing community feedback to guide their future actions. This is described in the case study "Restoring the Strong People: The Lower Elwha Klallam Tribe and the Elwha River" (Chapter 8).

The Way Forward

Building inclusive communities through breaking down silos, turfs, and mistrust as well as finding common ground is essential. It is essential for a local community that wishes to work together to clean up its rivers, to grow its local economy, or to build resilience and support adaptation to the climate crisis. The guiding principles for building communities that I have shared and illustrated, with examples from different communities and cultures from around the word, are also transcultural and interrelated. Drawing upon all of the principles can help transform a local community from surviving to thriving. Building inclusive communities is also essential if we are going to save the earth's ecosystems and humanity. I close this book by sharing a story on how these same principles can be applied at a larger scale—building a collaborative and connected global community.

In 2019 I participated in the United Nations 4th Environmental Assembly in Nairobi, Kenya. Participants were young and old, from all continents including national leaders, scientists, religious leaders, students, business leaders, artists, and social and environmental activists. The 4,500 participants, from 149 countries, were there to build a healthier global community. I was not surprised by the large formal plenary meetings with too many speeches from global leaders, encouraged by the international media coverage. However, what was both surprising and exhilarating was the hundreds, perhaps thousands, of different types of communities that were represented here, all dedicated to building a healthier global community. Many of these, with active volunteers, had been working throughout the previous two years in order to complete their research and present their findings or recommendations at this global gathering.

Despite the historic and ongoing economic rivalries, cultural differences, and political conflicts, delegates and participants were committed to working together to make decisions that would protect resources and benefit people around the world. For example, the representatives of faith-based communities shared insights from their traditions on "environmental challenges related to poverty and natural resources management, including sustainable food systems, food security and halting biodiversity loss."[7] I was encouraged to witness an imam, a rabbi, and a Catholic sister working together to address the challenge of the climate crisis. Local government representatives from some of the world's largest urban areas shared their ideas on "ways to reduce the 'weight of cities' by using our resources more efficiently through urban systems integration and circularity, and thereby harnessing climate and societal benefits, including health and jobs."[8] Every morning the civil sector (NGOs) met in the Green Tent to share their efforts from the previous day of discussions and meetings to enhance environmental protection and conservation, promote social justice and

Figure 14.7. Waste plastic boat at the UN Environmental Assembly, 2019.

Credit: James Gruber

gender equity, encourage green jobs, and support implementation of the UN sustainable development goals. Youth and school communities demonstrated their innovative ideas for pollution prevention and resource conservation that they had developed at their schools. And artists came together to build a boat made from marine plastic waste, that welcomed all of the delegates entering the assembly.

There were those representing State Departments that were negotiating the language for new international agreements. During lunch there were numerous small gathering of these colleagues from countries in Africa, Europe, Asia, and the Americas who greeted one another like old friends re-uniting and sharing hugs, prior to later sitting down at the negotiation tables. I saw hope (in spite of the bluster from some national leaders) that many scientific, advocacy, and business communities were growing their trust, awareness of different cultures, shared values, and dedication to work together to build a healthier global community, a global community that is linked with the local communities in their country. I was truly encouraged to see dynamic networks of local, national, and global communities that are working collaboratively for a healthier tomorrow. There is hope.

Notes

Introduction

1. For an excellent description of the period see Andrew Small, "The Wastelands of Urban Renewal," Feb. 13, 2017. citylab.com/equity/2017/02/urban-renewal-waste lands/516378/

2. Ronald A. Heifetz, *Leadership Without Easy Answers* (Cambridge, MA: The Belknap Press of Harvard University Press, 1994).

3. Ronald A. Heifetz and Martin Linsky, *Leadership on the Line: Staying Alive through the Dangers of Leading* (Boston: Harvard Business School Press, 2002).

4. Referred to as Vermont's first "Un-shopping Center," with the story in Chapter 3.

5. Published peer-review papers that discuss the foundation of the 12 Guiding Principles are available in the following publications: James S. Gruber, "Key Principles of Community-Based Natural Resource Management: A Synthesis and Interpretation of Identified Effective Approaches for Managing the Commons," *Environmental Management* 45 (2010): 52–66; James S. Gruber, "Characteristics of Effective and Sustainable Community Based Natural Resource Management: An Application of Q Methodology for Forest Projects," *Journal of Conservation and Society* 9, no. 2 (2011): 159–171; James S. Gruber, Jason S. Rhoades, et al., "Enhancing Climate Change Adaptation: Strategies for Community Engagement and University-community Partnerships," *Journal of Environmental Studies and Sciences* 7, no. 1 (2015), doi.org/10.1007/s13412-015-0232-1

Chapter 1: Challenges of Our Communities: Growing Local Leadership

1. Indicators of success that I use include: a) economics: external funding is either not needed or there is a reduced dependency on this funding; b) environment: natural resource systems are recovering and/or there is sustainable harvesting/management of natural resources; c) equity: the equitable sharing of financial and natural resources is recognized as important; d) empowerment: there is strong social and organizational capacity in the organization. My working definition of sustainability is that there is an effort within the organization to achieve a balance among four characteristics: ecological integrity, economic security, empowerment and responsibility, and social well-being.

2. Robert Putnam developed the term "social capital" and published research on building engaged communities.

3. Forum for the Future 2009, accessed August 10, 2019: forumforthefuture.org/the -five-capitals; North Central Regional Center for Rural Development, accessed

August 10, 2019: canr.msu.edu/ncrcrd/; Robert D. Putnam and Lewis M. Feldstein, *Better Together* (New York: Simon and Schuster, 2003); Cornelia Butler and Jan L. Flora, *Rural Communities: Legacy and Change, 3rd ed.* (Boulder, CO: Westview Press, 2007); Thomas Prugh, *Natural Capital and Human Economic Survival* (New York: Lewis Publishers, 1999); Mark Roseland, *Towards Sustainable Communities 4th Edition* (Gabriola Island, BC: New Society Publishers, 2012).

4. North Central Regional Center, accessed August 12, 2019.

5. See note 3.

6. Elinor Ostrom facilitated this 1998 World Bank Foundation Workshop.

7. James S. Gruber, "Key Principles of Community-Based Natural Resource Management: A Synthesis and Interpretation of Identified Effective Approaches for Managing the Commons," *Journal of Environmental Management* 45, no.1 (2008): 52–66, doi.org/10.1007/s00267-008-9235-y; James S. Gruber, "Characteristics of Effective and Sustainable Community Based Natural Resource Management: An Application of Q Methodology for Forest Projects," *Journal of Conservation and Society*, 9 no. 2 (2011): 159–171.

Chapter 2: Principle A—Involve Everyone

1. Lisa M. Campbell and Arja Vainio-Mattila, "Participatory Development and Community-Based Conservation: Opportunities Missed for Lessons Learned?" *Human Ecology* 31, no. 3 (2003): 417–437.

2. Kathryn Quick and John Bryson, "Public Participation," in *Handbook of Theories of Governance*, ed. Christopher Ansell and Jacob Torfing (Cheltenham: Edward Elgar, 2016).

3. Denise Scheberle, "Moving Toward Community-Based Environmental Management: Wetland Protection in Door County," *American Behavioral Scientist* 44, no. 4 (2000): 564–578, doi.org/10.1177/00027640021956387

4. James Gruber, "Building Sustainable Communities Through New Partnerships of Central and Local Governments: Lessons Learned from Eastern Europe and New England," 2000 International Conference on Sustainable Development, Environmental Conditions, and Public Management, published in *Sustainable Development, Environmental Conditions, and Public Management* (Tokyo, Japan: National Academy of Public Administration (US) and National Institute for Research Advance, 2002), 264–286.

5. Arian Spiteri and Sanjay Nepal, "Incentive-Based Conservation Programs in Developing Countries: A Review of Some Key Issues and Suggestions for Improvements," *Environmental Management* 37 (2006): 1–14.

6. *The World Bank Participation Sourcebook* (Washington, DC: World Bank, 1996).

7. Jeffrey D. Hackel, "Community Conservation and the Future of Africa's Wildlife," *Conservation Biology* 13 (1999): 726–734.

8. Sherry Arnstein, "A Ladder of Citizen Participation," *Journal of the American Planning Association* 35 (1969): 216–224.

9. Greater Upper Valley Solid Waste District, located in Vermont.

10. City of Keene, *Keene Comprehensive Master Plan* (Keene, NH: City of Keene, 2010): 10.

11. City of Keene, *Adapting to Climate Change: Planning a Climate Resilient Community* (Keene, NH: City of Keene, 2007): 6.

12. "Extreme Weather Can Threaten Water Supply," U.S. Climate Resilience Toolkit (2017), accessed June 30, 2019, toolkit.climate.gov/case-studies/addressing-water -supply-risks-flooding-and-drought

13. David Thomas and Chasca Twyman, "Equity and Justice in Climate Change Adaptation Amongst Natural Resource-Dependent Societies," *Global Environmental Change* 15 (2005): 115–124.

14. "EJSCREEN: Environmental Justice Screening and Mapping Tool," United States Environmental Protection Agency, accessed June 25, 2019, epa.gov/ejscreen

15. "Keene, NH Housing," USA.com, accessed July 24, 2019, usa.com/keene-nh -housing.htm

Chapter 3: Principle B: Work Together

1. This interesting article on social capital, accessed on October 22, 2018, can be found at robertdputnam.com/bowling-alone/social-capital-primer/

2. Citations include: Adam Barker, "Capacity Building for Sustainability: Towards Community Development in Coastal Scotland," *Journal of Environmental Management* 75 (2005):11–19; and D. Eade, "*Capacity-Building: An Approach to People-Centered Development*" (UK: Oxfam, 1997).

3. Robert D. Putnam and Lewis M. Feldstein, *Better Together* (New York: Simon and Schuster, 2003).

4. Lisa M. Campbell and Arja Vainio-Mattila, "Participatory Development and Community-Based Conservation: Opportunities Missed for Lessons Learned?" *Human Ecology* 31, no. 3 (2003): 417–437.

5. Barker, "Capacity Building," 11–19; Kelly F. Butler and Tom M. Koontz, "Theory into Practice: Implementing Ecosystem Management Objectives in the USDA Forest Service," *Environmental Management* 35 (2005): 138–150; Paul M. Thompson, Parvin Sultana, and Nurul Islam, "Lessons from Community-Based Management of Floodplain Fisheries in Bangladesh," *Journal of Environmental Management* 69 (2003): 307–321.

6. Denise Scheberle, "Moving Toward Community-Based Environmental Management: Wetland Protection in Door County," *American Behavioral Scientist* 44, no. 4 (2000): 564–578, doi.org/10.1177/00027640021956387

7. The Hartford Un-Shopping Center was designed and built in Hartford, Vermont, in 1993. It has served a region of five Vermont towns for over 25 years. Its innovative approach was cited in the US Congressional Record.

8. The Montshire Museum of Science in Norwich, Vermont, provided a leadership role in involving local youth in the artwork of the new center.

9. Ranjan Datta, "Community Garden: A Bridging Program Between Formal and Informal Learning," *Journal of Cogent Education* 3 (2016)

10. Tina Moffat, Charlene Mohammed, and K. Bruce Newbold, "Cultural Dimensions of Food Insecurity Among Immigrants and Refugees," *Human Organization* 76, no. 1 (2017): 15–27, dx.doi.org/10.17730/0018-7259.76.1.15

11. Government of Canada, Immigration, Refugees, and Citizenship Canada, 2018 Annual Report to Parliament on Immigration, canada.ca/en/immigration-refugees-citizenship/corporate/publications-manuals/annual-report-parliament-immigration-2018/report.html

12. FAO, IFAD, UNICEF, WFP and WHO. 2018. The State of Food Security and Nutrition in the World 2018. Building climate resilience for food security and nutrition. Rome, FAO, fao.org/3/i9553en/i9553en.pdf (p. 1–2).

13. David A. Boult, "Hunger in the Arctic: Food (In)Security in Inuit Communities A Discussion Paper," Ajunnginiq Centre, NAHO (2004), foodsecurecanada.org/sites/foodsecurecanada.org/files/2004_inuit_food_security.pdf

14. Boult, "Hunger."

15. Jane W. Njeru, Eugene M. Tan, Jennifer St. Sauver, Debra J. Jacobson, Amenah A. Agunwamba, Patrick M. Wilson, Lila J. Rutten, Swathi Damodaran, and Mark L. Wieland, "High Rates of Diabetes Mellitus, Pre-diabetes and Obesity Among Somali Immigrants and Refugees in Minnesota: A Retrospective Chart Review," *Journal of Immigrant and Minority Health* 18, no. 6 (2016): 1343–1349, doi.org/10.1007/s10903-015-0280-3

16. Ibid.

17. Samantha Artiga and Petry Ubri, "Living in an Immigrant Family in America: How Fear and Toxic Stress are Affecting Daily Life, Well-Being, & Health," *The Henry Kaiser Family Foundation* (2017), kff.org/disparities-policy/issue-brief/living-in-an-immigrant-family-in-america-how-fear-and-toxic-stress-are-affecting-daily-life-well-being-health/

18. Ranjan Datta, Nyojy U. Khyang, Hla Kray Prue Khyang, Hla Aung Prue Kheyang, Mathui Ching Khyang, and Jebunnessa Chapola, "Participatory Action Research and Researcher's Responsibilities: An Experience with an Indigenous Community," *International Journal of Social Research Methodology* 18, no. 6 (2015): 581–599, doi.org/10.1080/13645579.2014.927492

19. Tina Moffat, Charlene Mohammed, and K. Bruce Newbold, "Cultural Dimensions of Food Insecurity among Immigrants and Refugees," *Human Organization* 76, no. 1 (2017): 15–27, dx.doi.org/10.17730/0018-7259.76.1.15

20. Moffat et al, "Cultural Dimensions," 15–27.

21. Kristin Smith and Ann Tickamyer (ed.), *Economic Restructuring and Family Well-Being in Rural America*, (University Park, PA: Penn State University Press, 2011).

22. Elyzabeth W. Engle, "Coal Is in Our Food, Coal Is in Our Blood: Everyday Environmental Injustices of Rural Community Gardening in Central Appalachia," *Local Environment* 24, no. 8 (2019): 746–761.

23. Michele Morrone and Geoffrey Buckley (ed.), *Mountains of Injustice: Social and Environmental Justice in Appalachia*, (Columbus, OH: Ohio University Press, 2011).

24. Ronald Eller, *Uneven Ground: Appalachia Since 1945* (Lexington, KY: University Press of Kentucky, 2013).

25. Susan Keefe, *Participatory Development in Appalachia: Cultural Identity, Community, and Sustainability*, (Knoxville, TN: The University of Tennessee Press, 2009).

26. Stephen Fisher and Barbara Smith (ed.), *Transforming Places: Lessons from Appalachia*, (Champaign, IL: University of Illinois Press, 2012).

27. Appalachian Regional Commission, "The Appalachian Region," accessed June 10, 2019, arc.gov/appalachian_region/TheAppalachianRegion.asp

28. Elizabeth Catte, *What You Are Getting Wrong About Appalachia*, (Cleveland, OH: Belt Publishing, 2018).

29. Eller, *Uneven Ground*.

30. Fisher and Smith, *Transforming Places*.

31. Grow Appalachia, *Planting the Seeds for a Sustainable Future*, accessed April 23, 2018, growappalachia.berea.edu/#

32. Grow Appalachia, *Site Coordinator Manual*, (2016).

33. Grow Appalachia, *2016 Annual Report*, (2017).

34. Grow Appalachia, *Planting the Seeds*.

Chapter 4: Principle C—Protect Resources and Promote Fairness

1. Ruth Meinzen-Dick and Anna Knox, "Collective Action, Property Rights, and Devolution of Natural Resource Management: A Conceptual Framework" *International Food Policy and Research Institute* (Capri Working Paper no. 11, Vision Initiative, 1999).

2. Melissa Leach, Robin Mearns, and Ian Scoones, "Environmental Entitlements: Dynamics and Institutions in Community-Based Natural Resource Management," *World Development* 27, no. 2 (1999): 225–247.

3. Jessica Brown, Nora Mitchell, and Michael Beresford, "The Protected Landscape Approach: Linking Nature, Culture, and Community," IUCN–The World Conservation Union (2005), Gland, Switzerland, and Cambridge, UK.

4. Arian Spiteri and Sanjay Nepal, "Incentive-Based Conservation Programs in Developing Countries: A Review of Some Key Issues and Suggestions for Improvements" *Environmental Management* 37 (2006): 1–14, doi.org 10.1007/s00267-004-0311-7

5. Jeffrey D. Hackel, "Community Conservation and the Future of Africa's Wildlife," *Conservation Biology* 13 (1999): 726–734.

6. Adam Barker, "Capacity Building for Sustainability: Towards Community Development in Coastal Scotland," *Journal of Environmental Management* 75 (2005): 11–19.

7. Nicolas Gerber, Ephraim Nkonya, and Joachim Von Braun, "Land Degradation, Poverty and Marginality," *Marginality*, (Dordrecht: Springer, 2014), 181–202.

8. Jared Diamond, *Collapse: How Societies Choose to Fail or Succeed*, (New York: Viking Press, 2005).

9. Thomas Homer-Dixon, *The Upside of Down: Catastrophe, Creativity, and the Renewal of Civilization*, (Washington, DC: Island Press, 2006).

10. Note, my role was limited, but others in this initial advisory group, such as Emeritus Professor Mary Watzin of University of Vermont, were seminal to providing the needed knowledge, resources, and skills of fisheries ecological management and collaborating with these communities.

11. Mexico Forest—Electronic Journal of the National Forest Commission, accessed March 17, 2009, conafor.gob.mx

12. Heidi Asbjornsen and Mark Ashton, "Community Forestry in Oaxaca, Mexico," *Journal of Sustainable Forestry* 15, no. 1 (2002).

13. Kansas University webpage accessed 2009, ku.edu/ixtlandejuarez

14. Unidad Comunal Forestal Agropecuaria Y De Servicios, 2008, Community Brochures of Ixtlán de Juárez, Oaxaca, Mexico.

15. I was fortunate to interview one of the community partners (Sarah Hines) about this multidimensional urban initiative. Sarah works for the US Forest Services and was directly involved in the project.

16. Ibid, Sarah Hines interview.

17. Sarah Hines, Neha Srinivasan, Lauren Marshall, Morgan Grove, "Reclaiming Wood, Lives, and Communities: How Do We Turn a Waste Stream into an Asset That Revitalizes Cities?" learngala.com/cases/urbanwood/ (2017): 3–4

18. Hines et al., "Reclaiming," 3.

19. Ibid, 3.

20. Ibid, 4.

21. Redlining was a common method used in the 20th century as a method to discriminate against the African American population by denying federal mortgages in certain minority neighborhoods or communities. This practice started in Baltimore in the 1930s.

22. "Reclaiming," 4.

23. "Reclaiming," 5.

24. Bob Falk and David McKeever, "Generation and Recovery of Solid Wood Waste in the U.S." *BioCycle* 53 (2012): 30–32, biocycle.net/2012/08/15/generation-and -recovery-of-solid-wood-waste-in-the-u-s/

25. In the context of the urban revitalization initiative—and sustainable management of natural resources (wood, bricks, etc.) in Baltimore—the application of the triple bottom line framework will help address both social, environmental, and economic (financial) problems created by urban vacancy.

26. "Reclaiming," 5.

27. Co-production ensures that concrete and practical research suits decision makers.

28. Sarah Hines interview by Jacques Kenjio.

29. Hines, interview.

30. Hines, interview.

31. "Reclaiming," 8.

32. Ibid, 9.

33. Ian Duncan, "In 2010 Baltimore Had 16,800 Vacants. Eight Years and Millions of Dollars Later, the Number Is Down to 16,500" Baltimore Sun (2018): 1, baltimore

sun.com/maryland/baltimore-city/bs-md-ci-vacant-demolition-blocks-201802
27-story.html

34. Hines, interview.
35. Dipa Sharif, "Why We're Excited about Bricks and Boards," Quantified Ventures (2018): 2, medium.com/@QuantifiedVTS/why-were-excited-about-bricks-and-boards-c981d37c3233
36. Mutual of America, *Baltimore City Deconstruction Project*, 2018, youtube.com/watch?v=Drmgd33IRrs
37. "Reclaiming," 10.
38. Mutual of America, *Baltimore City Deconstruction Project.*
39. Hines interview.
40. Hines interview.
41. Mutual of America, *Baltimore City Deconstruction Project.*
42. Tushar Gandhi, amu.ac.in/about3.jsp?did=6284
43. Personal communication with the coordinator of the Center, Mrs. S. Lari.
44. Charity camp, amu.ac.in/about3.jsp?did=8563

Chapter 5: Principle D—Be Transparent

1. Sissela Bok, *Secrets: On the Ethics of Concealment and Revelation*, (Oxford: Oxford University Press, 1984).
2. Bok, *Secrets.*
3. John Rawls, *Theory of Justice*, (Cambridge, MA: Harvard University Press, 1971, Revised 1999).
4. Per Olsson, Carl Folke, and Filkret Berkes, "Adaptive Co-management for Building Resilience in Social-Ecological Systems," *Environmental Management* 34, no. 1 (2004): 75–90; Malcolm Newsom and Liz Chalk, "Environmental Capital: An Information Core to Public Participation in Strategic and Operational Decisions—The Example of River 'Best Practice' Projects," *Journal of Environmental Planning and Management* 47 (2004): 899–920.
5. Catherine Allan and Allan Curtis, "Nipped in the Bud: Why Regional Scale Adaptive Management Is Not Blooming," *Environmental Management* 36 (2005): 414–425; Lisa M. Campbell and Arja Vainio-Mattila, "Participatory Development and Community-Based Conservation: Opportunities Missed for Lessons Learned?" *Human Ecology* 31, no. 3 (2003): 417–437.
6. Derek Armitage, "Adaptive Capacity and Community-Based Natural Resource Management," *Environmental Management* 35 (2005): 703–715.
7. R. Edward Grumbine, "What Is Ecosystem Management?" *Conservation Biology* 8 (1994): 27–38; Newsom and Chalk, "Environmental Capital," 899–920.
8. Mihail Staynov, Bulgarian Project Director, Ministry of Environment. Public statement given at the first public hearing in Veliko Tarnovo, Bulgaria, 1997.
9. In October 1997, the Bulgarian National Assembly passed the Act for the Reduction of the Harmful Impact of Waste Upon the Environment, which developed a comprehensive solid waste program, addressing solid waste management through

programs for pollution abatement and prevention, as well as materials resource management.

10. This case study draws upon published accounts of this organization's work, outcomes from the 2019 Flavors of the Valley event, and a series of interviews.

11. This organization was formed in 1993. Betty Porter and Charlotte Faulkner were the project co-chairs and Delia Clark was the coordinator and later became the founding executive director.

12. Vital Communities' other programs are available on their website, vitalcommunities.org/

13. Interview with Allison Furbish, communications manager for Vital Communities, April 2019.

14. Furbish, interview.

15. Furbish, interview.

16. Interview with a vendor at the Flavors of the Valley 2019.

17. Interview with a resident attending the Flavors of the Valley 2019.

18. Staff member of Vital Communities during the Flavors of the Valley 2019.

19. A Panchayat is a village council that has an elected head and five reputable villagers acknowledged by the community as its governing body. This case study draws upon published accounts of Hiware Bazar's village council and interviews with community members.

20. Village Committees are comprised of villagers and officers to monitor various activities and regulations in the village.

21. *Shramdaan* is a traditional concept that means voluntary contribution involving physical effort.

22. Interview of Popatrao Baguji Pawar, who has been the village head *(Sarpanch)* for the past 25 years.

Chapter 6: Principle E—Support Research

1. Today, we all need to be cautious about our responses to the plethora of sensationalism, conspiracy theories, and click bait that invades our phones, emails, and social media accounts. Unfortunately, I have found that all too frequently this information exists to confuse and manipulate individuals, and society, into making poor decisions that benefit the promoters' self-serving interests.

2. Kelly F. Butler and Tom M. Koontz, "Theory into Practice: Implementing Ecosystem Management Objectives in the USDA Forest Service," *Environmental Management* 35 (2005): 138–150.

3. Ruth Meinzen-Dick and Anna Knox, "Collective Action, Property Rights, and Devolution of Natural Resource Management: A Conceptual Framework" *International Food Policy and Research Institute* (Capri Working Paper no. 11, Vision Initiative, 1999); Malcolm Newsom and Liz Chalk, "Environmental Capital: An Information Core to Public Participation in Strategic and Operational Decisions—The Example of River 'Best Practice' Projects," *Journal of Environmental Planning and Management* 47 (2004): 899–920.

4. Adam Barker, "Capacity Building for Sustainability: Towards Community Development in Coastal Scotland," *Journal of Environmental Management* 75 (2005): 11–19.

5. Earnest L. Boyer, "The Scholarship of Engagement," *Bulletin of the American Academy of Arts and Sciences* (1996): 18–33.

6. In the United States this approach has been endorsed by the EPA, CDC, NOAA, and other agencies. The United Nations UNESCO 2015 report *Global Trends in Support Structures for Community University Research Partnerships* describes where this approach is being applied around the globe.

7. Crystal Tremblay, Budd Hall, and Rajesh Tandon, *Global Trends in Support Structures for Community University Research Partnerships* (UNESCO, 2014).

8. Ibid.

9. Claudia Pahl-Wostl, Marc Craps, Art Dewulf, Erik Mosert, David Tabara, and Tharsi Taillieu, "Social Learning and Water Resources Management," *Ecology and Society* 12, no.2 (2007): 5.

10. D. Sanches and S. Rivera-Mills, "Engaged Scholarship: A Promising Road-Less-Travelled for STEM Science Cultures," *Society for Advancement of Hispanics /Chicanos and Native Americans in Science* (2014).

11. US Environmental Protection Agency, "A Review of Health Impact Assessments in the U.S: Current State-of-Science, Best Practices, and Areas for Improvement," (Cincinnati, OH: National Exposure Research Laboratory Office of Research and Development, 2013).

12. These partnerships are through the Environmental Studies Department, Antioch University New England, Keene, NH.

13. Team members include: Mohammad Bulle, Mohammad Taiea, Yves Pacifique Gakunde, and Lisa Yeaw; Community client: Hannah Grimes business incubators programs, Keene, NH.

14. Team members include: Chelsea Coombes and Chelsey Gorczyca. This co-op is located in Walpole, NH.

15. Livia Bizikova, Marcus Moench, Marius Keller, and Daniella Echeverria, "Climate Resilience and Food Security in Central America: A Practical Framework," *Climate and Development* 8, no. 5 (2016): 397–412, doi/10.1080/17565529.2015.106 4806

16. This study does not represent the views of the United States Peace Corps.

17. Encyclopedia Britannica, "Togoland," accessed August 2017, britannica.com/place /Togoland

18. The World Bank, "The World Bank in Togo," Last modified March 22, 2019, worldbank.org/en/country/togo/overview

19. Togo, BTI 2020—Togo Country Report, *Togo: Political and Economic Development (2013 to 2016) [Author's extended and up-dated version of "BTI 2016—Togo Country Report"]*, (Gütersloh, Germany: Bertelsmann Stiftung, 2016).

20. Prabhu Pingali, Luca Alinovi, and Jacky Sutton, "Food Security in Complex Emergencies: Enhancing Food System Resilience," *Disasters* 29, no. 1 (2005): 5–24, doi .org/10.1111/j.0361-3666.2005.00282.x

21. The World Bank, "The World Development Indicators Database—Country Profile: Togo," last modified April 24, 2019, databank.worldbank.org/data/views/reports/reportwidget.aspx?Report_Name=CountryProfile&Id=b45ofd57&tbar=y&dd=y&inf=n&zm=n&country=TGO

22. Divyanshi Wadhwa, "The Number of Extremely Poor People Continues to Rise in Sub-Saharan Africa," The World Bank, accessed September 19, 2018, blogs.world bank.org/opendata/number-extremely-poor-people-continues-rise-sub-saharan-africa

23. Rome, Food and Agriculture Organization of the United Nations, "The State of Food and Agriculture: Climate Change, Agriculture, and Food Security," (Food and Agricultural Organization of the United Nations, 2016).

24. Rüdiger Wittig et al., "A Study of Climate Change and Anthropogenic Impacts in West Africa," *Environmental Science Pollution Research* 14, no. 3 (2007): 182–189, doi.org/10.1065/espr2007.02.388

25. Frank Willett, "The Introduction of Maize into West Africa: An Assessment of Recent Evidence," *International African Institute* 32, no. 1 (1962): 1–13.

26. Photo with the participants' verbal consent to take and distribute.

27. Anne-Wil Harzing and Martha Maznevski, "The Interaction Between Language and Culture: A Test of the Cultural Accommodation Hypothesis in Seven Countries," *Language and Intercultural Communication* 2, no. 2 (2002): 120–139, doi.org/10.1080/14708470208668081

28. Seed funding gifted by Rachel Marshall, a long-time and much-respected Keene teacher, who presented the city with the opportunity to kick-start the lab activities that this partnership envisioned. The RMOLL was managed by Paul Bocko, Project Director of Antioch New England Institute.

29. David Sobel, *Beyond Ecophobia: Reclaiming the Heart in Nature Education* (Great Barrington, MA: Orion Society, 1999).

30. IUCN, "Commission on Environmental, Economic and Social Policy," accessed July 13, 2019, iucn.org/commissions/commission-environmental-economic-and-social-policy

31. Jeremy S. Brooks, "Design Features and Project Age Contribute to Joint Success in Social, Ecological, and Economic Outcomes of Community-Based Conservation Projects," *Conservation Letters* 10, no. 1 (2017): 23–32.

32. Grazia Borrini-Feyerabend, Jim Johnston, and Diane Pansky, "Governance of Protected Areas," in *Managing Protected Areas: A Global Guide*, ed. Michael Lockwood, Graeme Worboys, and Ashish Kothari, (London: Earthscan, (2006): 116–45.

33. Michael C. Gavin et al., "Defining Biocultural Approaches to Conservation," *Trends in Ecology & Evolution* 30, no. 3 (2015): 140.

34. Two manuscripts are in preparation for publication.

35. Mike Green, Henry Moore, and John O'Brien, *When People Care Enough to Act*, (Toronto: Inclusion Press, 2006).

36. Alison Mathie and Gord Cunningham, "From Clients to Citizens: Asset-Based

Community Development as a Strategy for Community-Driven Development,"
Development in Practice 13, no.5 (2003): 474–486.

37. John Kretzmann and John McKnight, *Building Communities from the Inside Out: A Path Toward Finding and Mobilizing a Community's Assets*, (Chicago: ACTA Publications, 1993).

38. Kretzmann and McKnight, *Building Communities*, 345.

39. Of the 94 participants, there were 40 females (F) and 54 males (M). The breakdown by village is a follows: (Magombera (F=10, M=15), Katurukila (F=8, M=12), Kanyenja (F=11, M=14), and Msolwa Station (F=11, M=13).

40. Questions used to guide the community visioning: How will you, meaning the individual village, manage the resources, and who will hold the community accountable? (Broken down by resource); In the case of a shared governance structure, which outside stakeholder would you want to partner with and why?; What measures do you think would improve communication and transparency with an outside stakeholder/partner?

41. Grazia Borrini-Feyerabend and Rosemary Hill, "Governance for the Conservation of Nature," in *Protected Area Governance and Management*, ed. Graeme Worboys et al., (Canberra: ANU Press, 2015): 169–206.

42. The most populous city in Tanzania.

43. Mathie and Cunningham, "From Clients," 474–486.

44. Mark S. Reed, "Stakeholder Participation for Environmental Management: A Literature Review," *Biological Conservation* 141, no. 10 (2008): 2417–2431.

45. Juliette Young et al., "Does Stakeholder Involvement Really Benefit Biodiversity Conservation?" *Biological Conservation* 158 (2003): 359–370.

Chapter 7: Principle F — Delegate and Empower

1. Derek Armitage, "Adaptive Capacity and Community-Based Natural Resource Management," *Environmental Management* 35, no. 6 (2005): 703–715; R. Edward Grumbine, "What Is Ecosystem Management?" *Conservation Biology*, 8, no. 1 (1994): 27–38; B. Child, "Lessons, Experiences, and Critical Conditions for CBNRM: Can Communities Conservation Bring International Goals Down to Earth?" Chairman's report from a workshop on the Millennium Ecosystem Assessment, Nordic Council of Ministers, Copenhagen, Denmark, from 29 October 2007 to 2 November 2007.

2. Armitage, "Adaptive capacity," 703–715; Grumbine, "What Is Ecosystem Management," 27–38; B. Child, "Lessons."

3. Per Olsson, Carl Folke, and Fikret Berkes, "Adaptive Co-management for Building Resilience in Social-Ecological Systems," *Environmental Management* 34, no. 1 (2004): 75–90.

4. Arun Agrawal and Clark C. Gibson, "Enchantment and Disenchantment: The Role of the Community in Natural Resource Conservation," *World Development* no. 4 (1999): 629–649; John M. Anderies, Marco A. Janssen, and Elinor Ostrom, "A Framework to Analyze the Robustness of Social-Ecological Systems," *Ecology and*

Society 9, no. 1 (2004): 18 [online] ecologyandsociety.org/vol9/iss1/art18/; Ruth Meinzen-Dick and Anna Knox, "Collective Action, Property Rights, and Devolution of Natural Resource Management: A Conceptual Framework" *International Food Policy and Research Institute* (Capri Working Paper no. 11, Vision Initiative, 1999).

5. Grumbine, "What Is Ecosystem Management?" 27–38.
6. Olsson, "Adaptive Co-management," 75–90.
7. Melissa Leach, Robin Mearns, and Ian Scoones, "Environmental Entitlements: Dynamics and Institutions in Community-Based Natural Resource Management," *World Development* 27, no. 2 (1999): 225–247, doi.org/10.1016?S0305-750X(98)00141-7
8. Denise Scheberle, "Moving Toward Community-Based Environmental Management: Wetland Protection in Door County," *American Behavioral Scientist* 44, no. 4 (2000): 564–578, doi.org/10.1177/00027640021956387
9. The institute, formed in 1993, was named Antioch New England Institute.
10. See Chapter 6, "Local Community-University Partnerships" for other examples of types of community assistance from universities.
11. M. Fuseina, interview by CRI staff, March 2019.
12. Fuseina interview.
13. Leslie Yetka of MCWD was a key leader in this public engagement and participation process.
14. Cities of Minneapolis and Lake Victoria.
15. University of Minnesota and Antioch University New England (AUNE).
16. The public engagement and participation process was a part of the Minnehaha Creek Watershed Stormwater Adaption Study. The co-principle investigators were Michael Simpson, from AUNE and Latham Stack, from Synthetic International. It received funding support from the Climate Program Office of NOAA.
17. Antioch New England Institute Annual Report.
18. See Chapter 14.

Chapter 8: Principle G—Earn Trust

1. Denise Scheberle, "Moving Toward Community-Based Environmental Management: Wetland Protection in Door County," *American Behavioral Scientist* 44, no. 4 (2000): 564–578, doi.org/10.1177/00027640021956387
2. Brian Walker et al., "Resilience Management in Socio-Ecological Systems: A Working Hypothesis for a Participatory Approach," *Conservation Ecology* 6, no.1 (2002): 14. consecol.org/vol6/iss1/art14/
3. Lisa M. Campbell and Arja Vainio-Mattila, "Participatory Development and Community-Based Conservation: Opportunities Missed for Lessons Learned?" *Human Ecology* 31, no. 3 (2003): 417–437.
4. Adam Barker, "Capacity Building for Sustainability: Towards Community Development in Coastal Scotland," *Journal of Environmental Management* 75, no. 1 (2005): 11–19.
5. Per Olsson, Carl Folke, and Filkret Berkes, "Adaptive Co-management for Build-

ing Resilience in Social-Ecological Systems," *Environmental Management* 34, no. 1 (2004): 75–90.

6. R. Edward Grumbine, "What Is Eccosystem Management?" *Conservation Biology* 8, no. 1 (1994): 27–38.

7. "Three Ways to Rebuild Citizens' Trust through Open Government," Web Foundation 2018, accessed May 15, 2019, webfoundation.org/news/?au=48

8. "Building Trust in Communities," University of Minnesota Extension (1994), accessed May 15, 2019, extension.umn.edu

9. "The Role and Importance of Building Trust," Penn State, College of Agricultural Sciences, Department of Agricultural Economics, Sociology, and Education, Center for Economic and Community Development, accessed May 16, 2019, aese.psu .edu.

10. "Three Ways."

11. "Building Trust in Communities."

12. Randolph Community Forest website includes the Forest Stewardship Plan, accessed June 10, 2019, randolphforest.org

13. B. Child and M. W. Lyman, "Natural Resources as Community Assets," *The Sand County Foundation*, Madison, WI, and The Aspen Institute (Washington, DC, 2005).

14. Randolph Community Forest website randolphforest.org

15. Ronald A. Heifetz and Martin Linsky, *Leadership on the Line: Staying Alive through the Dangers of Leading*, (Boston: Harvard Business School Press, 2002).

16. Russell W. Busch, "Tribal Advocacy for Elwha River Dams Removal on Washington's Olympic Peninsula," *Golden Gate University Environmental Law Journal*, no. 2 (2008): 5.

17. Laurence J. Kirmayer et al., "Rethinking Resilience from Indigenous Perspectives," *The Canadian Journal of Psychiatry* 56, no. 2 (February 2011): 84–91.

18. Research team includes Lower Elwha Klallam Tribe, US Geological Survey, NPS, University of Washington, National Oceanic and Atmospheric Administration (NOAA), Washington Sea Grant, Bureau of Reclamation, US Fish and Wildlife (WSFWS), Washington Department of Fish and Wildlife (WDFW), and the Elwha Research Consortium.

19. West Coast Environmental NGO that connects young people to the wonder and science of the natural world.

Chapter 9: Principle H—Embrace Feedback

1. Violet Mbit and Esther Kiruja, "Role of Monitoring and Evaluation on Performance of Public Organization Projects in Kenya: A Case of Kenya Meat Commission," *International Journal of Innovative Development & Policy Studies* 3, no. 3, (2015): 12–27.

2. John M. Anderies, Marco A. Janssen, and Elinor Ostrom, "A Framework to Analyze the Robustness of Social-Ecological Systems," *Ecology and Society* 9, no. 1 (2004): 18, ecologyandsociety.org/vol9/iss1/art18/; Jeffrey D. Hackel, "Community Conservation and the Future of Africa's Wildlife," *Conservation Biology* 13

(1999): 726–734; Malcolm Newsom and Liz Chalk, "Environmental Capital: An Information Core to Public Participation in Strategic and Operational Decisions— The Example of River 'Best Practice' Projects," *Journal of Environmental Planning and Management* 47 (2004): 899–920.

3. Derek Armitage, "Adaptive Capacity and Community-Based Natural Resource Management," *Environmental Management* vol. 35, no. 6 (2005): 703–715.

4. Per Olsson, Carl Folke, and Filkret Berkes, "Adaptive Co-management for Building Resilience in Social-Ecological Systems," *Environmental Management* 34, no. 1 (2004): 75–90.

5. Lisa M. Campbell and Arja Vainio-Mattila, "Participatory Development and Community-Based Conservation: Opportunities Missed for Lessons Learned?" *Human Ecology* 31, no. 3 (2003): 417–437; Anderies et al., 2004; B. Child and M. W. Lyman, "Natural Resources as Community Assets," *The Sand County Foundation,* Madison, WI, and The Aspen Institute (Washington, DC, 2005); Chairman's report from a workshop on the Millennium Ecosystem Assessment, Nordic Council of Ministers, Copenhagen, Denmark, from 29 October 2007 to 2 November 2007.

6. Olsson et al. 2004; Ruth Meinzen-Dick and Anna Knox, "Collective Action, Property Rights, and Devolution of Natural Resource Management: A Conceptual Framework" *International Food Policy and Research Institute* (Capri Working Paper no. 11, Vision Initiative, 1999).

7. A B-Corp is a Certified B Corporation. They are a "new kind of business that balances purpose and profit. They are legally required to consider the impact of their decisions on their workers, customers, suppliers, community, and the environment," bcorporation.net/

8. In 2017, Alanya's population was 299,464 per the *2017 Economic Report* (Alanya Chamber of Commerce, 2018): 24.

9. İbrahim Atalay, "The Effects of Mountainous Areas on Biodiversity: A Case Study from the Northern Anatolian Mountains and the Taurus Mountains," *Grazer Schriften der Geographie und Raumforschung* 41 (2006): 17–26. The Taurus Mountains are known for their rich biodiversity, especially flora native to the area.

10. Tourists visiting Alanya in 2017: 3,166,001 (*2017 Economic Report*: 25).

11. Mustafa Çakır (vice-chairman of the co-operative S.S. Alanya Su Ürünleri Kooperatifi), [interview] Can Yeniley, April 2019.

12. Gianpaolo Coro et al., "Forecasting the Ongoing Invasion of *Lagocephalus sceleratus* in the Mediterranean Sea," *Ecological Modelling* 371 (2018): 37–49. The silver-cheeked toadfish (*Lagocephalus sceleratus*) is native to the Pacific and Indian Oceans. Due to climate change it has entered Mediterranean Sea via the Suez Canal.

13. Nili Liphschitz and Cemal Pulak, "Wood Species Used in Ancient Shipbuilding in Turkey: Evidence From Dendroarchaeological Studies," *Skyllis* (2007): 73–82.

14. John L. Innes and Anna V. Tikina, *Sustainable Forest Management: From Concept to Practice* (Routledge: New York, 2017): 17.

15. Janice J. Gabbert, "Piracy in the Early Hellenistic Period: A Career Open to Talents," *Greece & Rome* 33, No. 2 (1986): 156–63.

16. Adrian Nicholas Sherwin-White, "Rome, Pamphylia and Cilicia, 133–70 B.C.," *The Journal of Roman Studies* 66 (1976): 1–14.

17. Philip de Souza, "Romans and Pirates in a Late Hellenistic Oracle from Pamphylia," *The Classical Quarterly*, 47, no. 2 (1997): 477–481.

18. G. E. Bean and T. B Mitford, "Sites Old and New in Rough Cilicia," *Anatolian Studies* 12 (1962): 185–217.

19. Even today the locals talk about how Cleopatra loved to swim at this beach that is known for its large-grain sand.

20. Çakır, 2019.

21. Çakır, 2019. Currently out of 94 registered fishermen, only 58 of them are co-op members.

22. Çakır, 2019.

23. In 2017, the tourism industry in Alanya generated approximately 2.2 billion dollars (US) in revenue for the local economy (*2017 Economic Report*, p. 25).

24. Mihai Macovei, *Growth and Economic Crises in Turkey: Leaving Behind a Turbulent Past?* Economic Papers 386 (Brussels: Economic and Financial Affairs, European Commission, 2009).

25. Michael M. Gunther, "Political Instability in Turkey During the 1970s," *Conflict Quarterly* (Winter 1989): 63–77.

26. Fikret Berkes, "Local-Level Management and the Commons Problem: A Comparative Study of Turkish Coastal Fisheries," *Marine Policy* 10, no. 3 (1986): 215–229.

27. Çakır, 2019.

28. Elinor Ostrom, *Governing the Commons* (United Kingdom: Cambridge University Press, 2015), p.19.

29. Berkes, "Local-Level," 215–229.

30. Çakır, 2019.

31. Çakır, 2019.

32. Berkes, "Local-Level," 215–229.

33. Ostrom, *Governing*, 19.

34. Ibid, 19.

35. Coro, Vilas, Magliozzi, Ellenbroek, Scarponi, and Pagano, "Forecasting the Ongoing," 37–49.

36. Çakır, 2019,

37. Garrett Hardin,"Tragedy of the Commons," *Science* 162, no. 3859 (1968), 1243–1248.

38. John M. Anderies and Marco A. Janssen, Sustaining the Commons, (Tempe, Arizona: Center for the Study of the Institutional Diversity, Arizona State University, 2013) V.

39. Ibid, 8.

40. Roy Morrison, *Ecological Democracy*, (Boston, MA: South End Press, 1995): 181.

41. Big Numbers Project (BNP), *Small-Scale Capture Fisheries: A Global Overview with Emphasis on Developing Countries*, (Big Numbers Project—FAO, World Fish Center, and PROFISH: World Bank, 2008).

42. World Bank, *Hidden Harvest: The Global Contribution of Capture Fisheries*, (Washington, DC: World Bank, 2012).

Chapter 10: Principle I—Practice Leadership

1. Malala Yousafzai, after nearly dying from an assassination attempt, continued her leadership work that was recognized through the award of the Nobel Peace Prize in 2014.

2. Greta Thunberg is a Swedish activist who began protesting outside the Swedish parliament focusing on the need for immediate action to combat climate change. Her TED talk has received worldwide attention and promoted critical global discussions.

3. James S. Gruber, "Key Principles of Community-Based Natural Resource Management: A Synthesis and Interpretation of Identified Effective Approaches for Managing the Commons," *Environmental Management* 45 (2010): 52–66.

4. Ronald A. Heifetz and Martin Linsky, *Leadership on the Line: Staying Alive through the Dangers of Leading* (Boston: Harvard Business School Press, 2002).

5. Ronald A. Heifetz, *Leadership Without Easy Answers* (Cambridge, MA: The Belknap Press of Harvard University Press, 1994).

6. Per Olsson, Carl Folke, and Filkret Berkes, "Adaptive Co-management for Building Resilience in Social-Ecological Systems," *Environmental Management* 34, no. 1 (2004): 75–90.

7. Peter M. Senge, *The Fifth Discipline Fieldbook: Strategies and Tools for Building a Learning Organization* (New York: Currency, Doubleday, 1994) and as discussed by others: Kelly F. Butler and Tom M. Koontz, "Theory into Practice: Implementing Ecosystem Management Objectives in the USDA Forest Service," *Environmental Management* 35 (2005): 138–150; A. R. Poteete and D. Welch, "Institutional Development in the Face of Complexity: Developing Rules for Managing Forest Resources," *Human Ecology* 32 (2004): 279–311.

8. Malcolm Newsom and Liz Chalk, "Environmental Capital: An Information Core to Public Participation in Strategic and Operational Decisions—The Example of River 'Best Practice' Projects," *Journal of Environmental Planning and Management* 47 (2004): 899–920; Brian Walker et al., "Resilience Management in Socio-Ecological Systems: A Working Hypothesis for a Participatory Approach," *Conservation Ecology* 6, no.1 (2002): 14, consecol.org/vol6/iss1/art14/

9. Derek Armitage, "Adaptive Capacity and Community-Based Natural Resource Management," *Environmental Management* vol. 35, no. 6 (2005): 703–715.

10. Denise Scheberle, "Moving Toward Community-Based Environmental Management: Wetland Protection in Door County," *American Behavioral Scientist* 44, no. 4 (2000): 564–578, doi.org/10.1177/00027640021956387

11. Melissa Leach, Robin Mearns, and Ian Scoones, "Environmental Entitlements:

Dynamics and Institutions in Community-Based Natural Resource Management," *World Development* 27 (1999): 225–247.

12. David Mathews, *For Communities to Work* (Ohio: The Kettering Foundation Press, 2002). The Kettering Foundation focuses on "basic political research—striving to understand how citizens and political systems can work together."

13. Horst W. J. Rittel and Melvin M. Webber, "Dilemmas in a General Systems Theory of Planning," *Policy Sciences* 4, no. 2 (1973): 155, doi.org/10.1007/BF01405730

14. Ronald Heifetz, "Eight Properties of Adaptive Work," adapted from the article "Adaptive Learning" in *Encyclopedia of Leadership*, edited by George R. Goethals, Georgia J. Sorenson, and James MacGregor Burns (MA: Berkshire Publishing Group, 2004).

15. Information in this case study was adapted from: *Sustainable Rural Development in Romania, Final Report*. Prepared by ISC and CET April 2003.

16. CET has the mission of supporting the sustainable development of the Cluj area.

17. ARDH has the goal of fostering communication and joint planning.

18. ISC helps communities in existing and emerging democracies, sustain.org/

19. Doctoral dissertation research (2009) by James Gruber.

20. Dan-Gabriel Parauan, previous President of CET, personal communication with James Gruber.

21. City of South Bend, *Vacant & Abandoned Properties Task Force Report* (South Bend: City of South Bend, 2013), 2. p. 2.

22. Ibid, 7.

23. "America's Dying Cities", *Newsweek*, January, 21, 2011, newsweek.com/americas-dying-cities-66873

24. *Vacant*, 3.

25. Ibid, 12.

26. Paige Ambord, telephone interview, April 2, 2019.

27. Jeff Parrot, "South Bend mayoral candidate says her code violations will help a push for 'equal protections,'" South Bend Tribune, March 28, 2019, southbendtribune.com/news/elections/south-bend-mayoral-candidate-says-her-code-violations-will-help/article_cbd0ec12-9dfe-5422-8b90-fa72b448258a.html

28. Timmy Broderick, "Pete Buttigieg tried to revive South Bend by tearing down homes. Did it work?," The Christian Science Monitor, April 5, 2019, csmonitor.com/USA/Politics/2019/0405/Pete-Buttigieg-tried-to-revive-South-Bend-by-tearing-down-homes.-Did-it-work

29. Ibid.

30. Danielle Fulmer, email interview, April 23, 2019.

31. Pam Myer, Elizabeth Maradik, email interview, April 23, 2019.

Chapter 11: Principle J—Decide Together

1. Thomas Dietz and Paul C. Stern (eds), "Public Participation in Environmental Assessment and Decision Making," *Division of Behavioral and Social Sciences and Education*, Committee on the Human Dimensions of Global Change (2009).

2. Thomas Dietz, Elinor Ostrom, and Paul C. Stern, "The Struggle to Govern the Commons," *Science* 302, no. 5652 (2003): 1907–1912; James Gruber and Delia Clark, "Building Sustainable Communities Through New Partnerships of Central and Local Governments: Lessons Learned from Eastern Europe and New England," 2000 International Conference on Sustainable Development, Environmental Conditions, and Public Management. *Sustainable Development, Environmental Conditions, and Public Management*, National Academy of Public Administration (US) and National Institute for Research Advancement (Japan), Tokyo, Japan, 2002 p. 264–286; Malcolm Newsom and Liz Chalk, "Environmental Capital: An Information Core to Public Participation in Strategic and Operational Decisions—The Example of River 'Best Practice' Projects," *Journal of Environmental Planning and Management* 47 (2004): 899–920; Denise Scheberle, "Moving Toward Community-Based Environmental Management: Wetland Protection in Door County," *American Behavioral Scientist* 44, no. 4 (2000): 564–578, doi.org/10.1177/00027640021956387; B. Child, "Lessons, Experiences, and Critical Conditions for CBNRM: Can Communities Conservation Bring International Goals Down to Earth?" Chairman's report from a workshop on the Millennium Ecosystem Assessment, Nordic Council of Ministers, Copenhagen, Denmark, from 29 Oct 2007 to 2 Nov 2007.

3. Brian Walker et al., "Resilience Management in Socio-Ecological Systems: A Working Hypothesis for a Participatory Approach," *Conservation Ecology* 6, no. 1 (2002): 14. consecol.org/vol6/iss1/art14/; Thomas Dietz, Elinor Ostrom, and Paul C. Stern, "The Struggle to Govern the Commons," *Science* 302, no. 5652 (2003): 1907–1912.

4. Arian Spiteri and Sanjay Nepal, "Incentive-Based Conservation Programs in Developing Countries: A Review of Some Key Issues and Suggestions for Improvements" *Environmental Management* 37 (2006): 1–14.

5. Arun Agrawal and Clark C. Gibson, "Enchantment and Disenchantment: The Role of the Community in Natural Resource Conservation," *World Development* 27, no. 4 (1999): 629–649; Dietz, Ostrom, and Stern, 2003; Paul M. Thompson, Parvin Sultana, and Nurul Islam, "Lessons from Community-Based Management of Floodplain Fisheries in Bangladesh," *Journal of Environmental Management* 69 (2003): 307–321.

6. Dietz and Stern "The Struggle to Govern the Commons."

7. Walker et al, 2002.

8. Published information and journal articles that describe the social and ecological research include: Universidad Técnica Particular de Loja (UTPL); Memorias del Taller "Trabajando juntos para la conservación de los páramos y lagunas de Oña, Saraguro y Yacuambi"; Proyecto descentralización y gestión de la conservación: un análisis de las decisiones que afectan a los humedales altoandinos y páramos de Oña, Saraguro y Yacuambi; Sandra Lee Pinel, Fausto López Rodriguez, Ramiro Morocho Cuenca, Diana Astudillo Aguillar and Danie Merriman, "Scaling down or scaling up? Local actor decisions and the feasibility of decentralized environmental governance: a case of Páramo wetlands in Southern Ecuador,"

Scottish Geographical Journal, (2018), doi.org/10.1080/14702541.2018.1439522; Iñiguez, M., J. Helsley, S. Pinel, J. Ammon, F. López, and K. Wendland, "Collaborative Community-based Governance in a Transboundary Wetland System in the Ecuadorian Andes" (2013).

9. A. Forsgren, S. Pinel, et al.,"The Social and Cultural Importance of High Andean Wetlands: Addressing the Stewardship Approach for Wetland Management," *The International Journal of Social Sustainability in Economic, Social, and Cultural Context* 10, no 1 (2015), doi.org/10.18848/2325-1115/CGP/v10i01/55255

10. State institutions include: SENAGUA, SENPLADES, MAE.

11. Agrawal and Gibson, "Enchantment"; John M. Anderies, Marco A. Janssen, and Elinor Ostrom, "A Framework to Analyze the Robustness of Social-Ecological Systems," *Ecology and Society*, vol. 9, no. 1 (2004): 18, ecologyandsociety.org/vol9 /iss1/art18/; Derek Armitage, "Adaptive Capacity and Community-Based Natural Resource Management," *Environmental Management* 35 (2005): 703–715; James S. Gruber, "Key Principles of Community-Based Natural Resource Management: A Synthesis and Interpretation of Identified Effective Approaches for Managing the Commons," *Environmental Management* 45 (2010): 52–66.

12. James S. Gruber, Jason L. Rhoades, Michael Simpson, Latham Stack, Leslie Yetka, and Robert Wood, "Enhancing Climate Change Adaptation: Strategies for Community Engagement and University-Community Partnerships," *Environmental Studies and Science* 7, no. 1 (2015), doi.org/10.1007/s13412-015-0232-1

13. Gruber, "Key Principles."

Chapter 12: Principle K—Strengthen the Foundation

1. Jeffrey Linkenbach, "The Positive Community Norms Workbook," (2012), accessed July 8, 2019, montanainstitute.com; static1.squarespace.com/static/51c386a4e4b 0c275d0a5bbf2/t/58e7b96dff7c5020c21121b5/1491581302087/INTRO+TO+POSI TIVE+COMMUNITY+NORMS.pdf

2. "Norm," WebFinance, Inc., accessed July 04, 2019, businessdictionary.com/defini tion/norm.html

3. Ibid.

4. Linda Lear, *Rachel Carson: Witness for Nature* (New York, NY, Mariner Books, 2009).

5. Thomas A. Heberlein, *Navigating Environmental Attitudes* (New York, NY: Oxford University Press, 2012), Chapter 6.

6. Paul M. Thompson, Parvin Sultana, and Nurul Islam, "Lessons from Community-Based Management of Floodplain Fisheries in Bangladesh," *Journal of Environmental Management* 69 (2003): 307–321.

7. Arun Agrawal and Clark C. Gibson, "Enchantment and Disenchantment: The Role of the Community in Natural Resource Conservation" *World Development* 27, no. 4 (1999): 629–649.

8. Ruth Meinzen-Dick and Anna Knox, "Collective Action, Property Rights, and Devolution of Natural Resource Management: A Conceptual Framework,"

International Food Policy and Research Institute (Capri Working Paper no. 11, Vision Initiative, 1999).

9. Brooke A. Zanetell and Barbara A. Knuth, "Participation Rhetoric or Community-Based Management Reality? Influences on Willingness to Participate in a Venezuelan Freshwater Fishery," *World Development* 32, no. 5 (2004): 793–807, doi.org/10.1016/j.worlddev.2004.01.002

10. Denise Scheberle, "Moving Toward Community-Based Environmental Management," *American Behavioral Scientist* 44, no. 4 (2000): 564–578, doi.org/10.1177/00027640021956387

11. John M. Anderies, Marco A. Janssen, and Elinor Ostrom, "A Framework to Analyze the Robustness of Social-Ecological Systems," *Ecology and Society*, 9, no. 1 (2004): 18 ecologyandsociety.org/vol9/iss1/art18/; Elinor Ostrom, *Governing the Commons* (United Kingdom: Cambridge University Press, 2015), p.19.

12. Jeff Linkenbach, "An Introduction to Positive Community Norms," accessed June 20, 2019, static1.squarespace.com/static/51c386a4e4b0c275d0a5bbf2/t/58e7b96dff7c5020c21121b5/1491581302087/INTRO+TO+POSITIVE+COMMUNITY+NORMS.pdf.

13. This religious community is Eglise Liloba Na Nzambe, Sous L'Inspiration Du Saint-Esprit.

14. This cooperative is Ou Allons Nous—Oan, a non-governmental organization (NGO) in the DRC.

15. Beginning by asking about strengths and accomplishments is important both for assessment and to build trust and confidence. This is central to an approach to positive change called "Appreciative Inquiry." David L. Cooperrider, Diana Whitney, and Jacqueline M. Stavros, *Appreciative Inquiry Handbook: For Leaders of Change*, (Brunswick, OH: Crown Custom Publishers, 2008) and Mark Branson, *Memories, Hopes and Conversations: Appreciative Inquiry, Missional Engagement and Congregational Change, Second Edition*, (Landham, MD: Rowan and Littlefield Publishers, 2016).

16. Marvin Weisbord and Sandra Janoff, *Future Search: An Action Guide to Finding Common Ground in Organizations and Communities*, (Oakland, CA: Barret and Koehler Publishers, 2000).

17. Dr. M. Gail Jones is Alumni Distinguished Professor of science education and Fellow at the Friday Institute for Educational Innovation.

18. Brett Bruyere, Ethan Billingsley, and Lori O'Day, "A Closer Examination of Barriers to Participation in Informal Science Education for Latinos and Caucasians," *Journal of Women and Minorities in Science and Engineering* 15, no. 1 (2009): 1–14.

19. Kimberly Shinew, Myron Floyd, and Diana Parry, "Understanding the Relationship Between Race and Leisure Activities and Constraints: Exploring an Alternative Framework," *Leisure Sciences* 26, no. 2 (2004): 181–199.

20. This work was supported by the National Science Foundation (Grant No. DGE-1252376 and ITEST Grant No. 1614468). Any opinions expressed in this material are those of the authors and do not necessarily reflect the views of NSF.

21. Bruyere, Billingsley, and O'Day, "Closer."
22. My colleagues who were seminal in completing this work included Delia Clark, Jessica Brown, Jacqueline K.S. Truesdale, and Sietske Smith.
23. Community foundations are local community philanthropy organizations that provide a long-term sustainable mechanism for community support.
24. The Baltic American Partnership Fund: Ten Years of Grantmaking to Strengthen Civil Society in Estonia, Latvia, and Lithuania, 2008.
25. Antioch New England Institute (ANEI) of Antioch University New England, a nonprofit consulting group with the mission: "Engaging people in the process of creating environmentally healthy, culturally rich, and economically strong schools and communities through leadership training, environmental education, and applied research."
26. ANEI partnered with The Quebec-Labrador Foundation's Atlantic Center for the Environment for this project.
27. Quote from program assessment.

Chapter 13: Principle L—Resolve Conflicts

1. Thomas Dietz, Elinor Ostrom, and Paul C. Stern, "The Struggle to Govern the Commons," *Science* 302, no. 5652 (2003): 1907–1912; Ruth Meinzen-Dick and Anna Knox, "Collective Action, Property Rights, and Devolution of Natural Resource Management: A Conceptual Framework" *International Food Policy and Research Institute* (Capri Working Paper no. 11, Vision Initiative, 1999); Elinor Ostrom, *Governing the Commons* (United Kingdom: Cambridge University Press, 2015), p.19.
2. Arian Spiteri and Sanjay Nepal, "Incentive-Based Conservation Programs in Developing Countries: A Review of Some Key Issues and Suggestions for Improvements," *Environmental Management* 37 (2006): 1–14.
3. Melissa Leach, Robin Mearns, and Ian Scoones, "Environmental Entitlements: Dynamics and Institutions in Community-Based Natural Resource Management," *World Development* 27 (1999): 225–247.
4. Denise Scheberle, "Moving Toward Community-Based Environmental Management," *American Behavioral Scientist* 44, no. 4 (2000): 564–578, doi.org/10.1177/00027640021956387
5. Jeffrey D. Hackel, "Community Conservation and the Future of Africa's Wildlife," *Conservation Biology* 13 (1999): 726–734.
6. John M. Anderies, Marco A. Janssen, and Elinor Ostrom, "A Framework to Analyze the Robustness of Social-Ecological Systems," *Ecology and Society*, vol. 9, no. 1 (2004): 18, ecologyandsociety.org/vol9/iss1/art18/
7. Simon Fisher, Dekha I. Abdi, Jawed Ludin, Richard Smith, Sue Williams, and Steven Williams, *Working with Conflict: Skills and Strategies for Action* (London, UK: The Bath Press, 2000).
8. The city manager of Keene at the time was John Maclean.
9. Wicked problems are discussed in Chapter 10.

10. CTAP was initiated in 2005. Ansel Sanborn of NH-DOT was the director of the CTAP program. James Gruber served as the director of Antioch New England Institute.

11. Ghana's Environment Protection Agency/Ministry of Environment, Science, Technology, and Innovation (2000). Northern Savannah Biodiversity Conservation Project. EPA/Ghana.

12. Caroline Abel and Kofi Busia, "An Exploratory Ethnobotanical Study of the Practice of Herbal Medicine by the Akan Peoples of Ghana," *Alternative Medicine Review* 10, no. 2 (2005): 112–122.

13. Komla Tsey, "Traditional Medicine in Contemporary Ghana: A Public Policy Analysis," *Social Science & Medicine* 45, no. 7 (1997): 1065–1074.

14. Ghana Statistical Service, 2000 Population and Housing Census: Summary Report of the Final Report.

15. Tsey, "Traditional Medicine," 1065–1074.

16. Kofi B. Barimah, "Traditional Healers in Ghana: So Near to the People, yet so Far Away From the Basic Health Care System," *TANG Humanitas Medicine* 6, no. 2 (2016): 1–7, doi.org/10.5667/tang.2016.0004

17. Debra Hassig, "Transplanted Medicine: Colonial Mexican Herbals of the Sixteenth Century," *Anthropology and Aesthetics* 17/18 (1989): 30–53.

18. Abel and Busia, "An Exploratory Ethnobotanical Study," 112–122.

Chapter 14: A Toolbox of Leadership Strategies

1. One visioning approach is effectively described in Marvin Weisbord and Sandra Janoff, *Future Search: An Action Guide to Finding Common Ground in Organizations and Communities*, (Oakland, CA: Barret and Koehler Publishers, 1995).

2. National Research Council, 2010 Report: "Adapting to the Impacts of Climate Change," accessed August 24, 2019, nap.edu/catalog/12783/adapting-to-the-impacts-of-climate-change

3. Stefka Tzekova, 1998, at a forum of the Bulgarian National Solid Waste Program.

4. Climate Change Initiative managed by Antioch University New England; M. Simpson director; NOAA funded.

5. National Research Council 2010 Report.

6. Two exceptional books on planning and facilitating a participatory decision-making meeting are Sam Kaner with Lenny Lind, Catherine Toldi, Sarah Fisk, and Duane Berger, *Facilitator's Guide to Participatory Decision Making*, New Society Publishing (1996), and Marvin Weisbord and Sandra Janoff, *Future Search*.

7. UN Environment Assembly 2019: A programme of events.

8. UN Environment Assembly 2019.

Index

A

abandoned properties, 9, 76–86, 207–212
accountability. *See* Embrace Feedback
  (Principle H)
action plans, 296–297
actions
  feedback, 299, 301
  implementation of, 298–299
adaptive leadership, 5–6, 198, 199–200,
  283–284
  See also Practice Leadership
  (Principle I)
adaptive transformative leadership, 169
agendas, setting, 285–286
agriculture
  local food, 99–103, 115
  resource management, 9–10, 103–109
Alanya, Turkey, 187–195
Albania, 63–66
Alhassan, Walisu, 143
Aligarh, India, 87–91
Ambord, P., 207–212
Andes, Ecuador, 225–233
Antioch New England Institute, 6
Antioch University New England, 6, 114,
  252
Appalachia, 53–58
Apuseni Mountains, Huedin, Romania,
  201–207
Arnstein, Sherry, 21
Arora, Shilpy, 103–109
assessment of issue, 286–288
asset mapping, 130–131
Asset-Based Community Development
  (ABCD), 126–135, 287

Association for Rural Development of
  Huedin, 201–207
Astudillo, Diana, 225–233
Atlantic Center for the Environment, 252
authority devolution. *See* Delegate and
  Empower (Principle F)
awareness of issue, 285–286

B

Baltic-American Partnership Fund, 252
Baltimore, Maryland, USA, 9, 76–86
Baltimore Office of Sustainability, 80
Banoenoma, Mr., 272–273, 277, 279–280
barriers, identification of, 290–292
"Barriers and Solutions" process, 291–292
Be Transparent (Principle D)
  case studies: main, 98–109
  case studies: supplemental, 28, 29, 50,
    57, 69, 70, 75, 82, 120, 121, 132, 149, 150,
    151, 152, 163, 165, 166, 172, 183, 185, 191,
    204, 209, 222, 228, 229, 230, 244, 245,
    246, 255, 271
  characteristics/research, 94
  effective communication, 93, 95–98
  suggestions/best practices, 110
Beg, Mirza I., 87–91
Beg, Tazeen, 87–91
Belmonte, Jesus Alberto, 72
benefit distribution. *See* Protect Resources
  and Promote Fairness (Principle C)
bike path development, 139–142
Bikotiba, Togo, 116–124
Bissonnette, Chad, 32–38
Bocko, Paul, 125–126
Boston, Massachusetts, USA, 219–225

Boston Nature Center, 223–224
Boult, David, 47
Brick & Board, 84
built capital, 12, 14
Bulgaria, 20–21, 95
Bureau of Indian Affairs, 115–116
business management, 181–187
Buttigieg, Pete, 207–210

C
Camp Small, 81
Capacity Rural International, 142–148
Carson, Rachel, 237
change, implementation of, 200–201,
    298–299
Chapola, Jebunnessa, 47–53
Chase's Mill, 217–219
church community, 242–249
citizen participation. *See* Involve Everyone
    (Principle A)
citizen scientists, 113
citizens, levels of involvement, 137
Clark, Delia, 6, 140
Clean Energy Team, 28
climate change adaptation plan, 148–153
climate change planning, 25–32
climate crisis, 11
Clubul Ecologic Transylvania, 201–207
collaborative partnerships. *See* Work
    Together (Principle B)
collaborative planning approach
    action plan, 296–297
    actions, 298–299
    agenda setting, 285–286
    barriers and solutions, 290–292
    convening and assessing, 286–288
    feedback and base of support, 299, 301
    impact vs. feasibility, 292–294
    legitimation, 298
    partners and resources, 295–296
    visioning and objectives, 288–290
Collapse (Diamond), 62
co-management, 198, 199–200
communication. *See* Be Transparent
    (Principle D)

communities
    building inclusiveness, 301–303
    challenges, 11
    health and vitality of, 1–3, 9–10
    values, 238
community capital, 6, 12–14
community forests, 159–169, 277–278
community foundations, 251–257
community gardens, 9, 47–58, 272–280
community leaders
    accountability, 180
    building trust, 158–159
    involvement of, 298
community meetings
    organizing, 300
    See also collaborative planning approach
community members
    mobilizing, 197, 199
    soliciting feedback from, 179–180
community norms, 235–237
community participation. *See* Delegate
    and Empower (Principle F); Involve
    Everyone (Principle A)
community philanthropy, 251–257
Community Technical Assistance
    Program, 265–272
community visioning, 131–133, 267–268,
    288–290
community-based resource management.
    See Protect Resources and Promote
    Fairness (Principle C)
community-led development, 32–38, 142–148
conflicts. *See* Resolve Conflicts
    (Principle L)
congregations, 242–249
conservation agencies, 260
control. *See* Delegate and Empower
    (Principle F)
convening event, 286–288
cooperation. *See* Resolve Conflicts
    (Principle L)
cooperatives, 115
core values, 238
cross-cultural participatory activities,
    49–50

cultural capital, 14
curbside recycling program, 157–158

D

dam removal, 169–175
Datta, Ranjan, 47–53
Decide Together (Principle J)
  case studies: main, 219–233
  case studies: supplemental, 29, 33, 48,
    50, 70, 71, 106, 107, 120, 121, 122, 129,
    130, 147, 149, 153, 164, 165, 166, 172,
    191, 203, 204, 209, 243, 246, 248, 253,
    254, 255, 266, 275
  characteristics/research, 216
  effective participatory approach, 217–219
  suggestions/best practices, 234
  "us" vs. "them," 215
decision making
  in collaborative planning approach, 298
  See also Decide Together (Principle J);
    Delegate and Empower (Principle F)
Delegate and Empower (Principle F)
  case studies: main, 142–153
  case studies: supplemental, 38, 50, 56, 70,
    71, 82, 88, 106, 107, 120, 121, 130, 166,
    172, 191, 203, 204, 205, 222, 229, 230,
    231, 244, 246, 247, 248, 253, 270, 271, 275
  characteristics/research, 138
  citizen involvement, 137
  devolution of authority, 139–142
  suggestions/best practices, 154
democracy
  accountability and, 180
  characteristics of, 95
  citizen role in, 10, 21
dessert bake-off, 295
Details Deconstruction, 80, 84
Diamond, Jared, 62

E

Earn Trust (Principle G)
  case studies: main, 159–175
  case studies: supplemental, 29, 37, 70,
    82, 89, 103, 107, 120, 121, 150, 184, 185,
    191, 204, 227, 228, 243, 244, 274, 275

characteristics/research, 156
  credibility of neighbors, 157–158
  elements of, 158–159
  in healthy communities, 155
  suggestions/best practices, 176
economic development, 201–207, 278–279
ecosystems
  changing community norms, 237
  feedback model, 177
  restoration, 169–175
ecotourism, 74–75, 205
education
  community participation, 219–225
  ecological research, 125–126
  family science program, 249–251
  for girls, 87–91
  herbalist training, 272–280
  sustainable development of, 143–145
Elofson, Patricia, 170
Elwha River, Washington, USA, 169–175
Embrace Feedback (Principle H)
  case studies: main, 181–195
  case studies: supplemental, 28, 29, 70,
    74, 82, 103, 106, 107, 120, 121, 130, 131,
    132, 151, 172, 173, 205, 209, 221, 228,
    230, 232, 244, 246, 247, 248, 255, 275
  characteristics/research, 178
  leader accountability, 180–181
  nature's model, 177
  soliciting responses, 179–180
  suggestions/best practices, 196
employment opportunities, 9, 76–86
empowerment. *See* Delegate and Empower
  (Principle F)
Engage Globally, 142–148
engaged scholarship, 112, 114
Engle, Elyzabeth W., 53–58
Ennes, Megan, 249–251
environmental protection, livelihoods and,
  63–66, 201–207, 225–233
Estonia, 251–257
Expanded Learning Time grant program,
  221–223
expert-driven approaches, 3–4, 10–11, 21,
  115–116

F

"fake news," 93

family science program, 249–251

feasibility, assessing, 292–294

feedback, 299, 301

    See also Embrace Feedback (Principle H); Involve Everyone (Principle A)

feedback advisory groups, 299

Fian, Ghana, 272–280

Fifth Discipline (Senge), 198

financial capital, 14

fisheries management, 187–195

Flavors of the Valley, 99–103

food, local, 99–103

Food Secure Canada, 47

food security, 9, 47–58, 116–124

forests, management, 66–76, 126–135, 159–169, 277–278

furniture factory, 71–74

future, vision for, 288–290

G

Gandhi, Tushar, 87

Ghana, 142–148

Gilsum, New Hampshire, USA, 181–187

global community, development of, 301–303

government, participatory, 106

government secrecy, 95

Graff, Walter, 162–169

Gran Sous, La Gonave, Haiti, 32–38

Great River Consumer Cooperative Society, 115

greenhouse construction, 43

Grove, J. M., 76–86

Grow Appalachia, 53–58

Guiding Principles

    development of, 13, 15–17

    research into, 7–8

    See also *specific principles*

H

Hannah Grimes Center, 114

Hardin, Garrett, 194

Hartford, Vermont, USA, 5–6, 44–46

health care, 272–280

Heckel, Heather, 32–38, 142–148

Heifetz, Ron, 5, 200

herbal garden, 272–280

highway expansion, effect on communities, 265–272

Hines, S., 76–86

Hiware Bazar, India, 9–10, 103–109

Homer-Dixon, Thomas, 62

Hoppin, Bo, 219–225

human capital, 14

Humanim Inc., 80, 84

I

immigrant communities, food security, 9, 47–53

Impact vs. Feasibility process, 293–294

Indigenous communities

    ecosystem restoration, 169–175

    expert-driven approaches, 115–116

    food security, 116–124

    natural resource management, 66–76

    relationships with, 49

    wetlands conservation, 225–233

information development. *See* Support Research (Principle E)

information sharing. *See* Be Transparent (Principle D)

Institute for Sustainable Communities, 204

international aid dependency, 32–38, 142

Involve Everyone (Principle A)

    case studies: main, 25–38

    case studies: supplemental, 48, 56, 70, 71, 75, 79, 82, 102, 105, 106, 107, 120, 121, 122, 129, 130, 132, 147, 148, 149, 151, 152, 163, 164, 165, 166, 170, 172, 173, 183, 185, 191, 203, 204, 205, 209, 222, 227, 228, 229, 230, 232, 245, 246, 253, 255, 266, 273, 275

    characteristics/research, 20

    public participation, 19, 21–24

    suggestions/best practices, 39

Ismat Literacy and Handicraft Centre, 87–91

Ixtlán de Juárez, Oaxaca, Mexico, 66–76

J

Jones, M. Gail, 249–251

K

Keene, New Hampshire, USA, 25–32, 125–126, 140–142, 179, 262–264
Kenjio, Jacques, 76–86, 99–103, 207–212
Kentucky, USA, 53–58
Kibler, K. M., 116–124
Kinshasa, Democratic Republic of the Congo, 239–241
Kiriscioglu, Tanju (TK), 187–195
Kretzmann, John, 129

L

Lake Ohrid, Albania/Macedonia, 63–66
landfill site, 23–24
landlords, 29–30, 262–264
Lari, Sabiha, 87
Latvia, 21, 251–257
leaders
    accountability, 180
    building trust, 158–159
    involvement of, 298
leadership. *See* adaptive leadership; collaborative planning approach; Practice Leadership (Principle I)
Leadership without Easy Answers (Heifetz), 5
legitimacy. *See* Earn Trust (Principle G)
legitimation, 298
Lithuania, 251–257
local food, 99–103
Lopez, Fausto, 225–233
Lower Elwha Klallam Tribe, 169–175

M

Macedonia, 63–66
Magombera Forest, Tanzania, 126–135
marginalized groups, 20, 47–53, 66–76, 87–91, 138–139, 159, 286
Markowitz, Paul, 201–207
Marshall, L., 76–86
Maryland Department of Housing and Community Development, 80

Maryland Department of Natural Resources, 80
material reclamation, 9, 76–86
Mathews, David, 199
Mauer, K. Whitney, 169–175
McKnight, John, 129
meetings
    organizing, 300
    stakeholder, 134–135
    See also collaborative planning approach
Mestiza people, 225–233
Mill Hollow Heritage Association, 218–219
Mill Hollow, New Hampshire, USA, 217–219
Minnehaha Creek Watershed District, 148–153
Minnesota, USA, 148–153
misinformation, 93
monitoring. *See* Embrace Feedback (Principle H)
Morocho, Ramiro, 225–233
museums, 249–251

N

Nabón people, 225–233
National Forest Commission, 76
National Park Service, 173, 175
National Research Council, 295
natural capital, 13, 14, 63
natural resource management
    fisheries, 187–195
    forests, 66–76, 126–135, 159–169, 277–278
    herbal medicine, 272–280
    protection and economic development, 201–207
    water, 9–10, 103–109
    See also Protect Resources and Promote Fairness (Principle C)
neighborhoods
    complaints, 262–264
    revitalization, 9, 76–86, 207–212
New Hampshire Department of Transportation, 265–272
New Hampshire, USA, 99–103, 265–272
Newsweek, 208

North Carolina, USA, 249–251
Norwich, Vermont, USA, 242–249
Nyerengen, J., 276

O
objectives, setting, 288–290
Ohrid, Macedonia, 63–66
1,000 Houses in 1,000 Days initiative,
    209–211
outdoor family science program, 249–251

P
Pacheco Rodriguez, C. Luis, 68
Parks & People Foundation, 81, 82, 83, 85
participatory conservation, 260
participatory decision making. *See* collab-
    orative planning approach; Decide
    Together (Principle J); Delegate and
    Empower (Principle F)
partners, leveraging assistance, 295–296
partnerships. *See* Work Together
    (Principle B)
Pawar, Popatrao Baguji, 103–104
Peasant Association for the Development
    and Advancement of Gran Sous, 32–38
philanthropy, 251–257
Phillips, Charlene, 265–272
Pinel, Sandra, 225–233
plan, formulation of, 296–297
Pogradec, Albania, 63–66
political capital, 14
power
    secrecy and, 95
    See also Delegate and Empower
    (Principle F)
Practice Leadership (Principle I)
    case studies: main, 201–212
    case studies: supplemental, 37, 38, 50, 70,
        71, 82, 83, 107, 120, 129, 130, 131, 148,
        149, 151, 152, 164, 166, 170, 185, 187, 192,
        221, 222, 231, 232, 243, 245, 253, 254, 275
    change implementation, 200–201
    characteristics/research, 198
    critical actions, 197, 199–200
    suggestions/best practices, 213

Principle A. *See* Involve Everyone
Principle B. *See* Work Together
Principle C. *See* Protect Resources and
    Promote Fairness
Principle D. *See* Be Transparent
Principle E. *See* Support Research
Principle F. *See* Delegate and Empower
Principle G. *See* Earn Trust
Principle H. *See* Embrace Feedback
Principle I. *See* Practice Leadership
Principle J. *See* Decide Together
Principle K. *See* Strengthen the
    Foundation
Principle L. *See* Resolve Conflicts
principles
    development of, 13, 15–17
    research into, 7–8
    See also *specific principles*
problem solving, participatory. *See* Decide
    Together (Principle J)
Protect Resources and Promote Fairness
    (Principle C)
    case studies: main, 66–91
    case studies: supplemental, 29, 38, 48,
        50, 102, 103, 105, 106, 107, 130, 132, 164,
        165, 166, 170, 191, 192, 203, 230, 232,
        245, 273, 274, 276
    characteristics/research, 62
    community-based resource
        management, 61, 63–66
    suggestions/best practices, 92
protected areas, 126–135
public hearings, 96–98
public participation. *See* Involve Everyone
    (Principle A)
Putnam, Robert, 11, 43
"pyramid scheme," 157–158

Q
Quantified Ventures, 81
Quebec-Labrador Foundation, 252

R
Rachel Marshall Outdoor Learning Lab,
    125–126

Ramsar Wetland designation, 229–231
Randolph Community Forest, New
    Hampshire, USA, 159–169
recycling centers, 5–6, 44–46
refugee communities, food security, 9,
    47–53
rental housing complaints, 262–264
research. *See* Support Research
    (Principle E)
Resolve Conflicts (Principle L)
    case studies: main, 264–280
    case studies: supplemental, 29, 48, 50,
        83, 106, 107, 120, 121, 164, 165, 192, 229,
        230, 231, 244, 248, 255
    characteristics/research, 260
    preventing conflict, 259, 261
    suggestions/best practices, 281
    understanding and addressing conflict,
        261–264
resource management. *See* natural
    resource management; Protect
    Resources and Promote Fairness
    (Principle C)
resource-dependent groups, 138
resources, leveraging, 44–45, 295–296
Reyes, Francis (Paco), 67
Room & Board, 81, 85
Roots of Development, 32–38
rural communities, food security, 53–58

S
Salas, Shaylin, 25–32, 99–103, 207–212
Sanborn, Ansel, 266
Saraguro people, 225–233
Saraguro-Oña-Yacuambi Wetlands,
    225–233
Saskatoon, Saskatchewan, Canada, 9, 47–53
Scarinza, John, 162–169
schools, participatory decision making,
    225–233
science centers, 249–251
Senge, Peter, 198
Shuar people, 225–233
Siddiqui, Jamila Majid, 87
Silent Spring (Carson), 237

social capital
    about, 14, 42, 43
    building, 228
    See also Strengthen the Foundation
        (Principle K); Work Together
        (Principle B)
social foundation, 217
    See also Strengthen the Foundation
        (Principle K)
solid waste management, 23–24, 96–98
solutions, identification of, 290–292
South Bend, Indiana, USA, 207–212
Srinivasan, N., 76–86
S.S. Alanya Su Ürünleri Kooperatifi,
    191–195
St. Jude Herbal Centre and Garden,
    272–280
stakeholder meetings, 134–135
stakeholder mobilization. *See* Involve
    Everyone (Principle A)
Stoddard, Patience, 242–249
stormwater adaptation project, 148–153
Strengthen the Foundation (Principle K)
    case studies: main, 241–257
    case studies: supplemental, 28, 29, 48,
        74, 79, 102, 103, 105, 106, 107, 121, 129,
        130, 147, 164, 165, 204, 210, 222, 227,
        228, 230, 274
    characteristics/research, 236
    community norms, 237
    social foundation, 235, 238–241
    suggestions/best practices, 258
Struga, Macedonia, 63–66
Sullivan County, New Hampshire, USA,
    96–98
Sumani, John Bosco, 272–280
Support Research (Principle E)
    case studies: main, 116–135
    case studies: supplemental, 29, 33, 50, 71,
        72, 79, 82, 105, 107, 149, 150, 151, 152,
        164, 170, 172, 173, 184, 191, 204, 209,
        227, 228, 232, 245, 247, 254, 255, 267, 275
    characteristics/research, 112
    partners for, 113–116
    questions, 111

suggestions/best practices, 136
workshop assessment of, 233–234
sustainable community development,
     142–148
sustainable economic development, 63,
     201–207, 225–233
Swansea, Massachusetts, USA, 139–140

T
Thunberg, Greta, 199
toilet design, 21
top-down approaches, 3–4, 10–11
town report cards, 180–181
"The Tragedy of the Commons" (Hardin),
     194
transparency. *See* Be Transparent
     (Principle D)
trust. *See* Earn Trust (Principle G)
12 Guiding Principles
     development of, 13, 15–17
     research into, 7–8
     See also *specific principles*

U
Udzungwa Forest Project, 128
underrepresented groups, 249–251
United Nations 4th Environmental
     Assembly, 301–303
United Nations Food and Agriculture
     Organization (FAO), 47
United States Forest Service (USFS),
     76–86
Universidad Técnica Particular de Loja,
     225–233
university partnerships, 114
Un-Shopping Center, 5–6, 44–46
Upper Valley region, New Hampshire/
     Vermont, USA, 99–103
The Upside of Down (Homer-Dixon), 62
urban redevelopment, 9, 76–86, 207–212
urban renewal efforts, 4

V
vacant homes, 9, 76–86, 207–212
Veliko Tarnovo, Bulgaria, 96–98

Vermont, USA, 23–24, 99–103
vision maps, 288–290
visioning, 131–133, 267–268, 288–290
Vital Communities, 99–103
vocational training, 87–91, 143–144
voluntary community contributions, 106

W
washing machines, 115–116
water
     dam removal, 169–175
     management, 9–10, 103–109
     stormwater management, 148–153
     system construction, 32–38
Wengerd, Nicole, 126–135
wetlands conservation, 225–233
Whyte, Bill, 181–187
wicked problems, 200
Willcox, David, 160, 162–169
Women in Democracy, 35
Work Together (Principle B)
     case studies: main, 47–58
     case studies: supplemental, 28, 29, 37, 38,
          70, 71, 75, 82, 102, 103, 105, 106, 120,
          121, 129, 131, 132, 147, 149, 150, 151, 152,
          153, 163, 164, 165, 166, 170, 172, 173, 183,
          185, 191, 192, 204, 205, 209, 222, 227,
          228, 229, 230, 232, 243, 244, 245, 246,
          253, 254, 266, 267, 272, 273, 275, 276
     characteristics/research, 42
     collaborative partnerships and social
          capital, 41, 43–46
     suggestions/best practices, 59
     workshop assessment of, 233–234
working groups, 295–296
W.S. Badger Company, 181–187

Y
Yetka, Leslie, 148–153
Young Achievers Science and Mathematics
     Pilot School, 219–225
Yousafzai, Malala, 199

Z
Zapotec community, 66–76

About the Author and the
Contributing Case Study Authors

JAMES S. GRUBER, PhD, PE: Director of the PhD Program in Environmental Studies at Antioch University New England, a member of the Commission on Environmental, Economic, and Social Policy, and a recent delegate to the UN Environmental Assembly in Nairobi, Kenya. Jim has consulted for governments and non-governmental organizations (NGOs) in North America, Eastern Europe, South America, and Africa on environmental issues and local governance focusing on citizen engagement in developing and implementing policy and programs. His work over the past three decades as a consultant, town manager, and professor has had a strong focus on facilitating positive adaptive change. He is a civil engineer and holds graduate degrees from MIT, Harvard Kennedy School of Government, and University of Zagreb. He resides in Alstead, New Hampshire.

Case Study Authors

The following are the primary authors of the case studies. Additional contributing authors are listed with each case study.

PAIGE AMBORD. Research fellow with the City of South Bend and a PhD candidate in Sociology at the University of Notre Dame.

SHILPY ARORA. Journalist in India writing extensively on issues of environment, climate change, wildlife, health, green technology, resource management, and sustainable development over the last ten years. Blogger and photographer.

MIRZA I. BEG. Environmental education specialist and faculty member at Stony Brook University, New York. Environmental consultant in Environmental and Sustainability Education.

TAZEEN BEG, MD. Anesthesiologist, assistant professor of Clinical Anesthesiology. Division chief, Non-Operating Room Anesthesia; Renaissance School of Medicine at Stony Brook University, New York.

PAUL BOCKO. Education Department faculty, Antioch University New England, with teaching, research, and professional practice focus on sustainability and place-based education.

JOHN BOSCO BAGURI SUMANI. PhD in Environmental Studies at Antioch University New England. Lecturer at the University for Development Studies, Ghana.

CHAD BISSONNETTE. Co-founder and executive director of Roots of Development, a nonprofit organization emphasizing community empowerment in Haiti. Author, speaker, and consultant.

JEBUNNESSA CHAPOLA. PhD candidate, Women's, Gender, and Sexualities Studies, University of Saskatchewan, Canada.

RANJAN DATTA, PhD. Banting Postdoctoral Fellow at the Johnson Shoyama Graduate School of Public Policy (JSGS), University of Regina, Canada.

ELYZABETH W. ENGLE. Assistant professor of Environmental Studies at McDaniel College. Research areas: community food systems, regenerative agriculture, sustainability, and environmental justice.

MEGAN ENNES, PhD. Assistant curator of Museum Education at the Florida Museum of Natural History, University of Florida.

HEATHER HECKEL. Co-founder and director of Engage Globally, a nonprofit organization supporting community-driven sustainable development, and an assistant professor at American University.

SARAH HINES. Works for the US Department of Agriculture Forest Service in Baltimore, with a BA from Harvard and MS and MBA degrees from the University of Michigan.

BO HOPPIN. Executive director, Hurricane Island Center for Science and Leadership, integrating science education and science research.

JACQUES KENJIO. PhD student in Environmental Studies, Antioch University New England. Teaching and research interests include land acquisitions, land tenure, politics in the environment, community engagement, and social justice.

KATRYNA M. KIBLER. PhD student in Environmental Studies, Antioch University New England. Synthesizes feminist and Indigenous theories to conduct ethical research on Indigenous food systems.

TANJU KIRISCIOGLU. PhD student in Environmental Studies, Antioch University New England. Guest teacher at Clark County School District, Las Vegas, Nevada.

FAUSTO LÓPEZ RODRIGUEZ. Instructor, researcher, and director of research group on governance, biodiversity, and protected areas, Universidad Técnica Particular de Loja, Ecuador.

CHARLENE PHILLIPS. MS candidate in Conservation Biology at Antioch University New England. Writing tutor and ESL instructor with an MA in English, TESOL.

PAUL MARKOWITZ. Independent consultant with over 30 years of experience in energy and environmental project management, as well as community engagement.

K. WHITNEY MAUER. PhD in Development Sociology, assistant professor in the Environmental Studies Program at Hobart & William Smith Colleges.

SHAYLIN SALAS. MS candidate in Environmental Advocacy at Antioch University New England. Climate justice and equitable community engagement specialist.

PATIENCE STODDARD, D. Min. Unitarian Universalist minister, organizational consultant, hospital and hospice chaplain, psychotherapist, and adjunct faculty, Antioch University New England.

NICOLE WENGERD. PhD in Environmental Studies, Antioch University New England. Lecturer at Keene State College in the Sociology and Environmental Study departments.

BILL WHYTE. Owner and founder of Badger Balm. Artist and creative writer with an interest in architecture and Aikido.

LESLIE YETKA, MS, MPA. Municipal natural resources manager experienced in community engagement and resilience planning.

ABOUT NEW SOCIETY PUBLISHERS

New Society Publishers is an activist, solutions-oriented publisher focused on publishing books for a world of change. Our books offer tips, tools, and insights from leading experts in sustainable building, homesteading, climate change, environment, conscientious commerce, renewable energy, and more—positive solutions for troubled times.

We're proud to hold to the highest environmental and social standards of any publisher in North America. When you buy New Society books, you are part of the solution!

- We print all our books in North America, never overseas

- All our books are printed on 100% post-consumer recycled paper, processed chlorine-free, with low-VOC vegetable-based inks (since 2002)

- Our corporate structure is an innovative employee shareholder agreement, so we're one-third employee-owned (since 2015)

- We're carbon-neutral (since 2006)

- We're certified as a B Corporation (since 2016)

At New Society Publishers, we care deeply about *what* we publish — but also about *how* we do business.

Download our catalog at https://newsociety.com/Our-Catalog or for a printed copy please email info@newsocietypub.com or call 1-800-567-6772 ext 111.

ENVIRONMENTAL BENEFITS STATEMENT

New Society Publishers saved the following resources by printing the pages of this book on chlorine free paper made with 100% post-consumer waste.

TREES	WATER	ENERGY	SOLID WASTE	GREENHOUSE GASES
71	5,700	30	240	30,600
FULLY GROWN	GALLONS	MILLION BTUs	POUNDS	POUNDS

Environmental impact estimates were made using the Environmental Paper Network Paper Calculator 4.0. For more information visit www.papercalculator.org.

Certified **B** Corporation

FSC — MIX Paper from responsible sources FSC® C016245 www.fsc.org

new society
PUBLISHERS
www.newsociety.com